Conversations with Gary Snyder

Literary Conversations Series
Monika Gehlawat
General Editor

Conversations with Gary Snyder

Edited by David Stephen Calonne

University Press of Mississippi / Jackson

www.upress.state.ms.us

The University Press of Mississippi is a member of the
Association of American University Presses.

"Riprap" from *Riprap and Cold Mountain Poems*; "Fixing the System"
and "This Present Moment" from *This Present Moment*; and "How" from
Danger on Peaks © Gary Snyder. Reprinted with permission.

First printing 2017
∞

Library of Congress Cataloging-in-Publication Data

Names: Snyder, Gary, 1930– | Calonne, David Stephen, 1953– editor.
Title: Conversations with Gary Snyder / edited by David Stephen Calonne.
Description: Jackson: University Press of Mississippi, [2017] | Series:
   Literary conversations series | Includes bibliographical references and
   index. |
Identifiers: LCCN 2017019629 (print) | LCCN 2017030980 (ebook) | ISBN
   9781496811639 (epub single) | ISBN 9781496811646 (epub institutional) |
   ISBN 9781496811653 (pdf single) | ISBN 9781496811660 (pdf institutional)
   | ISBN 9781496811622 (hardback)
Subjects: LCSH: Snyder, Gary, 1930-—Interviews. | Snyder, Gary,
   1930-—Criticism and interpretation. | Poets, American—20th
   century—Interviews. | Beat generation—Interviews. | BISAC: BIOGRAPHY &
   AUTOBIOGRAPHY / Literary. | LITERARY CRITICISM / Poetry. | LITERARY
   CRITICISM / American / General.
Classification: LCC PS3569.N88 (ebook) | LCC PS3569.N88 Z46 2017 (print) |
   DDC 811/.54 [B]—dc23
LC record available at https://lccn.loc.gov/2017019629

British Library Cataloging-in-Publication Data available

Books by Gary Snyder

Riprap. Ashland, MA: Origin Press, 1959.

Myths & Texts. New York: Totem Press/Corinth Books, 1960.

Riprap & Cold Mountain Poems. San Francisco: Four Seasons Foundation, 1965.

Six Sections from Mountains & Rivers Without End. San
    Francisco: Four Seasons Foundation, 1965.

A Range of Poems. London: Fulcrum Press, 1966.

The Back Country. New York: New Directions, 1968.

*Earth House Hold: Technical Notes & Queries to Fellow Dharma
    Revolutionaries*. New York: New Directions, 1969.

Regarding Wave. New York: New Directions, 1970.

Cold Mountain Poems: Twenty Four Poems by Han Shan.
    Translated by Gary Snyder. Portland: Press 22, 1970.

Manzanita. Bolinas: Four Seasons Foundation, 1972.

The Fudo Trilogy. Berkeley: Shaman Drum, 1973.

Turtle Island. New York: New Directions, 1974.

The Old Ways: Six Essays. San Francisco: City Lights Books, 1977.

Little Songs for Gaia. Port Townsend: Copper Canyon Press, 1979.

He Who Hunted Birds in His Father's Village. Bolinas: Grey Fox Press, 1979.

The Real Work: Interviews & Talks, 1964–1979. New York: New Directions, 1980.

Axe Handles. San Francisco: North Point Press, 1983.

Passage Through India. San Francisco: Grey Fox Press, 1983.

Left Out in the Rain: New Poems 1947–1985. San Francisco: North Point Press, 1986.

The Practice of the Wild: Essays by Gary Snyder. San Francisco: North Point Press, 1990.

No Nature: New and Selected Poems. New York: Pantheon, 1992.

A Place in Space: Ethics, Aesthetics and Watersheds. Berkeley: Counterpoint, 1995.

Mountains and Rivers Without End. Washington, D.C.: Counterpoint, 1996.

*The Gary Snyder Reader: Prose, Poetry, and Translations, 1952–
    1998*. Washington, D.C.: Counterpoint, 1999.

Look Out: A Selection of Writings. New York: New Directions, 2002.

The High Sierra of California: Poems and Journals by Gary Snyder,
    with Tom Killion. Berkeley: Heyday Books, 2002.

Danger On Peaks: Poems. Washington, D.C.: Shoemaker and Hoard, 2004.

Back on the Fire: Essays. Berkeley: Counterpoint, 1996.

Passage Through India: An Expanded and Illustrated Edition. Shoemaker & Hoard, 2007.

The Selected Letters of Allen Ginsberg and Gary Snyder. Berkeley: Counterpoint, 2009.

*The Etiquette of Freedom: Gary Snyder, Jim Harrison, and The Practice
    of the Wild*, ed. Paul Ebenkamp. Berkeley: Counterpoint, 2010.

Tamalpais Walking: Poetry, History, and Prints. Berkeley: Heyday, 2013.

Nobody Home: Writing, Buddhism, and Living in Places, in conversa-
   tion with Julia Martin. San Antonio: Trinity University Press, 2014.

Distant Neighbors: The Selected Letters of Wendell Berry and
   Gary Snyder. Berkeley: Counterpoint, 2014.

California's Wild Edge: The Coast in Prints, Poetry, and History. (Tom
   Killion author, with Snyder) Berkeley: Heyday, 2015.

This Present Moment: New Poems. Berkeley: Counterpoint, 2015.

The Great Clod: Notes and Memoirs on Nature and History
   in East Asia. Berkeley: Counterpoint, 2016.

Contents

Introduction

Gary Snyder was born in San Francisco in 1930 and two years later his family moved to a farm in Lake City near Seattle, Washington where they kept cows, chickens, ducks, geese as well as an orchard with a dozen fruit trees.[1] It was the Depression, Snyder's family was poor and the boy learned self-discipline and hard work early, doing chores, delivering milk to neighbors. By age ten his father Harold had taught him to use a crosscut saw and clean its blade—prefiguring Snyder's later deep respect for patiently accomplishing tasks with the proper tools, illustrated in one of his best-known poems, "Axe Handles": "Chen was an axe, I am an axe/And my son a handle, soon/To be shaping again, model/And tool, craft of culture,/How we go on."[2] Ernest Thompson Seton (1860–1946)—who founded the American youth outdoor program The League of Woodcraft Indians—was a great influence and by the age of eleven, Seton's *The Book of Woodcraft and Indian Lore* (1912) had become one of Snyder's most beloved books. He early parted company with Christianity's hierarchical view of creation in which humans occupied the evolutionary summit: the Native American and Buddhist respect for Nature he found more congenial. Rather than a unique creature made in "God's image," humans—as the Native Americans believed—appeared at the same time as all other beings and possessed no claim to special status.

At age twelve he had already begun to journey into the woods alone to camp for a night or two and at fifteen, scaled Mt. St. Helens. Mountains became his teachers, places of transcendent clarity where the quest for the deep Self might be undertaken. Snyder sought contact with a primal, archaic mystery seemingly lost to technologized urbanized humanity. Though he has been reluctant to reveal secrets regarding his spiritual experiences, he was obviously seeking what the Native Americans had also pursued on their visionary quests, when the shaman's epiphanic encounter with a tutelary animal marked one's initiation into a sacred zone. Snyder shifted away from an anthropocentric viewpoint and began to see life on earth in cosmic terms: time in large swaths of geologic eras. He typically spoke of the Neolithic, Paleolithic, Mesolithic—rather than in decades or centuries. For example, he dates the "Introduction" he wrote for the 1978 edition of *Myths and Texts* as "GS 13.X. 40077" —he views the year 1977 not as the twentieth century, but rather employs a "Homo sapiens calendar" which begins forty thousand years before the present "in the Gravettian/Aurignacian era"— thus 40077.[3]

Following graduation from Lincoln High School in Portland, Snyder earned a scholarship to Reed College where he studied anthropology and literature from 1947–1951: "It was the first time I had met affluent radicals. I had a hard time putting that together. I wasn't aware of class distinctions—took me years to figure that out. A part of the style of the impoverished intellectual left was that they assumed they were equal to everybody because they had politically correct ideas. Just like Marxists who wanted to figure they were right. 'History is on our side.' Part of the confidence of the left in those days was that sense of destiny."[4] At Reed he became friends with poets Philip Whalen and Lew Welch, took courses in anthropology with David French, studied poetry and Chinese calligraphy with Lloyd Reynolds and wrote his Senior Thesis on the mythology of the Haida people, thus continuing his profound engagement with Native American culture which had begun during his childhood: the thesis was subsequently published as *He Who Hunted Birds in His Father's Village: The Dimensions of a Haida Myth* (1979). Following his graduation from Reed, Snyder worked at a number of jobs in the forests and mountains. In mid-1951 while sitting near the Willamette River he experienced a *satori*—Zen Buddhist *awakening*—that "the entire universe is alive."[5] He traveled to the University of Indiana to study, however he had by now encountered D.T. Suzuki and Buddhism. Instead of pursuing an academic career in anthropology, he prepared to go to Japan to study Zen by learning Chinese and Japanese at UC Berkeley. Snyder's turn towards ecology, Native American and Asian culture signaled a wholesale rejection of Christianity as well as the vacuity and materialism of 1950's American society. Snyder found fellow pacifists and anarchists in the San Francisco Renaissance—West Coast poets such as Kenneth Rexroth, William Everson, and Robert Duncan—and he now also met Allen Ginsberg and Jack Kerouac who on the East Coast had been creating the Beat Movement. Ginsberg, Kerouac, as well as Diane di Prima would follow Snyder's example in their subsequent deep engagement with Buddhism.[6] Snyder read "After the Berry Feast" —a finely wrought poem decrying modern "civilization" in four sections based on two Native American mythic cycles involving Bear and the trickster Coyote—at the famous Six Gallery Reading in October, 1955 at which Ginsberg read "Howl," while Michael

McClure recited his poem about the killing of the great whales. Snyder was thus at the vanguard of the ecological movement at a time when few voices were being raised in opposition to the progressive despoiling of the planet. Kenneth Rexroth—along with Robinson Jeffers and D.H. Lawrence, an important early influence—declared that both Snyder and his friend Philip Whalen "have become, as poets, the most influential spokesmen, or even ideologists, of a new and revolutionary system of values, based on a constant, prayerful sense of the interlocking responsibilities of the community of all life on earth."[7]

Snyder would also spend time backpacking with Kerouac and many readers first encounter an engaging young man named Japhy Ryder in Kerouac's novel *The Dharma Bums* (1958) who climbs mountains, is physically tough and robust, an outdoorsman, handy with tools, familiar with Tibetan Tantric erotic practices, at once solitary and friendly, and deeply learned in Buddhist, Zen, and Native American lore. He is a wandering *bhikku*, and the beginnings of the "rucksack revolution" was now being launched. This engaging literary creation is actually—these same readers later learn—a real person named Gary Snyder. Snyder—while a character in a novel by the most famous "Beat" writer—has spent much of his career explaining why he would rather be known as a "Pulitzer-Prize winning poet" than as a Beat. He saw his poetic practice as essentially distinct from poets such as Ginsberg and Gregory Corso and in several of our later interviews, Snyder attempts to separate fact from fiction in Kerouac's portrait. Snyder was absent from the US during the tumultuous and thrilling years which marked the transition from the Beat to Hippy phase of the youth movement. He left for Japan on May 15, 1956 to study Zen Buddhism, returning permanently to America only in 1968. He also spent one year in the States teaching English composition at UC Berkeley in fall 1964-spring 1965. This period of Snyder's time in Japan and the birth of the counterculture of the mid-late fifties is chronicled by Al Aronowitz who would write a significant twelve-part series of articles on the Beats for the *New York Post* which ran in the March 9–March 22, 1959 issues. His portrait of Snyder was subsequently republished in *Swank* in 1961.

Snyder continued to evolve a unique syncretism of Native American—particularly the idea of the shaman who sets out on a quest to achieve a mystical vision and acts as the tribe's link to the deeper mysteries of being—Buddhism, and ecological awareness. In addition, a recurring theme in the early interviews of the sixties is Snyder's reimagining of family relationships. His training in anthropology and kinship systems is evident in his emerging ideas concerning the extended family and matrilineal descent. At a time when the American, heterosexual nuclear family was beginning to feel the pressures of greater divorce rates as well as the challenge of communal living and the emerging gay rights movement, Snyder's views seem eerily prescient. In his 1965 interview for *Ananke* he discusses his ideas concerning sexual freedom: "Most people do not have enough imagination to see where this will lead. They just say, 'I can't see where it will stop.' And the thing is, it won't stop. It will very possibly flip over into a possibility, a legal possibility, of people contracting marriages in any form they want to contract them." Recently the Supreme Court of the United States has ruled on the legality of same-sex marriage, thus vindicating Snyder's prediction of fifty years ago. Yet Snyder also saw the risks and dangers of the Socratic injunction to "know thyself" of some of the Beat and hippie approaches to life, and in the same *Ananke* interview, he explores a solution in terms of Buddhist ethics: "You come to see yourself in very limited ego-terms. Whereas, as the Buddhists say, 'When you discover yourself, you discover that there is no self.' And that is ultimately a very moral discovery. Without having any ethical rules laid down for you, you find that you are enough of everything and everybody that you can naturally and silently lead a harmonious way of life, rather than a life of extreme self-expression, artificial self-expression, which causes pain and discomfort for others." Snyder consistently was seeking a healthy and centered approach to the tumultuous spiritual, sexual, social, and political revolution convulsing America.

During one trip back to the States from Japan, Snyder participated in *The Human Be-In: A Gathering of the Tribes* on January 14, 1967 in Golden Gate Park, San Francisco with Timothy Leary, Lenore Kandel, Lawrence Ferlinghetti, and Michael McClure. Snyder was astonished at the transformation American youth culture had undergone during his absence: "So I got to see the way all those kids looked, and they were a pretty sight. There was a lot of color in the clothing, a lot of invention and imagination in the way everyone was doing things. The girls were stunning. The guys looked great too. And they were all friendly with each other. So I imagine they had a really great summer, but I was back in Japan by then!"[8] A month after *The Human Be-In*, Snyder joined Timothy Leary, Allen Ginsberg, and Alan Watts on Watts' boat the S.S. Vallejo for the "Houseboat Summit" in February, 1967. The lively debate which ensued covers several of the key issues of the times: Leary's injunction to "turn on, tune in and drop out," the spiritual quest of the shaman, as well as Snyder's desire to "encourage extended families everywhere."

In several of the interviews of the seventies, Snyder's comments on many topics would prove prophetic over the next decades. At Wisconsin in 1970 he joined Dan Kozlovsky, author of *An Ecological and Evolutionary Ethic*, in exploring several of the countercultural themes of the seventies: over-population, Tantra (he mentions specifically Sir John Woodroffe's (1865–1936)—known by his pseudonym Arthur Avalon—*Tantra of the Great Liberation*, patriarchy, urban development, communes, the destruction of the environment.[9] Snyder also demonstrates his familiarity with the work of Claude Lévi-Strauss and his observations in *The Savage Mind* concerning the Australian aborigines who in their complex kinship discussions qualify as "intellectual dandies" and demonstrate a refined sensibility equal or superior to our own much-vaunted civilized mentality. He also noted the slow fading of the idealistic dreams of the sixties and "The Age of Aquarius," declaring that "for better or worse, flower power is dead": the eco-revolutionaries would have to take a new approach in their efforts to fight the despoliation of the planet. As we have seen, Snyder was seeking to live in accordance with the deep, archaic values of ancient humanity and found himself increasingly out-of-step with what was considered the "mainstream" of American life. He continued to imagine the history of life in terms of millennia and in *The Drummer* in 1972 he observed: "Listen . . . I consider society peripheral to my life. I consider America and modern civilization a temporary aberration on the mainstream of human life that's been going on for 50,000 years. I'm trying to live in the mainstream."[10] *Alcheringa* —edited by Dennis Tedlock and Jerome Rothenberg (Snyder served as coeditor) was a significant part of the new "ethnopoetics" movement: the "First Magazine of the World's Tribal Poetics."[11] Snyder returns in his interview in *Alcheringa* (the name derives from the Arunta of Australia—"The Eternal Dream Time, The Dreaming of a sacred heroic time long ago when man and nature came to be, a kind of narrative of things that once happened") to Lévi-Strauss whom he sees as a "genius" and all of whose works he read in translation. However, although Snyder found much to admire in structuralist theory, he ultimately believed its approach to myth to be reductive. Snyder was influenced by Lévi-Strauss, particularly in relation to his conception of "wild thinking"—which is preferable to the usual translation of *La Pensée Sauvage* as *The Savage Mind*. According to Lévi-Strauss , the relationship of national parks to urban life bears the same relationship as the wilds of the unconscious to the cultivated and civilized conscious urban world, and this is a notion Snyder would expand upon in his own essays.

Snyder sought to live out a life in one "bioregion" and to make a community of like-minded spiritual seekers, and in 1971 built with the help of his friends a house which he named "Kitkitdizze," after a native plant. The structure mirrored his spiritual syncretism for it became a blend of Spanish Californian, Japanese, and Mandan Native American architectural styles. And he added a Neolithic touch with a fire pit in the center with a smoke-house hole in the roof. With the publication of *Turtle Island* in 1974, Snyder was awarded the Pulitzer Prize and now attained national prominence. The title "Turtle Island" derives from the belief among the Maidu of northern California (the Iroquois and Seneca have similar myths) that at the beginning of Creation there were as yet no stars, moon, or sun: darkness and water were everywhere. From the sky "Earth-Initiate" descends and Turtle asks if he can create for him some dry land so he might be able to emerge from the water. The Earth-Initiate inquires where he might find some earth and Turtle volunteers to dive to the bottom of the water to find earth with which to create the dry land. He spends six years below and emerges with a small bit of soil "as large as a small pebble" out of which Earth-Initiate creates the world.[12] Just as Snyder seeks to re-conceptualize historical time in terms of geologic eras, so too he seeks to re-orient Americans to the world-view of the Native Americans who inhabited "Turtle Island" before it was colonized by the European invaders and named "America." The rampant consumerism ravaging the modern world needs to be challenged through a return to a respect for Planet Earth. In his discussion with Lee Bartlett, he advocates that Americans reduce their meat consumption and derive more protein from grains such as corn and soybeans. He argues the excess grain could be used to feed those suffering from famine in India. He rejects Western materialism as essentially destructive of self and environment, as Henry David Thoreau counseled, "Simplify, Simplify." The more you reduce your "needs," the better; Snyder opposes in every possible way modern American "consumerism."

During this period, Snyder also continued to refine his ideas about shamanism. He tells Bartlett: "It's said over and over again in different primitive contexts that the shaman is one-half in the human world, but one-half out of the human world. That he draws on visions, songs, powers gained from animals, trees, or from waterfalls for healing energy." He elaborates on this in an interview four years later in the magazine *River Styx*:

> Actually, I'm just calling for poets to fulfill one of their ancient functions, which happens to be very necessary right now, and that is to be interpreters from the

otherness realm of the wild and of nature, both as understood inside and outside of ourselves, because poets and certain kinds of artists are the people who stand on that margin, and in the past, it was via dance and song that animal life was brought into the circle of the human. It still needs to be done; more so than ever before in a world in which there is the largest population that's ever existed of people who don't know anything about nature and do not need to know anything about nature as far as their survival is concerned. Something has to come up from inside, to speak to them, to bring them that voice.[13]

The Beat and hippie movements had resuscitated in terms of the contemporary American scene several key aspects of the archaic visionary quest for ecstasy and deep spiritual experience: music—classical, rock and roll, jazz, folk music; entheogens—marijuana, LSD, peyote, ayahuasca, mescaline; sacralized sexual experiences; poetry and dance. Snyder, like virtually all of the Beats—Michael McClure, Ginsberg, Diane di Prima—experimented with peyote, perhaps the most widely known of the entheogens of the Native Americans.

As we encounter Snyder in these interviews, we note that he spontaneously demonstrates a virtuosic ability to cover an impressive range of subjects with consummate ease, discoursing eloquently on matters as diverse as Buddhism, meditation, preserving the wild, poetics, world mythology, Native American studies, anthropology, and the Yuba water shed. He is curious about everything, and vigorously committed to living an unalienated life even in a society from which he remains spiritually and philosophically isolated. We learn of books important to Snyder in his omnivorous readings in literature, history, biology, economics, anthropology, ecology: *The White Goddess* by Robert Graves,; *The Origins of the Family, Private Property and the State* by Friedrich Engels; *Poems of Love and War: From the Eight Anthologies and the Long Poems of Classical Tamil* by A.K. Ramanujan; R. Gordon Wasson's *Soma: Divine Mushroom of Immortality*; *The American Conservation Movement: John Muir and His Legacy* by Stephen Fox; *The Environmental Imagination: Thoreau, Nature Writing, and the Formation of American Culture* by Lawrence Buell; William Everson's *Archetype West*; *Stone Age Economics* by Marshall Sahlins; Richard K. Nelson's *The Island Within* as well as his groundbreaking study of the Native Americans of Alaska, *Make Prayers to the Raven: A Koyukon View of the Northern Forest*.

One also notes the often formal precision of Snyder's responses to questions, his effort to articulate carefully exactly what he has in mind as well as his lively sense of humor, how frequently the interviews are punctuated by laughter. We remember his years of Zen training in which both humor and the *koan*—"what is the sound of one hand clapping?"—are central, as well as the daily ritual of rising early in the morning in the cold to do his meditation. It would be true to say that Snyder sees the discipline of inner and outer activity as being equally central: *mens sana in corpore sano—a healthy mind in a healthy body*, as the Roman poet Juvenal noted in his *Satire X*. He speaks of the discipline of a "goal free" meditation in which one observes one's own thoughts as they pass through the mind without judging them— the notion of "mindfulness" which has become increasingly popular of late. He tells us in his 1979 *Interlochen Review* interview that

> it was actually anthropology that led me to do Zen study. It was the question of objectivity really, the fundamental scientific question. Can an anthropologist be objective about another culture? Is it possible to even think about a sub-atomic particle without affecting the "nature" of the particle? The act of measuring affects the thing being measured. Realizing that and wanting to see if it were possible to approach naked mind, I went into Zen—to take all of the cultural and psychological clothes off. . . . But the intention of Buddhist practice, or Zen practice, through meditation, is to go down into your mind to the place where it is truly universal and unconditioned and truly free. From that point you can see how it is that all of these different kinds of trappings are put on and how you take them off. And how you can freely play with them.

The effort to approach "naked mind"—to gradually peel away the multiple layers of familial, cultural and social controls to arrive at the interior place which "is truly universal and unconditioned and truly free—becomes the recurring theme throughout these discussions."

Yet this is not a selfish, purely egotistical undertaking for Snyder was devoted to Mahayana Buddhism, which as he tells us in 1980 in the *Cottonwood Review* "is the Buddhism of those who commit themselves to a vision of everybody becoming enlightened together." Snyder also celebrates a pantheistic, pagan, polytheistic reverence for Nature as alive and sacred, and argues that "people are raised in a secular myth that says the world is inanimate. It's not very hard to reanimate the world for young people, because they're up for it, but everything works against the animation of the world when they start getting on in school and are being influenced by the media and the consumer world."[14] In several of his later interviews, Snyder returns frequently to the concept of "bioregionalism" which as we have seen, informs his book *Turtle Island*. He tells Catherine Spretnak in

1987 that "bioregionalism is a fancy term for staying put and learning what's going on" and elaborates in *Western American Literature*:

> Of course, the term was borrowed from biogeographers to begin with. And we put a spin on it ourselves, which was social and cultural. But in a sense we were looking for any language that would help us clarify that there was a distinction between finding your membership in a natural place and locating your identity in terms of a social or political group. The landscape was my natural nation, and I could see that as having a validity and permanence that would outlast the changing political structures. It enabled be to be critical of the United States without feeling that I wasn't at home in North America.

One sees the way these ideas began to inhabit Snyder's poetry as in his poem "For All": "I pledge allegiance to the soil/of Turtle Island,/and to the beings who theron dwell/one ecosystem/in diversity/under the sun/With joyful interpenetration for all."[15] Loyalty is pledged here not to the flag of the United States but rather to the Earth itself, to the "soil" of Turtle Island. And in place of the "Republic," our allegiance should rightly be to the "beings" who live on the Earth. "Ecosystem" replaces "Nation," "under the sun" replaces "under God," and in place of a non-existent "liberty and justice" Snyder declares a "joyful interpenetration" of terrestrial and cosmic energies.

Snyder has kept up an energetic program of lectures and readings and has estimated that he has appeared at virtually every college and university in the United States. We witness here his trips to a variety of institutions: Interlochen Center for the Arts in Northern Michigan, the University of Kansas, Naropa University, De Anza College, and the University of Wisconsin. We can see his easy rapport with the young in these exchanges, his gift at summarizing and articulating his beliefs in an approachable and genial way. In the final interviews Snyder returns to earlier themes and offers thoughtful interpretations of the life and work of his friend Jack Kerouac. At age eighty-five, he has been giving numerous readings from his latest book *This Present Moment* (2015), and he has continued to add to his prolific oeuvre—his latest book, *The Great Clod: Notes and Memoirs on Nature and History in East Asia* appeared in 2016. *Conversations with Gary Snyder* is intended to acquaint new readers with the achievements of a distinguished American poet as well as provide fresh insights for students and scholars already familiar with his admirable work and life.

DSC

Notes

1. Gary Snyder, "The Path to Matsuyama" in *Back on the Fire: Essays* (Emeryville: Shoemaker & Hoard, 2007), 51.

2. John Suiter, *Poets on the Peak: Gary Snyder, Philip Whalen & Jack Kerouac in the North Cascades* (New York: Counterpoint, 2002), 3; "Axe Handles" in *The Gary Snyder Reader: Prose, Poetry, and Translations 1952–1998* (Washington, D.C.: Counterpoint, 1999), 489.

3. Gary Snyder, "Entering the Fiftieth Millenium," *Back on the Fire*, 73.

4. John Sheehy, *Comrades of the Quest: An Oral History of Reed College* (Corvallis: Oregon State University Press, 2012), 205.

5. Anthony Hunt, *Genesis, Structure, and Meaning in Gary Snyder's Mountains and Rivers Without End* (Reno & Las Vegas: University of Nevada Press, 2004), 4.

6. On Snyder and Buddhism, see Rick Fields, *How the Swans Came to the Lake: A Narrative History of Buddhism in America* (Boston & London: Shambhala, 1992); Richard Hughes Seager, *Buddhism in America* (New York: Columbia University Press, 1999).

7. Kenneth Rexroth, "Poetry into the '70's," *The Alternative Society: Essays from the Other World* (New York: Herder and Herder, 1970), 175.

8. *Bloomsbury Review*, July/August 2007, 24.

9. Dan Kozlovsky, *An Ecological and Evolutionary Ethic* (Englewood Cliffs: Prentice-Hall, Inc., 1974).

10. Al Robins, "Gary Snyder: Keeper of the Tales," *Drummer*, No. 219, Nov. 30, 1972, 9.

11. See Gary Snyder, "The Politics of Ethnopoetics," in *The Old Ways*, 15–43.

12. Roland B. Dixon, *Maidu Myths: Bulletin of the American Museum of Natural History, Volume XVII, Part II* (New York: 1902), 39, 40; also see Gary Snyder, "Foreword" to *The Maidu Indian Myths and Stories of Hanc'ibyÿgim*, ed. and trans. William Shipley (Santa Clara/Berkeley: Santa Clara University/Heyday Books, 1991), vii, x.

13. Michael and Jan Castro, "An Interview with Gary Snyder," *River Styx 4: American Mythmaking*, 1979, 54. Also see Michael Castro, *Interpreting the Indian: Twentieth-Century Poets and the Native American* (Albuquerque: University of New Mexico Press, 1983); Sherry L. Smith, *Hippies, Indians, and the Fight for Red Power* (New York: Oxford University Press, 2012), 43–44, 56–70.

14. Geeta Dardick, "An Interview with Gary Snyder: When Life Starts Getting Interesting," *Sierra*, September/October 1985, 70.

15. Gary Snyder, "For All," *The Gary Snyder Reader*, 504.

Chronology

1930   Gary Snyder is born May 8, 1930 in San Francisco, California. Parents are Harold and Lois Snyder and he has a younger sister Anthea born in 1932.

1932   Family moves to Lake City north of Seattle in Washington State where they have a small dairy farm.

1937   In June, Snyder's feet are injured when his father was burning brush and stumps and he ran over the ash, mistakenly believing it was safe to do so. He begins ravenous reading of books from the Public Library during his four-month convalescence.

1942   Family moves to Portland, Oregon. Encounters Native Americans at the Farmers' Market in Seattle. Already had a strong sense of Native Americans as the "prior people" and has a sense of "outrage" at the European desecration of the land and indigenous cultures. Begins to camp in woods by himself for one or two nights at a time.

1943–45 Attends high school in Portland. Parents separate. Works as copy boy at newspaper. Works at Mount St. Helens YMCA summer camp doing trail crew as well as carpentry work and in summer of 1945, climbs Mt. St. Helens with Mazamas, a climbing group from Portland, Oregon at age fifteen .

1946–47 Climbs Mt. Adams at age sixteen; Mt. Baker and Mt. Rainier at seventeen. Becomes member of Wilderness Society and subscribes to *The Living Wilderness*. "The Youngsteigers"—an essay on mountain climbing and one of Snyder's earliest publications— appears in *Mazama*, Vol. 29, no. 13 in December, 1947. Graduates from high school. He shows the poetry he has been writing to a teacher and on its strength he receives scholarship and attends Reed College where he becomes friends with Philip Whalen, Lew Welch, and Dell Hymes.

1948   Begins keeping a journal or "notebooks of essentials." In summer, ships out as galley man from New York.

1949   First job with Forest Service in the Columbia National Forest (now Gifford Pinchot Forest) where he does hand logging out of Spirit Lake.

1950   First poems published in Reed College magazine; marries Alison Gass. Works for Parks Service excavating archaeological site of Old Fort Vancouver; writes senior thesis "The Dimensions of a Haida Myth."

1951   Graduates from Reed College with a degree in anthropology/literature; works during the summer at a logging camp on Warm Springs Indian Reservation in eastern Oregon, collecting a Tsimshian folktale and a fragment of a flood myth. On banks of Willamette River, has a *satori* experience: "the entire universe is alive." Attends Indiana University Graduate School for a semester but leaves and returns to San Francisco.

1952   Lives with poet Philip Whalen. By early summer, finishes his poem "A Berry Feast" and works as lookout at Crater Mountain, the Mount Baker National Forest. Divorces Alison Gass. Intense mountain climbing continues: climbs on average eight to ten peaks each summer and by end of year, Snyder scales Mt. Hood fourteen times.

1953   Works as lookout on Sourdough Mountain, Mount Baker National Forest. During his stays in mountain huts, Snyder first practices *zazen*—Buddhist meditation sitting cross-legged, and visits the Berkeley Buddhist Church. Enters UC Berkeley to learn Chinese and Japanese, and studies *sumi*—ink wash brush painting—with Chiura Obata. Works on *Myths and Texts*, meets Kenneth Rexroth.

1954   Works at the Warm Springs Lumber Company as choker—responsible for attaching cables to logs for removal; continues work on Warm Spring Reservation in summer collecting Native American materials. Publishes two book reviews—on Ella Clark's *Indian Legends of the Pacific Northwest* and Jaime de Angulo's *Indian Tales in Midwest Folklore*.

1955   In April, Alan Watts (1915–1973) introduces Snyder to Ruth Fuller Sasaki (1892–1967) who prepares the way for Snyder's subsequent trip to Japan. At Yosemite National Park, works on trail crew in back country. Enters graduate school at Berkeley again and works on translation of *Cold Mountain Poems* by Han-shan. Meets Jack Kerouac and Allen Ginsberg in fall. On October 7, at the

Six Gallery Poetry Reading at which "Howl" is premiered, Snyder reads "A Berry Feast." In fall and following spring spends time with Kerouac in Mill Valley cabin. Snyder appears in Kerouac's novel *The Dharma Bums* as "Japhy Ryder."

1956   January and February, hitchhiking trip with Ginsberg. Completes *Myths and Texts* in an abandoned cabin in Marin County. At the Academy of Asian Studies, meets the artist Saburo Hasegawa and attends his lectures. Receives scholarship from First Zen Institute of America to study Japanese and Zen in Japan and leaves on May 6 by the freighter Anita Maru to Kyoto. He lives in Zen Temple Shokoku-ji, studying with Miura Isshu Roshi. Begins work on a long poem to be called "Mountains and Rivers Without End."

1957   Leaves Japan in August, works in engine room for eight months of the ship Sappa Creek, departing from Yokohama. Visits Persian Gulf, Italy, Turkey, Okinawa, Wake, Guam, Ceylon, Pago Pagao, Samoa, Hawaii.

1958   Leaves ship at San Pedro, California on April 15 and goes to San Francisco. Translation of Han-Shan published in *Evergreen Review*. With Lew Welch, shares cabin in Marin County. In mid-June meets Joanne Kyger.

1959   Returns to Kyoto, Japan, starts studies of traditional Linji Chan—Rinzai Zen—with Oda Sesso Roshi (1901–1966), abbot at the Daitoku-ji monastery. *Riprap* published.

1960   Asked by Hisao Kanaseki to provide an introduction for the Japanese intelligentsia to the new poetry of the Beats, Snyder writes "Notes on the Beat Generation" and "The New Wind" which are published in Japanese translation in January in *Chuo-Koron*. On February 23, marries Joanne Kyger in the American Consulate in Kobe. *Myths and Texts* published.

1961–62   Leaves Kyoto in early December by boat with Kyger to to Sri Lanka and Nepal, then to India. In New Delhi, meets with Allen Ginsberg and in Dharamshala with the Dalai Lama. Returns to Japan in April.

1963   Ginsberg comes to Kyoto. Snyder and Ginsberg meet Nanao Sakaki for the first time.

1964   Returns to United States. On June 12, gives poetry reading with Lew Welch and Philip Whalen in San Francisco. Teaches English composition UC Berkeley Fall 1964–Spring 1965. Separates from Kyger. Receives Bess Hoskin Prize.

1965   With Richard Baker, Snyder organizes a "protest meditation" at the Oakland Army Terminal. In summer, Berkeley Poetry Conference with Robert Duncan, Charles Olson, Jack Spicer, Ginsberg. Goes with Ginsberg to the North Cascades where they climb Glacier Peak. On October 22, does a ritual circumambulatory hike with Philip Whalen and Ginsberg of Mount Tamalpais—the Hindu-Buddhist *pradakshina*. In October, returns to Japan, funded by a grant from the Bollingen Foundation. *Six Sections from Mountains and Rivers Without End* published. Divorce from Kyger.

1966   Meets Masa Uehara. *A Range of Poems* published. Receives prize from National Institute of Arts and Letters. Reads on college campuses. With Allen Ginsberg, Richard Baker from the San Francisco Zen Center and J. Donald Walters, purchases a hundred acres of land twenty-five miles north of Nevada City, California where four years later he will build a home.

1967   On January 14, blows the conch to open and close the *Human Be-In* or *The Gathering of the Tribes* in Golden Gate Park, San Francisco and chants *dharanis* (invocations) in Sino-Japanese. Returns to Japan in March. Spends summer at Banyon Ashram on the volcanic island of Suwa-now-se and marries Masa there. Studies with Nakamura Sojun Roshi at Daitokuji.

1968   In April, son Kai born in Kyoto and *The Back Country* is published. Receives Levinson Prize (for "Eight Songs of Cloud and Water") from Poetry (Chicago) and Guggenheim Fellowship. Father Harold dies in December; Snyder returns permanently to the US.

1969   Son Gen born. *Earth House Hold* published. Distributes "Smokey the Bear Sutra" at Sierra Club in San Francisco; hikes with Nanao Sakaki.

1970   On April 22, delivers Earth Day lecture at Colorado State College. Gives paper "The Wilderness" at The Center for the Study of Democratic Institutions, Santa Barbara. Moves to San Juan Ridge and builds house "Kitkitdizze" at foothills of the Sierra Nevada. *Regarding Wave* published.

1972   Attends United Nations Conference on the Environment in June with Michael McClure in Stockholm, Sweden; in July travels in Japan. *Manzanita* published.

1973   *The Fudo Trilogy* published which includes "Spel Against Demons," "Smokey the Bear Sutra" and "The California Water Plan."

1974   In spring, gives lecture "The Yogin and the Philosopher" at the Conference on the Rights of the Nonhuman, Claremont, California. *Turtle Island* published.

1974–79 Member of the Board of the California Arts Council.

1975   Receives Pulitzer Prize for *Turtle Island.*

1977   *The Old Ways* published.

1978   With Robert Aitken and Joanna Macy, founds The Buddhist Peace Fellowship.

1979   *He Who Hunted Birds in His Father's Village: The Dimensions of a Haida Myth* published.

1980   *The Real Work: Interviews and Talks 1964–1979* published.

1981   Travels to Japan. Reads with Nanao Sakaki in Australia.

1982   Helps build Ring of Bone Zendo near his home. Reads in England, Sweden, Scotland.

1983   *Axe Handles* and *Passage Through India* published.

1984   Travels in China guest of Writers' Union with Allen Ginsberg, Maxine Hong Kingston, Toni Morrison, and others.

1986   *Left Out in the Rain* published. Begins sixteen-year teaching career at UC Davis. He teaches half-time in the creative writing program and courses such as "The San Francisco Poetry Renaissance and the Beginnings of the Beat Generation," as well as "Translations of Chinese and Japanese Poetry and their Effect on Twentieth-Century American Literature." Receives the American Poetry Society Shelley Memorial Award.

1987   Becomes member of the American Academy of Arts and Letters. Travels in Alaska.

1989   Divorce from Masa Uehara.

1990   On April 22, gives "Earth Day and the War Against the Imagination" at Bridgeport on the South Yuba River. Establishes Yuba Watershed Institute. Reads in Taiwan. *The Practice of the Wild* published.

1991   Marries Carole Koda, they travel in Japan.

1992   *No Nature* published. In September speaks at Ecology Center of the Upper Indus Watershed in Leh, India; reads in Spain.

1994   Travels to Africa—Botswana and Zimbabwe. Teaches literature and wilderness thought at The University of California at Davis.

1995   *A Place in Space* published. Reads in Ireland. In fall, goes to Nepal with Carole Koda and daughter, hikes to Base Camp on Sagarmatha (Everest).

1996   Visits Paleolithic sites Peche-merle, Cougnac, Niaux, El Portel, Lascaux and Trois-Frères in Dordogne and Pyrenees. *Mountains and Rivers Without End* published.

1997   Receives Bollingen Prize and John Hay Award for Nature Writing.

1998   In March, receives The Numata Foundation Cultural Award for furthering the appreciation and understanding of Buddhism in Tokyo. Reads in Greece and Czech Republic. Receives Lanna Award and Lila Wallace Reader's Digest Grant.

2004   In November, receives the Masaoka Shiki International Haiku Grand Prize from the Ehime Cultural Foundation in Matsuyama City, Japan.

2010   *Etiquette of Freedom*, documentary film and book with Jim Harrison published.

2015   *This Present Moment* published.

2016   *The Great Clod: Notes and Memoirs on Nature and History in East Asia* published.

Conversations with Gary Snyder

Visit with a Fellaheen Man

Alfred G. Aronowitz / 1961

From *Swank*, 8, no. 4 (September 1961), 49–52, 64–67. Reprinted by permission of Joel Aronowitz.

On the stone-edged dirt streets that led through Kyoto, a motorcycle guns through the Japanese night carrying a young man who, although he doesn't wear a black leather jacket, holds somewhat more valid credentials in the Beat Generation. He is, in fact, a character right out of one of Jack Kerouac's books, and, if that's not enough, he's actually the hero of it. He is Gary Snyder, the bearded but otherwise thinly disguised protagonist who climbs mountains without a second thought or a second wind; who translates ancient Oriental poetry into modern American idiom and, with equal ease and ecstasy, does the same with ancient Oriental sex customs; who shaves his head and hitchhikes through the West, dispensing, in return for rides, the Truth according to Buddha; who topples trees with the vigor of the lumberjack he once was, but with much more tenderness than he topples conventions; who strips to nakedness at genteel parties and yet remains more clothed in innocence than those still wearing their suits; who shares narcotics and visions with America's Indians and then sets those visions to verse with the free hand of beat prosody; who is a poet and who dominates Kerouac's *The Dharma Bums* with the name, as improbable as himself, of Japhy Ryder.

"The crack of the dying logs was like Japhy making little comments on my happiness," wrote Kerouac in one passage of the book, describing their camp during a climb up a mountain in search of exhilaration and other benefits. "I looked at him, his head was buried way under inside his duck-down bag. His little huddled form was the only thing I could see for miles of darkness that was so packed and concentrated with eager desire to be good. I thought: 'What a strange thing is man . . . like in the Bible it says, Who knoweth the spirit of man that looketh upward? This poor kid ten years younger than I am is making me look like a fool forgetting all the ideals and joys I knew before, in my recent years of drinking and disappointment, what does he care if he hasn't got any money, all he needs is his rucksack with those little plastic bags of dried food and a good pair of shoes and off he goes and enjoys the privileges of a millionaire in surroundings like this . . .'"

Snyder's present surroundings, of course, are no more surprising than he is. Kyoto, aside from its contributions to the post card, is also the site of Daikota Temple, that labyrinthine compound of crumbling mud-and-tile walls, incredible gardens, wooden gates, impassable bamboo grove, high-gabled structures and painted dragons which serves as the home office for one of the several great temple-systems of the Rinzai sect of Zen and in which, with his head unshaven and with his beard flashing the red-oranges and yellows of the Van Gogh self-portraits he resembles, Snyder participates in the meditations and rigors of a Zen student. As for the 244 pages of adulation directed at him by friend Kerouac, Snyder seems to be a young man with a tendency toward hard rather than swell-headedness and, anyway, Zen Buddhism has its own way of seeing that his heroics remain back home in the minds of the readers and not in his own.

"They really get at the ego," explains Snyder, describing the temple routine of *zazen*, those half-hour periods of cross-legged silence when the student monks mediate on their *koans*, little puzzles, semantic and irrational, to which there are no answers but to which they must find one, reciting it, finally, in the *sanzen*, a momentary but momentous interview with their Zen master, held often four times daily with the first at four in the morning, a confrontation which Snyder describes as "the fierce face-to-face moment where you spit forth truth or perish."

"I feel," says Snyder, telling about three such weeks of intensive meditation, "like I'd been through a dozen lives."

A recount of his adventures, many of which are not included in *The Dharma Bums*, makes it seem as if Snyder has been through a dozen lives. But the inevitable question of what is so highly ranked a member of the Beat Generation doing in a Zen Buddhist monastery is probably best answered by the question of what is Zen Buddhism doing in the Beat Generation. "*The decline of the West!*" proclaims Snyder with mock drama, but he adds, in all seriousness: "Zen is the most important thing in my life. The trouble is that nine-tenths of these other cats are hung up on these Christian notions and Judaic notions of right and wrong. They can't stand contradictions. And the idea that a religious and spiritual life is contradictory with a life of senses and yaking and enjoyment and so forth, this isn't so. Zen sees the world as one thing. American Zen, or the type practiced in San Francisco, at least, is not accurate Zen. The thing about Zen is that there's a hell of a lot of talk about it but it's generally misunderstood and misrepresented." Snyder, for his part, claims neither to misrepresent Zen nor to represent it, but it is quite obvious that he, for one, is no longer hung up on the Judeo-Christian notions with which he was endowed. He has, in fact, so liberated his own mind that he no longer associates it with the tradition that nurtured it. *"You Westerners!"* he often says, in a voice full of patent condescension, placing himself emphatically on the side of the Pacific where he now happens to be. Or else; with some derision, *"The Western mind!"* Or else in equally disparaging tones: "It's all these Westerners that think you can understand your world by reducing it to a manipulated simplicity!" And yet, in Snyder's case, his conversion to Zen Buddhism and the Oriental mind has been strangely enough, an almost purely American phenomenon, evolving from his preoccupation, literally, with the nature of the country. "Japhy Ryder," says poet Allen Ginsberg, looming in the background of *The Dharma Bums* behind the somewhat symbolic mask of Alvah Goldbook, "is a great new hero of American culture." And the fact of the matter is that he is also the hero of *The Dharma Bums* not, essentially, because of his and Kerouac's devotion to Buddha but because he represents, perhaps as perfectly as anyone can, a unity of the hipsterism, the Paul Bunyan travelogue and all the other spontaneous and classic forces that have helped created the Beat Generation.

" . . . I was amazed at the way he meditated with his eyes open," wrote Kerouac. "And I was mostly humanly amazed that this tremendous little guy who eagerly studied Oriental poetry and anthropology and ornithology and everything else in the books and was a tough little adventurer of trails and mountains should also suddenly whip out his pitiful beautiful wooden prayer-beads and solemnly pray there, like an oldfashioned saint of the deserts certainly, but so amazing to see it in America with its steel mills and airfields . . ."

Undismayed by contradiction, Snyder, of course, finds no need to reconcile the place he has established for himself within American culture and his place without it. "This is largely a big rural movement," he says, sounding, in fact, rural himself, with an affected country twang, Far Western, hayseed and cracker-barrel, but speaking also with an interlacing of hip colloquialisms and self-evident erudition that at the same time dispels any corn from what he has to say. "Like the kids coming into San Francisco and going down to North Beach these days, they're not from the cities, mostly, but from the farms or back woods, where they've been working in isolation, hatching, sort of, writing their poetry or reading or just thinking, picking up on all sorts of ideas, and now they're bringing this great rural culture to the urban centers. See, you city fellers don't have any monopoly on culture."

Actually, Snyder himself was born in San Francisco. "My parents were extremely poor—The Depression," he says. "So they went back to Seattle, my father's home town, and got a tar-paper shack and an acre of stumpland out north of town. Over the years, my father built the place up, fenced it, got another acre, fixed the house, built a barn and got cows and chickens. I was brought up a farmboy with chickens to feed and a milk route to our neighbors. My mother was, and is, a very high-strung, neurotic person with literary ambitions, and farm life and poverty wore her down. But she got me onto books and poetry at the age of five. When I was seven, I burned my feet badly while burning brush, and for four months couldn't walk. So my folks brought me piles of books from the Seattle public library and it was then I really learned to read and from that time on was voracious—I figure that accident changed my life. At the end of four months, I had read more than most kids do by the time they're eighteen. And I didn't stop. I was hung up on American Indians and nature all through childhood and hated civilization for having [screwed up] the Indians, as described in Ernest Thompson Seton's book of the Woodcraft Indians, my bible at eleven, and for ruining the woods and soil—which I could see going on all about me.

"So when I say I am anarchist today and don't have much use for Western culture, I guess it goes pretty far back. I spent most of my spare time as a kid in the woods around our place and, feeling at home there, always felt uncomfortable when we went into Seattle. In high school—we had moved to Portland on account of the war—I took to spending my summers in the Cascade mountains and did a lot of real mountaineering—glaciers and all that—Mount Hood, Baker, Rainier, Shasta, Adams, St. Helens, etc., and skied in the winters. Ran around with a gang of ex-ski-troopers; we called ourselves the *Wolken-schiebers*. My parents—and grandparents—were radicals and atheists, so when I got a chance to go to Reed College on a scholarship, I took it. With scholarships and odd jobs and greatly enjoyed tricks of living on nothing, I made it through college, making it summertime by trail-crew and logging and labor jobs. And in the summer of 1948, I hitched to New York and worked on a ship to South America. I had to wait until I got the ship and I was broke in New York. For a couple of days I panhandled and slept on park benches, while roaming through Greenwich Village.

"I was very Marxist in college, but couldn't make it with the regular Commie bunch because of my individualistic, bohemian, anarchist tendencies, all much looked down upon. Of course, being the only real member of the proletariat in the bunch of them, the others being upper middle class New York kids as a rule, they really couldn't say much. I took anthropology—Indians—and literature at Reed and got much involved with primitive religion, mythology, and primitive literature—song, ritual, dance—and at about the same time was beginning to read Far Eastern history and Chinese poetry. I was married for about six months then and my left-wing wife didn't dig this sudden interest in Oriental philosophy and Shoshone folktales.

"Out of college, I spent the summer of 1951 as a log-scaler on an Indian Reservation, where I dug the Berry Feast and later made up the poem about it, and then went on a long hike in the Olympic Mountains. Up in the mountains, all the notions that had been swarming in my head crystallized and sort of hung there until the fall of that year I picked up a copy of D. T. Suzuki, writing about Zen, and read it while hitch-hiking to a graduate fellowship in anthropology at Indiana. It finished the job, and although I stayed one semester at Indiana, I was through with the academic world and headed back West in '52 for what proved to be five years of mountain jobs, scenes in San Francisco, Chinese language study, writing poetry and so on, until I first came to Japan. Then I was at sea on a tanker for eight months, in San Francisco, and back in Japan again. I love to roam around and I like tough self-discipline, I don't mind hard work and being poor never bothered me. I guess that's what makes it possible to carry on like I do. Being free doesn't mean evading necessity, it means outsmarting it."

Snyder's emergence from the soil of America shows, of course, to what extent the roots of the Beat Generation are buried there. Whether by the romanticism which is another root or the realism which is still another, he has become a symbol of the fellaheen man that Kerouac keeps referring to—the farmers who give hitchhikers lifts in the rattletrap trucks that are the latter-day prairie schooners of the West, the Negroes who share their Saturday night wine in the bottle gangs of small-town alleys, the cowboys who spend the week telling about their weekend love rites that are sometimes grossly overstated if not overrated, the Mexicans who always offer a part of the nothing they have, sometimes no more than vermin hospitality and sometimes marijuana by candlelight. To Kerouac, as to other Beats, the fellaheen man, the man of the soil, the man of the great serf class, is creating his own culture. "Jack got that from Spengler," Snyder explains. "But Spengler applies it to mean a vast body of men without traditions, like they were dropped into history by a trick wave. The fellaheen man has no tradition behind him and no values and he just picks up on comic books. And there he is."

Snyder doesn't necessarily agree with the concept of the fellaheen man in its entirety and especially not with his own involvement as a symbol, but he does insist that Western culture is being overthrown by a cultural evolution either of the non-white races or influenced by them. "Of course, it's more realized out on the West Coast, where the people are closer to the Oriental and American Indian aspect," he says. And yet, Snyder's own poetry, although reflecting, as might be expected, this Oriental and American Indian aspect (as if the American Indian were a foreigner, anyway), also reflects, as might be expected, too, his attachment to the soil. Sometimes, in fact, he sounds as if he is to the Northwest what Robert Frost was to the Northeast. In the title poem of his book *Riprap*, which he defines as "a cobble of stone laid on steep slick rock to make a trail for horses in the mountains," Snyder writes for example:

Lay down these words
Before your mind like rocks.
    placed solid, by hands
In choice of place, set
Before the body of the mind
    in space and time:
Solidity of bark, leaf, or wall
    riprap of things:
Cobble of milky way,
    straying planets,
These poems, people,
    lost ponies with
Dragging saddles
    and rocky sure-foot trails.
The worlds like an endless
    four-dimensional
Game of *Go*.
    ants and pebbles
In the thin loam, each rock a word
    a creek-washed stone
Granite: ingrained
    with torment of fire and weight
Crystal and sediment linked hot
    all change, in thoughts,
As well as things.

Probably it was inevitable that Snyder, the farmboy bringing his culture to the city, should meet with Kerouac and Ginsberg, the city boys in search, among other things, of rural America. "I could tell right away that his poetry was good," recalls Ginsberg, describing their meeting in 1955 at Berkeley, California, where Snyder lived in a shack, one of the many in his life. "I'd expected to find him writing poetry that *rhymed*, but as soon as he took it out to show me I could see from the way the lines were spaced out that he knew what he was doing." Until then, Snyder's almost sole companion had been Philip Whalen, whom Snyder had met at Reed College and who, like Snyder, was also a poet of the back woods. The Warren Coughlin of *The Dharma Bums*, in which Kerouac describes him as "a hundred and eighty pounds of poet meat," Whalen had come from Portland but had made his home in the entire Northwest, not going, perhaps, to the lumberjack extremes of Snyder but working as a forest lookout in the solitude of the Cascade mountain peaks and, more recently, as a bailiff for a country judge, traveling the circuit of an endless Oregon county. "The Sierras are more spectacular than the Cascades, but the tourists have ruined them," complains Whalen, who has shared views with Snyder as well as viewpoints. "Everywhere you go in the Sierras, you find tin cans." Inducted, willingly or not, into the Beat Generation, Whalen, too, has become one of its major poets, living, often in San Francisco. "I wrote poetry in total isolation for ten years with only Whalen to talk to," Snyder recalls, but the advent of Kerouac and Ginsberg has, of course, lessened his isolation. There is a question, nevertheless, of whether they have proved as strong an influence on him as he on them: Kerouac, for his part, has written: "But I can't recreate the exact (will try) brilliance of all Japhy's answers and come-backs and come-ons with which he had me on pins and needles all the time and did eventually stick something in my crystal head that made me change my plans in life." As for Ginsberg, it was Snyder who persuaded him to abandon any last hope of gaining wisdom from the academic world and to give up the graduate courses he had been taking at the University of California. A short time later, Ginsberg completed "Howl," the poem which has been both hailed and damned as the manifesto of the Beat Generation.

"Actually, Allen and I were very close, too," says Snyder commenting on how his friendship with Kerouac was portrayed in *The Dharma Bums*. "Well, Jack has a funny ambivalence toward Ginsberg. He says that Allen is really the devil. You know, Kerouac's mother won't let Ginsberg into the house. That's really so. She says that he's a bad influence. And Kerouac, when he's home, won't let Ginsberg come either because he says, 'It makes my mother mad.' But Allen and I had a very exciting relationship, actually, and when we hitchhiked up to the Northwest we fought all the way. We argued constantly because his urban, what seems to me sort of sentimental thing, was very different from my stony mountain outlook at that time. I'd say: 'All right, Ginsberg, read your Howl to them mountains and trees and see if you can make them cry and take their clothes off. You've got to face up to them, too.' That was in February of '56, and he read "Howl" at the University of Washington and I read my poems and then we also read them at Reed College during that little hitchhiking tour. And we managed to stir up both of the schools into quite a storm, which got them going on what was going on in San Francisco. And the interest still hasn't died down up there.

"There were several times that Allen took his clothes off. Once he did it at some poetry gathering in Venice West and he walked around a put his arm around a little old lady. Another time, at a party, Kenneth Rexroth was lying beneath a table talking to somebody and stark naked Allen Ginsberg flung himself down on Rexroth and kissed him and said, 'I love you, Rexroth!' Allen was kidding, of course, and Rexroth kidded him back. Rexroth said, *'Get off me, you naked fairy!'* But there was a while there when we did go around taking our clothes off at parties. It was simply to shake up the scene, but we had to quit doing that because everybody began to expect it of us. One night Ginsberg and I went uninvited to a students' party in Berkeley— it was just a bunch of students in the English department and a couple of faculty members—we went totally uninvited, stripped off all our clothing and marched around in there. They were too damn well bred to throw us out, but they hated it. Ginsberg would go up and put his arm around these people and say, 'Don't you want to be naked and face us all the way you were born? Don't you love yourself?'"

The informality of both the parties and the party dress was, of course, well documented in *The Dharma Bums*, which, incidentally, also introduced another experience in nakedness to the reading public, Yabyum. And if the Greeks didn't have a word for it, the Romans did. " . . . Don't you know about yabyum, Smith?" Japhy asks in the book, arriving at the author's house with a girl named Princess. Whereupon the author, Kerouac, adds, " . . . couldn't believe my eyes when I saw Japhy and Alvah taking their clothes off and throwing them every which way and I looked and Princess was stark naked, her skin white as snow when the red sun hits it at dusk . . . 'Here's what yabyum is, Smith,' said Japhy, and he sat crosslegged on the floor and motioned to Princess, who came over and sat down on him facing him with her arms about his neck and they sat like that saying nothing for a while . . .

'This is what they do in the temples of Tibet. It's a holy ceremony, it's done just like this in front of chanting priests. People pray and recite Om Mani Pahdme Hum, which means Amen the Thunderbolt in the Dark Void. I'm the thunderbolt and Princess is the dark void, you see.'. . . Finally Japhy's legs began to hurt and they just tumbled over on the mattress where both Alvah and Japhy began to explore the territory. I still couldn't believe it. 'Take your clothes off and join in, Smith!'"

"Jack made me out to be quite a lover in the book, which is not so," Snyder insists with some excess of modesty, even if *The Dharma Bums* is supposed to be a novel. "It's a sort of strange feeling to be a hero of a book. People expect all sorts of things from you." In any event, Snyder seems to have been as much at home amid the Princesses and other eager femininity of San Francisco's North Beach as he was in the lonely barrenness of his wood stove shack halfway up a California mountain across the Golden Gate Bridge, or, for that matter, as he is in Japan. "The trouble with those North Beach girls," he says, "is they want—really—the security and family scene of middle class types but aren't willing to give in and make the compromises necessary for such a scene, playing a real female role and so on." And yet, Snyder has married one of them, Joanne Kyger, an admiral's daughter, who is also a poetess of some merit, at least in Snyder's opinion, and who belonged, it turns out, to an ephemeral group of San Francisco poets organized into the so-called "Dharma Committee," the by-laws of which contained a proviso limiting membership to persons who have not been able to get past page forty-six of *The Dharma Bums*.

"Well, I'm not the marrying kind, in the legal sense," Snyder comments. "I believe in the ritual and the witness of one's friends, but I wouldn't bother to register such a union with the state, in the US—it ain't their business. In Japan I imagine it would be convenient—passport and visa problems—to make it legal as well."

Snyder's new wife will have to put up with more than Shoshone folk tales. The obvious delight of a Japanese house in the country, where Snyder now lives, with a garden, strawberries and a well, somehow loses a bit of its obviousness with the Zen fate that has situated him there. "It isn't all fun," he says. "I have to get up at three every morning to go see my Zen master and tell him what I think about my koan and must spend three more hours every day meditating on it if I'm going to have any answer at all."

During the weeks of *Sesshin*, or "concentrating the mind," the routine at Daitohu Temple is even more demanding, and certainly even more demanding than a wife. With time marked by the dings and clangs of assorted bells and by the carbine-sounding whacks of one hardwood block upon another, the student Zen monks make their way through hours as austere as the cold temple mats on which they sleep, but hours that are also rich in thought, however enforced. In a continuum of ceremonies, the students file from one task to another, chant *sutras*, meditate in unison, or rush to kneel before the sanzen room in which the Zen master occasionally commemorates the answers they give to their koans with a menacing growl or a blow with a stick. "Zazen is a very tight thing."

Rooted as he is in America's soil, Snyder has flowered into Zen Buddhism through his own personal synthesis, but the process, mysterious as it is, is being duplicated elsewhere more and more, even if not in so perfect a form. "My parents—they're divorced now, my mother works for a newspaper— well, they were atheists and their parents were atheists before them," Snyder says. "I guess somewhere way back in the family, a hundred years or so ago, we must have been Lutherans. But my sister and I grew up in a tradition of no religion at all." Snyder's sister is Thea Snyder Bama, a small, young and beautiful woman with long, red-golden hair, who once was a fashion model in New York but who gave up her career, her husband and his fortune to return to San Francisco, where, the girlfriend of a scholarly longshoreman, she lives in a suburban Bohemia in Mill Valley, participating often in little theater productions and walking some nights through the streets of North Beach, arm-in-arm with her man and singing Hebrew liturgies in a flawless, mournful soprano. "I became a Zen Buddhist," he explains, "and my sister converted to Judaism."

Perhaps the search for spiritual experience which characterizes the Beat Generation, propelling some toward Buddhism, some toward Zen Buddhism and others toward other religions, is no more than the quintessence of one of the new cultural eruptions which characterizes our entire age and which, in its more popular forms, has provided Billy Graham with audiences as astronomical as his assumed sponsor, has inflated church memberships and masonry, has prompted boards of education to institute classroom Bible readings in defiance of the cultural eruptions of generations ago, and has encouraged state legislatures to enact new Sunday closing laws, creating some consternation among those other religions, also renascent, which observe the Sabbath on other days. Cultural eruptions, however, are never really quite as simple as that, and Snyder, who believes along with other Beat personages, that another cultural eruption of our age has come about in the assaying of culture itself, places the responsibility for the advent of Zen in America in all directions.

"Sociologically, the popularity of Zen in America is a manifestation of the growing influence of the non-white races, but so is the interest in any other non-Occidental tradition," Snyder insists, adding, incidentally, that he thinks cultural anthropology has become to this generation what Freud was to the twenties. "We're being besieged on all sides by non-Occidental things in art and philosophy and cultural objects, like even the eating of rice with chopsticks. The history of Zen in the West is very complicated and goes clear back to the 1890s. If you put it all in its perspective, it would be a big, complicated thing. But the essential part of it is that Suzuki, in the twenties, published these books which were read around and had some small influence, and then, in the forties, they were reprinted in England and they were read, widely. No the reason that they were read and the reason that they were picked up on is something else. That was part of the individualist, and anarchistic, and personalistic, and also religious interest that intellectuals picked up on after the war and a reaction against the idea that society and human beings can be changed by political means. Also, there are a lot of things in Zen that seem to tie in with the theories of the automatic psychologists, which are widely read. Karen Horney was influenced by Suzuki and practically all the others, like Erich Fromm, and so that's the literary thing behind it. Now why people pick up on Zen is a deeply personal thing for me. And the Zen that is moving to America is going to undercut Suzuki entirely because he's not an accurate representative of Zen. There are really no good books on Zen in European languages and Suzuki, from whom the others derive, actually knows very little traditional Zen practice and is a sloppy thinker to boot. Suzuki had very little Zen training, and, in his books over-stresses *satori*, or enlightenment, and gives no picture of the actual practice and time involved for a real Zen Buddhist. Kerouac? Jack doesn't know anything about Zen. He came onto it by reading the Sacred Books of the East series. I deeply respect Jack's insights in Buddhism, and I think they are very valid, but this is simply some of the American Buddhism as it's practiced. It's not the same as mine."

When he talks about Zen like this, his face loses its mountain grin, the friendliness evaporates from his eyes, leaving behind only their intensity, and he quits the countrified intonations that otherwise exaggerate his speech. He sits erect in his chair, often folding his legs beneath him in the half-lotus position and sometimes leaning forward only slightly with sparse, open-handed gestures to emphasize his arguments. Sometimes he picks on his beard, which grows like wisdom itself, framing him in the picture of the Oriental mystic that a number of his companions consider him to be, never saying a wrong thing or making an insignificant move. "I enjoy my beard," he says, gravely, but with mischievous whimsy, too. "Beards come out of your face, and it's just another thing that you can experiment with and enjoy having, cutting it different ways, letting it grow. Just to amuse you. I can't understand why people don't grow beards, really. A beard is an emblem of your rank and role like a mandarin's long fingernails. It shows that you don't do respectable work; it's a class thing—a mandarin had long, long fingernails because he didn't do manual labor, he was a scholar and that was a sign of his caste. I mean, with a beard, it shows that you don't have to go to an office." He tells of his "Small satoris"—"I've had several at various times in my life, but 'Great Satori,' the real enlightenment, I ain't had that yet." And of enlightenment below decks, in the engine room of a tanker, eight months without sunlight: "I needed a ship to get back to the States from Japan and I guess they needed someone pretty bad, too. I should have been suspicious when I signed up and I asked the exec how much time the ship had left at sea. 'Not much, not much,' he said, but it wasn't until we were underway that I found out it was eight months. Anyway, I made enough on that job to buy a little car, just a heap to get me between Mill Valley and San Francisco, and to live off for a year." He is sinewy of a height somewhere between medium and doughty and he wears the clothes of his ruggedness—a young man who doesn't remember owning a suit or any other garment that he didn't buy good-and-cheap and good-and-used at the Good Will store.

"Beat to me," he says, "means the state of mind people get into when they have gone down and been as far down and out and depressed and miserable as they possibly could get and discover that it isn't so bad as they think, so nothing worries them anymore. And so they can be gay about things because they aren't afraid of not making it because they've seen how bad it is and it isn't nearly as bad as the fear of it. As for the Beat Generation, well that applies to a few people only. As far as I'm concerned, it only exists in this period among a certain type of intellectual, creative person that has rejected attitudes of striving after success and prestige and is no longer trying to make it in the academies but still has a great concern with creative activity. It involves voluntary poverty and a decision to stay out of the mess and mix-up of advertising agencies and universities and all that bit and trying to make it being poor, if necessary, but trying to create and be yourself as best you can. No, we can't afford leather jackets.

"When Jack first started using the word *beat*, I said, 'Well, sure, that must mean me,' because I was thinking about the life I had led being poor and I mean really being poor, and I have been as poor as anybody can be in this country and continue to exist and then dug it. Hitchhiking, working on all kinds of jobs, riding on railroads and being around all kinds of hoboes and bums and not making a romantic thing out of it because it was of necessity, but at the same time not feeling that I was bugged and not feeling that I was wasting my life and that my creative, intellectual talents were being thrown away because I was digging it. And that's what beat means to me."

And then he adds:

"Aww, I'm too young to be in a book. And besides, I'm just getting warmed up. Wait about twenty-five years."

He's Living a Life of Zen and Poetry

Monique Benoit / 1964

San Francisco Chronicle (June 11, 1964), 29. Reprinted by permission of the *San Francisco Chronicle*.

Gary Snyder carefully put down the black cloth bag he was carrying.

"What do you have in that bag?" I asked with my usual curiosity.

"Everything I need," replied the poet.

"Notebooks and poetry. Actually it is a Buddhist bag. The monks carry everything in it including their razor.

"And you see this little side pocket? It's a fan pocket: monks use one all the time."

Gary recently came back from Japan where he spent the last three years. He had lived there before for five years as a lay monk in a temple.

"Are you back permanently?"

"No. I plan to return there next year. Actually I would prefer living in India or here, but my teacher is in Kyoto."

"Your teacher? What are you studying?"

"I keep working on Zen Buddhism."

"What do you mean by 'working on'? Do you plan to spend your life studying this philosophy?"

"I am not spending my life. I am 'living' it, and this is my way of doing it," explained Gary.

"There are several kinds of Zen Buddhism. The one I am interested in is not intellectual or philosophical, it is strictly intuitive. You have to solve riddles."

"Excuse my stupidity, but I don't quite understand," I said, thinking Gary was speaking in riddles.

"I'll give you an example. A student goes to his master and asks 'What is Zen?'

The master replies: 'You see that cypress tree at the bottom of the garden? That is Zen.'

Then the student must find the answer to this riddle."

"Have you found the answer?" I asked, hoping he'd let me in on the secret.

"No, I am still working on this one," replied Gary with a smile.

A native of San Francisco, Gary attended the University of California and studied anthropology.

It was during that time that he discovered Zen and decided to go and live in Japan to study it. After working for a while on a ranch and in forests, he left for the first time.

He spent the first year studying Japanese, which he speaks fluently, so he could participate in the teachings of Zen.

"What do you do in Japan?"

"Every day, I go to see my teacher, usually around five in the morning, then I go home, have breakfast, write poetry, work in the garden, meditate or talk with people."

"I don't suppose you are married. This life doesn't seem compatible with domesticity."

"I was, but am now separated. As a husband I am quite reliable and a good provider.

"A woman may have to do a lot of camping with me, but I'll see that she always has a sleeping bag, and if it rains I'll build a fire to keep her warm."

"Still it takes money to live. How do you manage?"

"I take jobs when I need money. I was a seaman for six months before coming back. I also do poetry readings and get paid for it."

Gary will have his next poetry reading tomorrow at the Longshoremen's Hall. In the fall he will teach poetry at the University of California. He has been writing since the age of five, and has had two volumes published. This summer, Gary will go mountain climbing.

"Are you a hermit?"

"No. Actually, I like people and enjoy talking with them. Since I came back I find it a little difficult to relate to women, though."

"Maybe you understand Oriental women better?"

"No, there is little to understand or talk about with the Japanese women. I prefer Western ones. They have a strength that is refreshing."

Maybe Gary's problem is not that he doesn't relate to women. Maybe it is hard for women to relate to him.

Interview with Gary Snyder

Anonymous / 1965

Ananke 4, no. 2 (May 1965), 6–13. Copyright Arizona Board of Regents for the University of Arizona.

Gary Snyder was born in San Francisco in 1930 and raised near Seattle. After his graduation from Reed College, where he majored in cultural anthropology, he did graduate work in anthropology at the University of Indiana, and in Chinese at the University of California. He is widely known for his association with the San Francisco poetry movement of the mid–1950's. Japhy Ryder, the hero of Jack Kerouac's *The Dharma Bums*, is based on Gary Snyder. Since 1956 he has spent much of his time in Japan, where he went to study formal Zen training. He is now teaching, for a year, at Berkeley.

In explaining himself, he said, "As a poet, I hold the most archaic values on earth. They go back to the Paleolithic: the fertility of the soil, the magic of animals, the power-vision in solitude, the terrifying initiation and rebirth, the love and ecstasy of the dance, the common work of the tribe."

Anonymous: The San Francisco movement of the mid-fifties was often thought of as a reaction against intellectualism. Do you think this is true?
Gary Snyder: Some of them were and some weren't. Ginsberg, in a sense, was reacting against his own intellectualism. And I suppose that is pretty much what it was, because we were all pretty much intellectuals. At the same time, more than being just a reaction, I think there really was a valid sense of new possibilities. That sense of it, for me and for the people I know personally, has continued to grow, in such a way that it is not necessary to make it that kind of revolt anymore. If you know where you stand, it's very easy to go back to books. All of us are reading now, but with our own sense of what we want to do, not being led around the nose by a library.

Anonymous: Some people who know you have described you as a revolutionist. What kind of revolution are you interested in?

Snyder: Like a lot of other people I know, I am very interested in the possibilities of radical social transformation, not only through allowing people to explore their own consciousness, but by the possibilities of radically altering all of our sexual attitudes and our family structure, by being permissive in the whole sexual area in ways which have not yet been imagined in this country. I am very much interested in the implications, for example, of polygamy and polyandry and group marriage as possible ways for people to live. And actually, in California, a lot of people are virtually living that way. There are families that are full of children from different families, different fathers, with different relations, different names. The whole traditional family structure has been breaking down in all sorts of interesting ways, and I take a positive view of it.

There seems to be a strong drift in our society toward a new system of family relationships. The whole drift in our society for the past three hundred years has been toward wider and wider concepts of sexual freedom, of sexual permissiveness. Most people do not have enough imagination to see where this will lead. They just say, "I can't see where it will stop." And the thing is, it won't stop. It will very possibly flip over into a possibility, a legal possibility, of people contracting marriages in any form they want to contract them. There is no reason why, within our own particular constitutional setup, it would not be possible for you to go down to the courthouse with three other people and get married, or five other people, or any combination you like. All that is needed, and I think this is very likely coming, although this is a very eccentric sounding idea, is that we move into matrilineal descent, you know, the name descending in the female line. Once we get back to matrilineal descent, dozens of things will alter, which aren't immediately apparent. But it would change a number of relationships.

As Engels pointed out, in a very interesting but little known book called *The Origins of Family, Private Property, and the State*, accumulation and transmission of wealth is possible only when you worry about problems like bastardy, and wealth is passed down in the male line. But if you have a system where the concept of the legitimate heir is impossible because all heirs are equally legitimate, that is to say, all the children of a woman are equally her children, the question of legitimacy never develops because the question of who the father is is irrelevant. In this kind of system, every generation redistributes its wealth. This does not imply matriarchy, which is something else. It does imply a different set of relationships within the family, a different set of power-and wealth-distributing patterns.

Anonymous: Do you feel that this system would be more natural than the one we have had?

Snyder: Put it this way: most of our problems come out of one or another forms of repression, and this could be a way in which human beings would be in more of a one to one relationship with themselves. They wouldn't have that interior split that some people suffer, partly because, as Freud pointed out, there is an enormous drive in everyone for multiple sexual experiences, which they at some point learn to repress, learn to think of as irresponsible, if not downright wrong. In the modern world it has come out in the open in a creepy way, in a sort of imaginary sex life of billboard advertising and consumer transformations. Sex drives are exploited to make you buy things. And there is a whole world of the drug, the novel, and moving pictures which give surrogate satisfaction to this. And this whole thing would be cut off at the roots, a whole edifice of illusion would immediately be wiped out if people were in a position to do whatever they wanted to do once in a while.

Anonymous: There is an increase in what seems to be unrepressed sex in modern poetry, for example, in Ginsberg. But how is this different from the surrogate sex in novels that you were talking about?

Snyder: Well, "unrepressed" sex doesn't necessarily mean unrepressed. We wouldn't talk about it if we were doing it. These people are still in the curious position of subconsciously verbalizing it. This is the point at which we are now, winning the right to verbalize it. The next step would be to put certain things into practice so that we would no longer have to verbalize it, and then we would be able to return more to poetry.

Anonymous: Is this perhaps why you do not write so much about sex, because you have gone beyond it in your own life?

Snyder: Perhaps that is part of it. Actually, this has not so much to do with poetry as it does with politics. I mean really revolutionary moral politics, say, of our future for the next two hundred years. You see, I was trained up in anthropology, and I tend to take a somewhat longer-range, anthropological view of social movements. And at the moment, what is revolutionary is not in ideology. What is revolutionary is the consciousness implications of racial integration, for example, the changes in peoples' ways of thinking that this gradually implies. Because, of course, racial integration does really mean intermarriage. And everybody in the South that says that this is going to lead to intermarriage, man, they know what they're talking about.

So, in that sense, the "sexual revolution" and the "civil rights revolution" and the "narcotics-hallucinogenics-marijuana revolution" are all the most significant things happening now, to my mind. They are much deeper than just intellectual-political changes, they are real changes in people's whole approach to life. Toynbee once said that it is very hard to estimate how great the changes will be on the Arabic world when they begin to drink alcohol. Whereas, man, the reverse is true. It was very naïve of him to say that. They're not drinking more. The real changes that are curious to see coming are as something like marijuana spreads out of the Islamic-Arabic world or the Mexican-Indian world into our white consciousness, which is an alcohol consciousness.

Anonymous: The pleasures of our culture are all relatively contained for the sake of civilization. Do you think the culture, as it is now, could stand this kind of individual liberation?

Snyder: I don't think that anything worthwhile is built by repression and frustration. I don't know what you mean by civilization. I don't think this is a particularly civilized situation. On the other hand, it is of some uses to us, in some senses. But nothing stands to be lost, finally.

Anonymous: Do you feel that, for many people, the risk of asking them to go beyond this kind of minimal life may be too much?

Snyder: What actually happens, and probably will always happen, is that those who want to take risks will take them, and those who do not want to will find safe niches to sit in. I'm not proposing that you will ever live in a situation where everybody is forced to go out and run all the risks. I am just suggesting that it should be left open to people that want to be more experimental or adventurous in exploring all of their potentialities. In Milton's essay "Areopagitica," he says something that is very significant. He says that God would prefer that ten men go to hell if one man can grow thereby. That is the kind of risk that we have to be able to run. Let ten beatniks commit suicide or become addicts if one young beatnik turns into something pretty great. That's my attitude. And the risks are real, of course. Right now, especially. A lot of people do fall by the wayside. But they may just as well fall by the wayside while running the risks in the Bay area as hiding in a split-level suburban house.

The real risk in individualism, the real risk, is being made into an ego-maniac. The real razor's edge that you have to walk when you are concerned with the Socratic maxim "know thyself," is that you know yourself in the wrong way. You come to see yourself in very limited ego-terms. Whereas, as the Buddhists say, "When you discover yourself, you discover that there is no self." And that is ultimately a very moral discovery. Without having any ethical rules laid down for you, you find that you are enough of everything and everybody that you can naturally and silently lead a harmonious way of life, rather than a life of extreme self-expression, artificial self-expression, which causes pain and discomfort for others.

Anonymous: What about particular, personal relations, like friendship and love, under these conditions?

Snyder: Everything I am thinking of would, among other things, make it possible for people to love each other more. The less you fear, the more you love, obviously. Love between two people is one of the most exciting and insight-causing types of relationships. In fact, the closest that people in our society now ever get to existential, spiritual insights, to real self-examination, is in periods of romantic and marital crisis. Like when some real estate broker is breaking up with his wife and she is going off with his two kids, that is the time, for maybe two or three months, when he will really examine his life.

Romantic love and sex are very important to us now because they are some of the few conditions under which people feel real, in what is otherwise a pretty ersatz existence, where nothing ever touches you very closely. That is the way we are living today. We very seldom see sickness, death or old age, and we very seldom are really in pain or really in danger. Nor do we feel the seasons go by. But love is one place where we are brought down to our flesh and emotions. That is another reason why we make such a big surrogate thing of it. Had we more danger and more reality, on all levels, surrogate love and surrogate sex would be less important.

There are lots of terms to love, but the most exciting term, to my mind, is when you get not only self-knowledge but knowledge of others. And that is very exciting to conceive of, because that is really when the Socratic and Buddhist idea of knowing yourself, and of being enlightened in yourself, becomes transferable. Then it becomes a possibility of mutual enlightenment. Which is, you know, how great.

To take it a step farther, mutual enlightenment has been possible not only with a girl, but with another man, not by sexual activities but by a meeting of minds, and then possible with trees and animals. And with the whole universe. That's when it really becomes the total world in mutual interaction, which is love in the highest sense.

Anonymous: You have said that you write with your body. What does that mean?

Snyder: I don't know how to verbalize it, except to say that it is simply a sensation of wholeness and oneness. It is the sensation of what I think I do. What my body feels is what I feel. That is very different from a sense of being a mind up here, separated from a body which is someplace else. While writing, it is a sense of rightness, as when you dive into water properly and feel the rightness of the way you have dived. And there is a sense of rightness in all kinds of physical things, especially things that you learn, like tennis or playing an instrument or writing poetry.

Anonymous: Is this a part of your ideas about projective verse?

Snyder: Yes, I don't know if it is Olson's ideas, but it's my ideas. I don't know if our ideas differ or not. I may be taking things where Olson implied them, but didn't articulate them, or it may be that I am taking them in a direction a little different. But it is so clearly implied in Olson when he says, "The center is the belly. The breath is the line. You breathe through your belly. And you write from the belly." Well, in physiological-neurological terms, as I translate that, it means writing and thinking with a complete body-mind consciousness, with a feeling of rightness and solidness that runs through the whole body, not playing with a dance of intellect only.

One of my poems is about doing a lot of little chores and jobs around the house. It is very close to what I am thinking of in a very obvious way, of the act and the thought being together. And, in that sense, the act is pervaded by mindfulness. For example, there is a body-mind dualism if I am sweeping the floor and thinking about Hegel. But if I am sweeping the floor and thinking about sweeping the floor, I am all one. And that is not trivial, nor is the sensation of it trivial. Sweeping the floor becomes, then, the most important thing in the world. Which it is.

Anonymous: Does this work to make the poem a part of you, so that your body and mind and your poem are one?

Snyder: That's the way I feel it. It can't be intellectually defended , but that is the feeling I have, and that is when I get the solidest kind of writing going. It just doesn't stop anywhere. It's all one piece.

My first start in this direction was at the same time I began writing all the poems I consider worthwhile. That was when I was working for a trail crew up in Yosemite Park. I found myself doing three months of hard, physical labor, out in the trails every day, living more or less in isolation, twenty-five miles from the nearest road. We never went out. We just stayed in there working on those trails week after week. At the beginning, I found myself straining against it, trying to exercise my mind as I usually exercise it. I was reading Milton, and I had some other reading, and I was trying to go out on the trails during the day and think about things in a serious intellectual way, while doing my work. And it was frustrating, although I had done the same thing before, on many jobs. Finally, I gave up trying to carry on an intellectual interior life separate from the work, and I said the hell with it, I'll just work. And instead of losing something, I got something much greater. By just working, I found myself being completely there, having the whole mountains inside of me, and finally having a whole language inside of me that became one with the rocks and with the trees. And that was where I first learned the possibility of being one with what you were doing, and not losing anything of the mind thereby.

Anonymous: Did it matter then how good the job was that you were doing, how well you worked?
Snyder: I did a good job. And the job was all I was doing. And it was great.

The Houseboat Summit: Changes

Alan Watts, Gary Snyder, Timothy Leary, and Allen Ginsberg / 1967

San Francisco Oracle 1, no. 7, (April, 1967), from *San Francisco Oracle Facsimile Edition*, 150–51, 154–56, 160–61, 163–65, 177. Reprinted by permission of Ann Cohen.

Alan Watts: . . . Look then, we're going to discuss where it's going . . . the whole problem of whether to drop out or take over.

Timothy Leary: Or anything in between, sure.

Watts: Or anything in between, sure.

Leary: Cop out . . . drop in . . .

Gary Snyder: I see it as the problem about whether or not to throw all your energies to the subculture or try to maintain some communication within the main culture.

Watts: Yes. All right. Now look . . . I would like to make a preliminary announcement so that it has a certain coherence. This is Alan Watts speaking, and I'm this evening, on my ferry boat, the host to a fascinating party sponsored by the *San Francisco Oracle*, which is our new underground paper, far-outer than any far-out that has yet been seen. And we have here, members of the staff of the *Oracle*. We have Allen Ginsberg, poet, and rabbinic sadhu. We have Timothy Leary, about whom nothing needs to be said (laughs). And Gary Snyder, also poet, Zen monk, and old friend of many years.

Allen Ginsberg: This swami wants you to introduce him in Berkeley. He's going to have a Kirtan to sanctify the peace movement. So what I said is, he ought to invite Jerry Rubin and Mario Savio, and his co-horts. And he said: "Great, great, great!" So I said, "Why don't you invite the Hell's Angels, too?" And he said: "Great, great, great! When are we gonna get hold of them?" So I think that's one next feature . . .

Watts: You know, what is being said here, isn't it: To sanctify the peace movement is to take the violence out of it.

Ginsberg: Well, to point attention to its root nature, which is desire for peace, which is equivalent to the goals of all the wisdom schools and all the Saddhanas.

Watts: Yes, but it isn't so until sanctified. That is to say, I have found in practice that nothing is more violent than peace movements. You know, when you get a pacifist on the rampage, nobody can be more emotionally bound and intolerant and full of hatred.

And I think this is the thing that many of us understand in common, that we are trying to take moral violence out of all those efforts that are being made to bring human beings into a harmonious relationship.

Ginsberg: Now, how much of that did the peace movement people in Berkeley realize?

Watts: I don't think they realize it at all. I think they're still working on the basis of moral violence, just as Gandhi was.

Ginsberg: Yeah . . . I went last night and turned on with Mario Savio. Two nights ago . . . aafter I finished and was talking with him, and he doesn't turn on very much . . . this was maybe the third or fourth time. He was describing his efforts in terms of the motive power for large mass movements. He felt one of the things that move large crowds was righteousness, moral outrage, and ANGER . . . righteous anger.

Leary: Well, let's stop right here. The implication of that statement is: we want a mass movement. Mass movements make no sense to me, and I want no part of mass movements. I think this is the error that the leftist activists are making. I see them as young men with menopausal minds. They are repeating the same dreary quarrels and conflicts for power of the thirties and forties, of the trade union movement, of Trotskyism and so forth. I think they should be sanctified, drop out, find their own center, turn on, and above all avoid mass movements, mass leadership, mass followers. I see that there is a great difference—I see complete incompatible difference—between the leftist activist movement and the psychedelic religious movement.

In the first place, the psychedelic movement, I think, is much more numerous. But it doesn't express itself as noisily. I think there are different goals. I think that the activists want power. They talk about student power. This shocks me, and alienates my spiritual sensitivities. Of course, there is a great deal of difference in method. The psychedelic movement, the spiritual seeker movement, or whatever you want to call it, expresses itself . . . as the Haight-Ashbury group had done . . . with flowers and chants and pictures and beads and acts of beauty and harmony . . . sweeping the streets. That sort of thing.

Watts: And giving away free food.

Leary: Yes . . . I think this point must be made straight away, but because we are both looked upon with disfavor by the Establishment, this tendency to group the two together . . . I think that such confusion can only lead to disillusion and hard feelings on someone's part. So, I'd like to lay this down as a premise right at the beginning.

Ginsberg: Well, of course, that's the same premise they lay down, that there is an irreconcilable split. Only, their stereotype of the psychedelic movement is that it's just sort of like the opposite . . . I think you're presenting a stereotype of them.

Snyder: I think that you have to look at this historically, and there's no doubt that the historical roots of the revolutionary movements and the historical roots of this spiritual movement are identical. This is something that has been going on since the Neolithic as a strain in human history, and one which has been consistently, on one level or another, opposed to the collectivism of civilization toward the rigidities of the city states and city temples. Christian utopianism is behind Marxism.

Leary: They're outs and they want in.

Snyder: . . . but historically it arrives from a utopian and essentially religious drive. The early revolutionary political movements in Europe have this utopian strain in them. Then Marxism finally becomes a separate, non-religious movement, but only very late. That utopian strain runs right through it all along. So that we do share this . . .

Ginsberg: What are the early utopian texts? What are the early mystical utopian political texts?

Snyder: Political?

Ginsberg: Yeah. Are you running your mind back through Bakunin or something?

Snyder: I'm running it back to earlier people. To Fourier, and stuff.

Watts: Well, it goes back to the seventeenth century and the movements in Flemish and German mysticism, which started up the whole idea of democracy in England in the seventeenth century. You have the Anabaptists, the Levellers, the Brothers of the Free Spirit . . .

Snyder: The Diggers!

Watts: The Diggers, and all those people, and then eventually the Quakers. This was the source. It was, in a way, a secularization of mysticism.

In other words, the mystical doctrine that all men are equal in the sight of God, for the simple reason that they ARE God. They're all God's incarnations.

When that doctrine is secularized, it becomes a parody . . . that all men are equally inferior. And therefore may be evil-treated by the bureaucrats and the police, with no manners.

The whole tendency of this equalization of man in the nineteenth century is a result, in a way, of Freud. But the absolute recipe for writing a best seller biography was to take some person who was renowned for his virtue and probity, and to show, after all, that everything was scurrilous and low down.

You see? This became the parody. Because the point that I am making—this may seem to be a little bit of a diversion, but the actual point is this: Whenever the insights one derives from mystical vision become politically active, they always create their own opposite. They create a parody.

Wouldn't you agree with that, Tim? I mean, this is the point I think you're saying: that when we try to force a vision upon the world, and say that everybody ought to have this, and it's GOOD for you, then a parody of it is set up. As it was historically when this vision was forced upon the West, that all men are equal in the sight of God and so on and so forth . . . it became bureaucratic democracy, which is that all people are equally inferior.

Snyder: Well, my answer to what Tim was saying there is that, it seems to me at least, in left-wing politics there are certain elements, and there are always going to be certain people who are motivated by the same thing I'm motivated by.

And I don't want to reject the history, or the sacrifices of the people in that movement . . . if they can be brought around to what I would consider a more profound vision of themselves, and a more profound vision of themselves and society . . .

Leary: I think we should get them to drop out, turn on, and tune in.

Ginsberg: Yeah, but they don't know what that means even.

Leary: I know it. No politician, left or right, young or old, knows what we mean by that.

Ginsberg: Precisely what do you mean by drop-out, then . . . again, for the millionth time?

Snyder: Drop out throws me a little bit, Tim. Because it's assumed we're dropping out. The next step is, now what are we doing where we're in something else? We're in a new society. We're in the seeds of a new society.

Ginsberg: For instance, you haven't dropped out, Tim. You dropped out of your job as a psychology teacher in Harvard. Now, what you've dropped into is, one: a highly complicated series of arrangements for lecturing and for putting on the festival . . .

Leary: Well, I'm dropped out of that.

Ginsberg: But you're not dropped out of the very highly complicated legal constitutional appeal, which you feel a sentimental regard for, as I do. You haven't dropped out of being the financial provider for Millbrook, and you haven't dropped out of planning and conducting community organization and participating in it.

And that community organization is related to the national community, too. Either through the Supreme Court, or through the very existence of the dollar that is exchanged for you to pay your lawyers, or to take money to pay your lawyers in the theatre. So you can't drop out, like DROP OUT, 'cause you haven't.

Leary: Well, let me explain . . .

Ginsberg: So they think you mean like, drop out, like go live on Haight-Ashbury Street and do nothing at all. Even if you can do something like build furniture and sell it, or give it away in barter with somebody else.

Leary: You have to drop out in a group. You drop out in a small tribal group.

Snyder: Well, you drop out one by one, but . . . you know, you can join the sub-culture.

Ginsberg: Maybe it's: "Drop out of what?"

Watts: Gary, I think that you have something to say here. Because you, to me, are one of the most fantastically capable drop-out people I have ever met. I think, at this point, you should say a word or two about your own experience of how to live on nothing. How to get by in life economically.

This is the nitty-gritty. This is where it really comes down to in many people's minds. Where's the bread going to come from if everybody drops out? Now, you know expertly where it's gonna come from—living a life of integrity and not being involved in a commute-necktie-strangle scene.

Snyder: Well, this isn't news to anybody, but ten or fifteen years ago when we dropped out, there wasn't a community. There wasn't anybody who was going to take care of you at all. You were really completely on your own.

What it meant was, cutting down on your desires and cutting down on your needs to an absolute minimum; and it also meant, don't be a bit fussy about how you work or what you do for a living.

That meant doing any kind of work. Strawberry picking, carpenter, laborer, longshore . . . well, longshore is hard to get into. It paid very well. Shipping out . . . that also pays very well.

But at least in my time, it meant being willing to do any goddam kind of labor that came your way, and not being fussy about it.

And it meant cultivating the virtue of patience—the patience of sticking with a shitty job long enough to win the bread that you needed to have some more leisure, which meant more freedom to do more things that you wanted to do. And mastering all kinds of techniques of living really cheap.

Like getting free rice off the docks, because the loading trucks sometimes fork the rice sacks, and spill little piles of rice on the docks which are usually thrown away.

But I had it worked out with some of the guards down on the docks that they would gather fifteen or twenty-five pounds of rice for me, and also tea . . . I'd pick it up once a week off the docks, and then I'd take it around and give it to friends. This was rice that was going to be thrown away, otherwise. Techniques like that.

Watts: Second day vegetables from the supermarket . . .

Snyder: Yeah, we used to go around at one or two in the morning, around the Safeways and Piggly Wigglies in Berkeley, with a shopping bag, and hit the garbage cans out in back. We'd get Chinese cabbage, lots of broccoli and artichokes that were thrown out because they didn't look sellable anymore.

So, I never bought any vegetables for the three years I was a graduate student at Berkeley. When I ate meat, it was usually horsemeat from the pet store, because they don't have a law that permits them to sell horsemeat for human consumption in California like they do in Oregon.

Ginsberg: You make a delicious horse meat sukiyaki. (laughter)

Watts: Well, I want to add this, Gary, that during the time you were living this way, I visited you on occasion, and you had a little hut way up on the hillside of Homestead Valley in Mill Valley and I want to say, for the record, that this was one of the most beautiful pads I ever saw. It was sweet and clean, and it had a very, very good smell to the whole thing. You were living what I consider to be a very noble life.

Now, then, the question that next arises, if this is the way of being a successful drop-out, which I think is true, can you have a wife and child under such circumstances?

Snyder: Yeah, I think you can, sure.

Watts: What about when the state forces you to send the child to school?

Snyder: You send it to school.

Leary: Oh no, c'mon, I don't see this as drop-out at all.

Snyder: I want to finish what I was going to say. That's the way it was ten years ago.

Today, there is a huge community. When any kid drops out today, he's got a subculture to go fall into. He's got a place to go where there'll be friends, and people that will put him up and people that will feed him—at least for a while—and keep feeding him indefinitely, if he moves around from pad to pad.
Leary: That's just stage one. The value of the Lower East Side, or of the district in Seattle or the Haight-Ashbury, is that it provides a first launching pad.

Everyone that's caught inside a television set of props, and made of actors . . . the first thing that you have to do is completely detach yourself from anything inside the plastic, robot Establishment. The next step—for many people—could well be a place like Haight-Ashbury. There they will find spiritual teachers, there they will find friends, lovers, wives . . .

But that must be seen clearly as a way station. I don't think the Haight-Ashbury district—any city, for that matter—is a place where the new tribal . . .
Snyder: I agree with you. Not in the city.
Leary: . . . is going to live. So, I mean DROP OUT! I don't want to be misinterpreted. I'm dropping out . . . step by step.

Millbrook, by the way, is a tribal community. We're getting closer and closer to the landing . . . We're working out our way of import and export with the planet. We consider ourselves a tribe of mutants. Just like all the little tribes of Indians were. We happen to have our little area there, and we have to come to terms with the white men around us.
Snyder: Now look . . . Your drop-out line is fine for all those other people out there, you know, that's what you've got to say to them. But, I want to hear what you're building. What are you making?
Leary: What are we building?
Snyder: Yeah, what are you building? I want to hear your views on that. Now, it's agreed we're dropping out, and there are techniques to do it. Now, what next! Where are we going now? What kind of society are we going to be in?
Leary: I'm making the prediction that thousands of groups will just look around the fake-prop-television-set American society, and just open one of those doors. When you open the doors, they don't lead you in, they lead you *out* into the Garden of Eden . . . which is the planet.

Then you find yourself a little tribe wandering around. As soon as enough people do this—young people do this—it'll bring about an incredible change in the consciousness of this country, and of the Western world.
Ginsberg: Well, that is happening actually . . .

Leary: Yeah, but . . .

Snyder: But that Garden of Eden is full of old rubber truck tires and tin cans, right now, you know.

Leary: Parts of it are . . . Each group that drops out has got to use its two billion years of cellular equipment to answer those questions: "Hey, how we gonna eat? Oh, there's no more paycheck, there's no more fellowship from the university! How we gonna eat? How we gonna keep warm? How we gonna defend ourselves? How we gonna eat? How we gonna keep warm?"

Those are exactly the questions that cellular animals and tribal groups have been asking for thousands of years. Each group is going to have to depend upon its turned on, psychedelic creativity and each group of . . .

I can envision ten M.I.T. scientists, with their families, they've taken LSD . . . They've wondered about the insane-robot-television show of M.I.T. They drop out.

They may get a little farm out in Lexington, near Boston. They may use their creativity to make some new kinds of machines that will turn people on instead of bomb them. Every little group has to do what every little group has done throughout history.

Snyder: No, they can't do what they've done through history. What is very important here is, besides taking acid, is that people learn the techniques which have been forgotten. That they learn new structures, new techniques. Like, you just can't go out and grow vegetables, man. You've gotta learn *how* to do it. Like we've gotta learn to do a lot of things we've forgotten to do.

Leary: I agree.

*

Voice from Audience: Let me throw in a word . . . the word is evil and technology. Somehow they come together, and when there is an increase in technology and technological facility, there is an increase in what we usually call human evil.

Snyder: I wouldn't agree with that . . . no, there's all kinds of non-evil technologies. Like, neolithic obsidian flaking is technology.

VFA: But in its advanced state it produces evil.

Watts: Yes, but what you mean, I think, is this: When you go back to the great myths about the origin of evil, actually the Hebrew words which say good and evil as the knowledge of good and evil being the result of eating the fruit of the tree of knowledge . . . these words mean advantageous and disadvantageous and they're words connected with technical skills. And the whole idea is this, which you find reflected in the Taoist philosophy that the moment you start interfering in the course of nature with a mind that is centered and one-pointed, and analyzes everything, and breaks it down into bits . . . the moment you do that you lost contact with your original know-how . . . by means of which you now color your eyes, breathe, and beat your heart. For thousands of years mankind has lost touch with his original intelligence, and he has been absolutely fascinated by this kind of political, god-like, controlling intelligence . . . where you can go ptt-ptt-ptt-ptt . . . and analyze things all over the place, and he has forgotten to trust his own organism. Now the whole thing is that everything is coming to be realized today. Not only through people who take psychedelics, but also through many scientists. They're realizing that this linear kind of intelligence cannot keep up with the course of nature. It can only solve trivial problems when the big problems happen too fast to be thought about in that way. So, those of us who are in some way or other—through psychedelics, through meditation, through what have you—are getting back to being able to trust our original intelligence . . . are suggesting an entirely new course for the development of civilization.

Snyder: Well, it happens that civilization develops with the emergence of a class structure. A class structure can't survive, or can't put across its principle, and expect people to accept it . . . if they believe in themselves. If they believe, individually, one by one, that they are in some way godlike, or Buddha like, or potentially illuminati. So it's almost ingrained in civilization, and Freud said this, you know "Civilization as a Neurosis," that part of the nature of civilization is that it must PUT DOWN the potential of every individual development.

This is the difference between that kind of society which we call civilized, and that much more ancient kind of society, which is still viable and still survives, and which we call primitive. In which everybody is potentially a chief and which everybody . . . like the Comanche or the Sioux . . . EVERYBODY in the whole culture . . . was expected to go out and have a vision one time in his life. In other words, to leave the society to have some transcendental experience, to have a song and a totem come to him which he need tell no one, ever—and then come back and live with this double knowledge in society.

Watts: In other words, through his having had his own isolation, his own loneliness, and his own vision, he knows that the game rules of society are fundamentally an illusion.

Snyder: The society not only permits that, the society is built on it . . .

Watts: Is built on that, right!

Snyder: And everybody has one side of his nature that has been out of it.

Watts: That society is strong and viable which recognizes its own provisionality.

Snyder: And no one who ever came into contact with the Plains Indians didn't think they were men! Every record of American Indians from the cavalry, the pioneers, the missionaries, the Spaniards . . . say that every one of these people was men. In fact, I learned sòmething just the other day. Talking about the Yurok Indians, an early explorer up there commented on their fantastic self-confidence. He said, " . . . Every Indian has this fantastic self-confidence. And they laugh at me," he said, "they laugh at me and they say: Aren't you sorry you're not an Indian? Poor wretched Indians!" (laughs) this fellow said.

Well, that is because every one of them has gone out and had this vision experience . . . has been completely alone with himself, and face to face with himself . . . and has contacted powers outside of what anything the society could give him, and society expects him to contact powers outside of society . . . in those cultures.

Watts: Yes, every healthy culture does. Every healthy culture provides for there being non-joiners. Sanyassi, hermits, drop-outs too . . . every healthy society has to tolerate this . . .

Snyder: A society like the Comanche or the Sioux demands that everybody go out there and have this vision, and incorporates and ritualizes it within the culture. Then a society like India, a step more civilized, permits some individuals to have these visions, but doesn't demand it of everyone. And then later it becomes purely eccentric.

Leary: We often wonder why some people are more ready to drop out than others. It may be explained by the theory of reincarnation. The people that don't want to drop out can't conceive of living on this planet outside the prop television studio, are just unlucky enough to have been born into this sort of thing . . . maybe the first or second time. They're still entranced by all of the manmade props. But there's no question that we should consider how more and more people, who are ready to drop out, can drop out.

Watts: If there is value in being a drop-out . . . that is to say, being an outsider . . . You can only appreciate and realize this value, if there are in contrast with you insiders and squares. The two are mutually supportive.

Leary: Yeah, if someone says to me, "I just can't conceive of dropping out . . ." I can say, "Well, you're having fun with this go around . . . fine! We've all done it many times in the past."

Ginsberg: The whole thing is too big because it doesn't say drop out of WHAT precisely. What everybody is dealing with is people, it's not dealing with institutions. It's dealing with them but also dealing with people. Working with and including the police.

Snyder: If you're going to talk this way you have to able to specifically say to somebody in Wichita, Kansas who says, "I'm going to drop out. How do you advise me to stay living around here in this area which I like?"

Leary: Let's be less historical now for awhile and let's be very practical about ways in which people who want to find the tribal way . . . How can they do it . . . what do you tell them?

Snyder: Well, this is what I've been telling kids all over Michigan and Kansas. For example, I tell them first of all: "Do you want to live here, or do you want to go someplace else?"

Leary: Good!

Snyder: All right, say I want to stay where I am. I say, okay, get in touch with the Indian culture here. Find out what was here before. Find out what the mythologies were. Find out what the local deities were. You can get all of this out of books. Go and look at your local archaeological sites. Pay a reverent visit to the local American Indian tombs, and also the tombs of the early American settlers. Find out what your original ecology was. Is it short grass prairie, or long grass prairie here? Go out and live on the land for a while. Set up a tent and camp out and watch the land and get a sense of what the climate here is. Because, since you've been living in a house all your life, you probably don't know what the climate is.

Leary: Beautiful.

Snyder: Then decide how you want to make your living here. Do you want to be a farmer, or do you want to be a hunter and food gatherer? You know, start from the ground up, and you can do it in any part of this country today . . . cities and all . . . For this continent I took it back to the Indians. Find out what the Indians were up to in your own area. Whether it's Utah, or Kansas, or New Jersey.

Leary: That is a stroke of cellular revelation and genius, Gary. That's one of the wisest things I've heard anyone say in years. Exactly how it should be done. I do see the need for transitions, though, and you say that there will be city people as well as country people and mountain people . . . I would suggest that for the next year or two or three, which are gonna be nervous, transitional, mutational years—where things are gonna happen very fast, by the way—the transition could be facilitated if every city set up little meditation rooms, little shrine rooms, where the people in transition, dropping out, could meet and meditate together. It's already happening at the Psychedelic Shop, it's happening in New York. I see no reason though why there should be ten or fifteen or twenty such places in San Francisco.

Snyder: There already are.

Leary: I know, but let's encourage that. I was just in Seattle and I was urging the people there. Hundreds of them crowd into coffee shops, and there is this beautiful energy. They are liberated people, these kids, but they don't know where to go. They don't need leadership, but they need, I think, a variety of suggestions from people who have thought about this, giving them the options to move in any direction. The different meditation rooms can have different styles. One can be Zen, one can be macrobiotic, one can be bhakti chanting, one can be rock and roll psychedelic, one can be lights. If we learn anything from our cells, we learn that God delights in variety. The more of these we can encourage, people would meet in these places, and AUTOMATICALLY tribal groups would develop and new matings would occur, and the city would be seen for many as transitional . . . and they get started. They may save up a little money, and then they head out and find the Indian totem wherever they go.

Snyder: Well, the Indian totem is right under your ground in the city, is right under your feet. Just like when you become initiated into the Haineph pueblo, which is near Albuquerque, you learn the magic geography of your region; and part of that means going to the center of Albuquerque and being told: There is a spring here at a certain street, and its name is such and such. And that's in a street corner in downtown Albuquerque. But they have that geography intact, you know. They haven't forgotten it. Long after Albuquerque is gone, somebody'll be coming here, saying there's a spring here and it'll be there, probably.

Leary: Tremont Street in Boston means "three hills."

Ginsberg: There's a stream under Greenwich Village.

*

Watts: Let's get back to a fundamental thing. I think that what you are really—all of you—are having the courage to say is that, the absolutely primary thing is that there be a change of consciousness in the individual: that he escape from the hallucination that he is a separate ego in an alien universe and that we all come to realize, primarily, that each one of us is the whole works.

Each one of us is what is real and has been real for always and always and always and will ever be . . .

And although the time language may not be appropriate there, nevertheless, we are that, and to the extent that it can't be spread around. That's what
you and I are, and we lose our anxieties and we lose our terror of death, and
our own unimportance.

That this is the absolutely essential ingredient, which if we get hold of
that point, all the rest will be added unto you, in the sense of, "Seek you first
the kingdom of God and all these things shall be added to you."
Snyder: Right.
Watts: Isn't that what you're saying? I mean, isn't that absolutely basic?
And even if this is only realized among a statistical minority (crash in back-
ground of photographer falling into woman's lap) minority of people.
Leary: That's a tender sight.
Watts: Even if this is only realized by a statistical minority, nevertheless, it's
IMMENSELY powerful.
Leary: It affects consciousness.
Watts: It affects everybody.
Leary: I would add to practical step number two that more celebrations be
set up all over . . . more Be-Ins . . . that April twenty-first, the solstice, be a
nice time to try to arrange—in as many cities as possible, because that'll be
spring in the northern cities where it's hard to have a . . .

And one thing I've learned is that all of these experiences should be out
of doors . . . what about April twenty-first?
Snyder: Yeah, sure.
Watts: And in Central Park, hah!
Snyder: . . . and then in July with the Indians in New Mexico—the big gath-
ering of the tribes.

It just occurred to me, the practical details . . . The mode of it is something
like the Maha-lila. Like, you're asking, how's it going to work?

Well, now, the Maha-lila is a group of about three different families who
have sort of pooled their resources, none of which are very great. But they
have decided to play together and to work together and to take care of each
other and that means all of them have ways of getting a small amount of
bread, which they share. And other people contribute a little money when it
comes in. And then they work together on creative projects . . . like they're
working together on a light show right now for a poetry reading that we're
going to give. And they consider themselves a kind of extended family or
clan. When they went to the Be-In, they had a banner which said Maha-lila.
Like, that was their CLAN banner.
Leary: Yeah, I saw that . . . that's the model.

Snyder: That's the model . . . and the model for the time is that breaking out of the smaller family organization we work in slightly larger structures, like clan structures, in which people do work at various jobs and bring in whatever bread they can from various jobs. But they're willing to pool it and share it and they learn how to work and play together. Then they relate that to a larger sense of the tribe, which is also loose . . . but for the time being everybody has to be able—from time to time—to do some little job.

But, the reference is . . . The thing that makes it different is . . . that you don't bring it home to a very tight individual or one monogamous family unit, but you bring it home to a slightly larger unit where the sharing is greater. I think that's where it starts.

Leary: The extended family is the key.

Snyder: The extended family is, I think, where it starts. And my own particular hobby horse on this is that the extended family leads to matrilineal descent and when we get matrilineal descent—then we'll have group marriage, and when we have group marriage we'll have the economy licked.

Because with the group marriage . . . capitalism is doomed and civilization goes out (laughter).

Leary: Practical step number three (laughter) which I would like to see . . . I would like to suggest that June twenty-first, which is the summer solstice, we try to have an enormous series of Be-Ins in which . . .

Ginsberg: June twenty-first?

Snyder: The summer solstice.

Leary: April twenty first we have Be-Ins in different cities.

Watts: No, March the twenty first is the spring . . .

Snyder: The equinox is on March twenty-first, solstice is June twenty-first.

Ginsberg: What's an equinox?

Snyder: That's when the nights and days are equal.

Leary: Wherever I said April, I want to take that back. I should have said March.

Ginsberg: Solstice?

Watts: The sun's standing still at Xmas and midsummer . . .

Snyder: Midsummer's night. I think we should encourage extended families everywhere.

Watts: Well, it's very practical to encourage extended families because the present mode of the family is a hopeless breakdown. Because, first of all, the family is an agrarian cultural institution, which is not suited to an urban culture.

All the family consists in a dormitory . . . where a wife and children are located, and the husband, who engages in a mysterious activity in an office or a factory, in which neither the wife nor the children have any part nor interest . . . From which he brings home an abstraction called money. And where there are lots of pretty secretaries in the scene in which he actually works.

And so, they have no relation whatsoever to what he does, and furthermore, the awful thing about the family, as it exists at the moment, is that the husband and the wife both feel guilty about not bringing up their children properly, and therefore they live for their children.

Instead of living out their own lives and doing their own interesting work in which the children would automatically become interested as participants and, watchers on the side.

As it is, they were doing everything, they say. We live, we work, we earn our money for you darlings, and these poor darlings feel all these things thrown at them and they don't know what to do with it.

And then they are sent away to school, shrilled off to school as Dylan Thomas put it, to be educated for everything and nothing.

Leary: By strangers.

Watts: By strangers.

Leary: Who are of dubious . . . ahh. . . .

Watts: Who would teach them all sorts of purely. . . .

Leary: . . . moral, intellectual and sexual characteristics.

Watts: Right (laughter) Abstract formulations and things they'll learn, and . . . the family has no reality.

And the greatest institution today in the American family is the babysitter. Someone just to take the children out of our consciousness while we enjoy ourselves.

VFA: And the DEATH sitter, to take the old people out of our consciousness . . . and even DEATH has been taken from the people.

Watts: And the DEATH sitter, exactly . . . the courtesy of the mortician, yes . . . a good death is no longer possible, practically . . .

Snyder: I have a four stage thing . . . uh, American Indian technologies.

Watts: Practical now . . .

Snyder: . . . meditation centers, group marriage, and periodical gatherings of the tribes.

Leary: I don't agree with group marriage . . . We are a tribal people. You cannot have infidelity in a tribe. Infidelity . . . ah, sexual freedom.

Snyder: Infidelity is defined as going outside the tribe.

Leary: . . . is anonymous, impersonal, anthill sexuality. Every woman . . .

Snyder: Now, wait a minute.

Leary: Let me finish . . . every woman is all women. If you can't find all women in one woman it's YOUR problem. Infidelity cannot be tolerated in a tribal, seed carrying . . .

Ginsberg: Who's tolerating!

Snyder: Infidelity is defined as living outside . . . .

Ginsberg: We're talking infidelity. What about homosexuality? We're . . . (laughter)

Snyder: . . . is living outside the areas of your commitments, Tim. Anthropologically . . . and actually. . . .

Ginsberg: What's going to happen to me?

Leary: You're going to have nine children.

Ginsberg: What if I don't want them?

Leary: You told me you wanted to . . .

Ginsberg: Sometimes, but not always . . .

Snyder: No, here's what I was driving at . . . uh . . . Tim

Ginsberg: But you're a Catholic . . . or something . . . (laughter)

Snyder: Let me say this . . . let me answer what he said there, Allen. (laughter)

Leary: I'm an Irish Catholic . . . may I have the wine, please? (laughter)

Ginsberg: What Mario Savio said . . . (chuckling)

Leary: What?

Ginsberg: That you were an Irish Catholic . . . (laughter)

Leary: Well, the Celts, of course, have . . . a long history of . . .

Ginsberg: What should Mario Savio do?

Snyder: I don't know.

Leary: Drop out, turn on, and tune in.

Watts: I think, Tim . . . you're being a little acceptive here. I do think it's possible for some of us to have found all women in one woman . . .

Snyder: I want to get back at something . . . Just let me say something with him . . . Infidelity means denying your commitments. Now if your commitments are within a group marriage, then fidelity is being true within your group marriage. And infidelity is being untrue or dishonest outside of that.

Now there are some cultures in South America in which all forms of marriage are permitted. There are group marriages, polyandrous marriages, polygamous marriages, AND monogamous marriages.

Watts: By group marriages . . . just a moment, let's get a question of definition here.

Snyder: Okay. A group marriage is where, a number of people—as a group—whatever the number is, announce . . . a marriage is a social announcement of commitment . . . announce that we will be responsible for the children we produce and for each other.

Watts: Now, in other words, all males and all females in this group can be in mutual intercourse with each other?

Snyder: But not outside the group.

Ginsberg: You make rules to take care of that. You gotta bring in . . .

Snyder: I'm not making rules. I'm just telling you what the anthropological precedences are in these things.

It happens that in this South American culture that the majority of the marriages are monogamous, but it also happens that there are some polyandrous, some polygamous, and a few group ones.

I think that what we can allow is people to combine in whatever combinations they wish.

Leary: Oh, I would certainly agree with that.

VFA: Can I illustrate that? If my old lady wants to fuck anybody in the room here it's alright with me, but if she fucks uh . . . J. Edgar Hoover, I'm going to get very upset. (laughter)

Snyder: She should get a prize. She'd be doing something for the nation, baby.

Leary: Yes, he'd be making love, not war. (laughter)

Watts: Well, you're simply saying that if she does that she's not at all the sort of person you thought she was. And that you've been deceived.

Snyder: What you're saying is endogamy. Within the tribe is okay, but outside the tribe . . .

Ginsberg: Why make rules?

Female VFA: I don't think it's possible, in the first place, for anybody's old lady to fuck J. Edgar Hoover.

VFA: That may be the problem!

Watts: Oh, that question is academic (laughter).

Snyder: But I wasn't . . . you know, like your idea of fidelity . . . fidelity is perfectly reasonable, but fidelity simply means: in terms of the areas of commitment you've established for yourself.

Leary: That is a beautiful . . . a beautiful model . . . and I think it requires a little consciousness, which I hope will come quickly to the human race, Gary.

Snyder: I think we've had it.

Watts: No, but I don't . . . I don't think that you should talk about . . . when people, just as Lao-tzu said, when the great Tao was lost there came talk of duty to man and right conduct, and so when the essential idea of love is lost there comes talk of fidelity.

That actually, the only possible basis for two beings—male and female—to relate to each other is to grant each other total freedom . . . and say, I don't put any bonds on you, you don't put any bonds on me because I want you, I love you THE WAY YOU ARE! And I want you to be that . . .

The minute you start making contracts and bonds and signing on the dotted line, you are WRECKING the whole relationship. And you just have to trust to the fact that human beings should be legally allowed to trust each other, and to enter into a fellowship that does not involve a contractual arrangement.

Leary: I think we all agree with that.

Watts: You know, because if you don't do that, YOU KILL IT!

Snyder: In primitive cultures marriage is not a contractual arrangement, it's a public announcement.

Watts: Yes!

Snyder: It's a relationship which is made public.

Leary: What was your fourth point, Gary?

Snyder: Occasional gatherings of the tribe . . . tribes! That wasn't a point . . . it was an activity.

Say rather than group marriage, extended families. Extended cooperation structures, in other words. American Indian technologies, meditation centers, extended cooperative clan type or extended family type structures with much more permissiveness in the nature of the family structure than is permitted, say, in Judeo-Christian tradition, and gatherings of the larger tribes periodically.

Gary Snyder

Dan Kozlovsky / 1970

Modine Gunch 3, 1970, 21–25. Reprinted by permission of Dan Kozlovsky.

On November 9, Gary Snyder visited Madison. Snyder is a poet and ecologist as well as an authority on anthropology and Zen Buddhism. He gave a fine reading in the Union and later participated in a discussion with UW faculty member Dan Kozlovsky (DK) and a small audience (A). The following is a shortened version of that discussion. At least two of Snyder's books are published by New Directions—*The Back Country* and *Earth House Hold.*

Gary Snyder: You can find out right away where anybody's head is by asking them, "What do you think the optimum population of the world would be?" In a sense, everything revolves from that.

Dan Kozlovsky: Half of what we have today?

GS: Maybe one tenth. To know the logic of that would indicate a person has thought it through. Otherwise they're saying, "Let's not grow anymore or let's try to slow down the birthrate or use hydroponics." That's all bullshit.

DK: One thing I try to show my ecology students is that we are already farming hydroponically. You see, the top soil in many parts of Wisconsin is gone. You get off the land just what fertilizers you put on it. There is no residual actual fertility in the soil anymore. Hydroponics is no real solution.

Audience: Boulding brings that out in one of his essays. Twenty-five percent of all the people that ever lived are alive today and ninety percent of all scientists are alive. But it appears that science is incapable or doesn't give a damn.

GS: Well, scientists say they don't know what to do. The public are the only ones that think science is going to solve things. It is an interesting commentary on the state of our culture that practically everybody on the street believes with blind faith that science will solve it. And it's going to be an enormous rude sudden shock when the public as a whole realizes that science isn't going to solve it. There'll be a real anxiety hysteria when people realize that something else may happen. It'll be like the death of God over again.

DK: A rapidly increasing proportion of our people are moving into urban environments. How can you teach ecology to anyone who lives eleven stories off the ground? It's possible, I think, to spend four years here as an undergraduate at the University of Wisconsin and never have your feet off the asphalt or concrete.

GS: Maybe I'm a pessimist but I think everyone going to the cities is one of these days going to be all choked up. They're going to wither on the vine. The cities are a lost cause, and the people who go to the cities are a lost cause along with it.

DK: We have all sorts of hotshot landscape architects and city planners that are going to prevent the deterioration of the cities by building many, many more cities. The plan is, before the year 2000, 110 new cities will be built in the US, ten of which will have more than one million and one hundred of which will be somewhere in the neighborhood of one hundred thousand.

GS: Anybody who plans things like that is of the nature of the enemy.

DK: The point is, it will either be that or the deterioration of the existing cities.

GS: It would be better that the existing cities simply deteriorated. I think that absolutely no plans should be made for future population growth. What is important is not providing for future population, what is important is keeping what we've got in terms of open space, soil wilderness, animal population, soil and water.

DK: Suppose that the conditions became so atrocious that we wake up one morning and three hundred thousand people in Chicago have choked to death. I don't think it will teach anybody any sort of lesson. We can afford to lose one hundred million people and it won't change the price of coffee in the Rathskeller one nickel.

GS: There is an exceedingly large number of young people who are very concerned about this sort of thing. And that's the sort of concern that can be educated to put some things in practice. I can only think of the old IWW slogan "Forming a new society within the shell of the old" and there's a lot of the old society that we can't hope to shore up and save so we let it fall.

I've talked to people who say we have the power to destroy the city. You can't believe that? The city has the capability of destroying itself. You destroy their water supply, the main routes of communication, and transportation going in and out their electrical system and then you just sit and wait. Right away their toilets don't flush and their garbage piles up.

DK: But we're not talking about guerilla warfare.

GS: Listen, that's just what we are talking about. Let's quit skirting around it. Everyone says that the problem is terrible and nothing can be done. What it comes down to finally is either we have complete totalitarianism, clamping down on the whole planet trying to manage things one way or another, or we have some kind of total chaos. I'm afraid the totalitarian protection of the planet's resources would be too political. It wouldn't be benevolent. The commitment of government is to growth, technology and civilization. Civilization is ultimately the enemy. The very order of the society that we have lived in for the last four thousand years has outlived its usefulness. At the moment I think a breakdown would be better than over-organization.

DK: I've argued with people to the effect that we need a violent revolution, but you can also make a case for that fact that it would be ecologically horrendous. The society we have now is making a real bloody mess, but it's possible to make a worse one.

GS: I only see chaos as a transitional thing. I don't see any ultimate chaos. Eventually nature will reassume its balances and I think man has a chance to end up in harmony with that balance. What I mean by chaos is the possibility that the technological thing will simply overload itself and break down. The machinery that we are dependent on might choke itself with garbage. It would be good for the soil and animals if people were thrown back on a lower level of economy. The whole revolutionary push and rhetorical intention has to be redefined in terms of ecology. The Marxist commitment to progress and industry is a reactionary commitment. There will be a change of consciousness in the younger people forcing us to redefine the expectation of the revolution. We must redefine justice and human rights to mean justice and natural rights. The revolution must be a revolution for bison too. It's unfortunate that Marx didn't take Malthus more seriously. The whole socialist movement has a rather unconsidered anti-population control bias and it has slowed down China fifteen years. Only in the last three years has China admitted there's a population problem.

People trying to live in communes are on the right track especially if they really have to get in and learn how the land works. The fact that they're doing it right now on marginal land, the land that agri-business has withdrawn from because it's not productive in capitalist terms means that they're having to learn all the finer details of farming that belong to real agriculture. There's an adaption in that that has definite survival value. And there's survival in the astonishing interest that people have out in the west in the American Indian technology. For example, I know of a number of people, myself included, who would prefer to be nonviolent if possible. If we were to read out a scenario of the country people with food and the city people without food and the city people swarming out and the country people having to defend their food supplies—the only way you can put yourself in that scenario without having to resort to violence is to voluntarily choose to live in any area of such low subsistence value that no one would come and compete with you for it. Your special knowledge and skill would remove you from competition. That would be to choose to live in the Great Basin or northern Nevada. You could keep your honor that way at least. It's amazing how many people are fascinated by jack-rabbit technology and lizards.

DK: If we take those who are genuinely concerned about the way human population is relating to its environment and stick them in communes then they're not solving the problem.
GS: Those people are part of the solution and part of the problem.

DK: No, no. They deliberately extract themselves from the main problem.
GS: That's the solution.

DK: That's a solution for themselves and not the general populace.
GS: There is no solution for the general populace. The only solutions offered are on the order of massive baling wire up to the point where finally it doesn't hold together or fear some totalitarianism will exist where you have to fill out a form months in advance if you want to have a baby. Some of the people who are going off to live in communes are very conscious of this type of thing and they don't consider what they're doing a withdrawal or retreat, but they consider it the establishment of a base camp from which to make forays—educational, political, confrontational—or ultimately as guerillas. For better or for worse, flower power is dead.

A: To what degree are communes organized on the West Coast?

GS: There isn't any total organization. Within themselves it depends entirely on the outfit. They try everything. Somebody like Black Bear on the forks of the Salmon in northern California, where they have a completely chaotic or anarchist premise and they have a lot of trouble getting the dishes washed. At the other end of it is Tassajara, which is the training school for the Zen Center in San Francisco, in the Los Padres National Forest. At Tassajara there's always about fifty people and they live an extraordinarily ordered life following the pattern of Zen monasteries. Men and women with kids are there, and they're up every morning at four a.m. meditating for two hours. And then there's all kinds of ranges in between, but I would say that the commonest model would be a combined economic base with a certain amount of local farming, local work, sawmill work, or whatever money you can make locally plus a certain amount of cash inflow from the outside of which dope trading is a big element. A lot of money there, many communes partially support themselves in dope running about which they feel no moralistic qualms because it's just grass and acid, hashish, and things like that.

There's usually a great interest in whatever the local Indians were up to in the past. So they do a lot of hunting but with an Indian kind of sense to it. They do a lot of things like tanning their own hides. There's a ranch in northern Marin that eats venison twice a month at least and it's all deer that have been killed alongside the highway. They've got their guts to the point where they won't let a dead deer on the highway go by. Even if it's a little old they'll skin it, clean it, hang it, and eat it. They consider that very righteous since they let nothing go to waste. Another kind of organization is the thirteen communes in San Francisco, all of them in old buildings, that own three pickup trucks jointly that make a daily run to meatpacking plants and bakeries and they get surplus, waste, and throwaway food which is redistributed. They live entirely off the waste.

There was an extraordinary thing in the newspaper a couple of weeks ago. In the Eureka Valley-Death Valley region which is a vast unoccupied area, the sheriff departments with the aid of helicopters had finally rounded up a band of twenty nomads, and women, who had been living for several years in that region with stolen jeeps and dune buggies living entirely by stealing. They had children and families, and the adults were practically naked, they just wore loincloths. They kept their pursuers at bay for months by making false camps and raiding auto campgrounds. They'd been living that way for about three years. They weren't intellectuals or hippies or anything like that. They were weird spin-offs from L.A. This may not be a solution to the general problems but it is a symptom of alternative possibilities. There will probably be a transitional period in which there will be predatory tribes living off the remnants of civilization.

A: What are the forms of communication between these people?
GS: They have little mimeographed newsletters that they send around to one another. And they get together for three or four days of camping someplace and talk and then split again. There are a lot of couriers.

A: Tell me something about the stability of these communes. I'm under the impression that they're increasingly more together.
GS: We should qualify this thing about communes. There aren't very many things that you would really call communes. That is to say, they're really large and trying to do something communistic. These are rare and are having lots of problems.

There's an intermediary thing beginning to develop which is probably more realistic and more hopeful. That is, lots of smaller situations wherein two or three households are combining their energies and living in a communal way in the country keeping in contact with a wider circle of people. The big communes are very difficult but a dozen people, which is the practical size of a hunting band, can develop something together that is very workable. I always have about eight people in my household. There are certain people who are stable and are always there. We have all the privacy we want but at the same time it's very practical for babysitting and cooking. It's best for the women. My wife is not saddled with all the work of child-raising, so she's able to sit zazen in the mornings with us instead of having to cook breakfast and change the baby's diapers. It's a very convenient and functional thing and also very educational. Now instead of talking about communes we should talk about the broader thing that's taking place. That's the gradual shift in the attitudes towards marriage, and life styles of all sorts. The commune is part of the transformation of marriage into something else.

A: What sort of things do you see happening to it?
GS: Well, I think monogamy is gradually being phased out, being replaced by a looser more permissive monogamy plus occasional group, polyandrous, or polygamous marriage. Various types of combinations will come to be accepted. With children from various liaisons under one roof, there is a tendency toward matrilineal descent, which is one of the natural and simple

ways of solving a child's surname—he is always the child of his mother. Legitimacy is a completely illusory concept. Our attitudes towards nature are deeply involved with our attitudes towards women. The patriarchal male oriented female subordinated family system or social organization comes with an attitude of exploitedness towards nature who is no longer the mother. There are hopeful indications that are moving towards a reverence for the feminine which may mean reverence for nature. I believe this strongly enough to try and put it into practice in my own spheres.

A: What about the birthrate in groups like this? It would seem to me that if you had this loose sort of organization you could have a smaller number of children per female but have everyone experience what it's like and participate in child-rearing.

GS: Precisely! In a thing called "The Four Changes" which I wrote with some people from Ecology Action—I'll be sending some copies to the Whole Earth Co-op when they're printed—in this we talk about population, pollution, consumption, and transformation. We ask what can be done in social-political action, community action, and inside your own head. Under the heading of population, talking about the action the community can do, we say: explore other social structures and marriage forms such as group marriage and polyandrous marriage which provide family life but which produce less children—share the pleasure of raising children widely so that all need not reproduce more than one child for the period of this crisis. Adopt children. Let reverence for life also mean reverence for femininity and for other species, most of which are threatened.

Everybody has had the attitude until very recently that human beings were just barely making it and we'd better keep reproducing. It's a very sudden change of affairs, and only very specialized people have ever had a sense of holding population down. People like the Eskimos and the Tibetans. They clearly recognized that their livelihood would be in danger if the population went beyond a certain level. These people practice exposure of infants. The tantric communities of Bengal, Assan, and Nepal controlled conception through Yoga. The women who are trained in Yoga can conceive or not conceive at will. What it amounts to is control of the autonomic nervous system. For them, of course, it's magic and ritual. It means going through certain meditation exercises and mantras which will cause a beautiful and intelligent child to be born. That is where we will be when we are living in harmony with nature. We'll be able to control ourselves. If you want to read about it, get the *Great Liberation Tantra* translated by Sir John Woodroffe.

I think it describes all the steps you have to go through starting with how you make love, how you orient everything, what you have in the room, then what you do at the fourth month and then at the eighth month. Ritual and magic with your wife, what you do when the child is being born, and finally what you do when you first introduce the child to the sun.

A: Did you try it?
GS: Yes.

A: Does it work?
GS: Well, my baby is beautiful.

A: Is the coming Buddhism going to be one that is going to be more violent? Is it going to take the American Frontiersman outlook—the man who took no shit from anyone? He was an honest God-fearing man all by himself with his family and no one swindled him because he just put his fist through their face when they tried.
GS: That's not the image I imagine. All this talk about violence is because we are talking about a difficult transitional period in history. But there is another kind of violence that is really not violence. It is inherent in being a member of a food chain which we all are. This Buddhism accepts and would transform into a sense of ceremony and sacrament rather than a sense of nature red in tooth and claw. The Buddhist view of nature is a great mutual sacrifice where we have to eat one another.

A: Most Americans just buy the Marlboros they buy and the cowboy shows they watch have this kind of image.
GS: We have to carry it several steps farther and with several steps of greater sophistication. For one thing I'd like to get rid of that frontiersman image right now because he is not my model. My model is the Indian. Take our heads back to where we are chopping our logs down to make our log cabin and my little blond child is playing in the clearing and my wife in her calico dress is gathering berries—stop! Look over the fence and see the Indians and say fuck it, I'll join them. The Indian is involved not as an ideal but as a practical thing. They had a depth of experience on this continent that we don't have. All primitive and archaic lifestyles are worth referring to for information on alternative ways of doing things and also checking on the problems they had and seeing what they did wrong. For example the Hopi deliberately chose to be where they are saying that a harsh environment is what we want.

DK: Was that the case or were they trying to get away from other warring tribes?

GS: In their own mythology they say they chose to stay there. It's interesting that they should phrase it that way. That's important whether that's the actual historical case or not. It puts their minds in a certain way. There's the possibility, which is further out, that the bushman and some of the American Indians were the highest point of human evolution so far. Suppose they had deliberately chosen not to develop the tool making side of things and developed other sides. It is conceivable that certain cultures had much more depth and complexity than we think, but we don't see it because they didn't do material things. Like the Australians with their elaborate kinship systems which are not visible to the observer unless you get into it so that Claude Lévi-Strauss says that actually the Australians are intellectual dandies. They sit around discussing the subtleties of kinship relations over and over again. They apparently have elaborate discussions on how one person relates on all different levels and across all different clan lines and they argue about the precise terminology for a person at a particular point in the network. This is one of their major fascinations and points of relationship in their culture.

A: Looking to the future, do you think that Christianity and the Protestant ethic will be able to cope with the changes in America?

GS: It can't even cope with the changes in itself. I think it will be replaced with a combination of the psychological insights, techniques, and devices that are in shamanism plus the metaphysics and disciplines that are in Mahayana Buddhism plus the science of biology and ecology.

DK: Why do we need the first two?

GS: Because they are practical. You can teach certain things about animals, but a shamanist can speak with animals.

DK: I'm not convinced of the need for this shamanism at all. As a matter of fact I think it can stand between man and nature just like contemporary religions. In other words, what's wrong with developing an evolutionary philosophy that doesn't depend on this at all?

GS: Nothing, as long as the evolutionary philosophy is more than philosophy, that it's in practice. Here's what practice is organically. Here's how it would emerge from your own consciousness and self-experimentation. You want to know how your mind works and what its contents are so you say I will put myself in a situation where there are no outside distractions. I will cut off inputs. I won't talk to anyone. I won't read. I will try not to look at anything in particular or hear anything. If you put yourself in that situation you get a sense of what is in your consciousness and how it flows from day to day. That's exercise one. Exercise two is, taking it for granted that I put my system through the same cycle of three meals a day and eight hours of sleep every night, how would it affect my nervous system and perception of things if I alter this cycle. So you try fasting for a while or trying changing your hours of sleep. These are experiments with the self. You try solitude. You don't have to be a shamanist to ask yourself what it would be like to spend four days in one spot in nature without budging from it and see what I see in that time. The science of the mind is arrived at by experiments with one's perceptions and one's own inner consciousness and extending that and seeing how one perceives and relates to the things in the world around him. The conditions of nature are very good for this. You can try bending your mind with psychedelics and see how that alters things. Now the reason shamanism is useful is that if you undertake a course of action systematically and with seriousness you'll find your head going off in several directions at once and you won't always know how to handle it so it's good to have a teacher to guide you through.

I've been talking on the farthest out level, usually about everything. That's because we don't have very much time and the farthest out level sort of sets a limit on what I think should be. But I don't mean to exclude everything that is possible within that. It's all valuable and should be done.

A: Have you been traveling a lot?

GS: A little bit in the West. I've only been back from Japan for ten months. In February my wife and I and a couple of friends ran the length of the Baja peninsula in a truck. That was interesting. It took twenty-five days driving at ten miles an hour. Then I've been seeing some Indian friends in the Red Power movement. Trying to find out what's been happening in Berkeley, which is always interesting and never too easy to understand. I've been up in the High Sierras with some friends sort of charting out the possibilities of starting some on-site schools with maybe three month periods to teach ecology, American Indian technology, and meditation.

Well, I have an appointment with a computer in a little while.

A: Seriously? What are you going to do?

GS: I'm going to chant some Sanskrit diranis to it.

A: The revolution is when the computer chants it.
A: Yah, and we've lost then.
GS: The computer is now your guru.

From Anthropologist to Informant:
A Field Record of Gary Snyder

Nathaniel Tarn / 1972

Alcheringa, No. 4 (Autumn 1972), 104–13. Reprinted by permission.

Poet Nathaniel Tarn, who interviews Gary Snyder, was himself an anthropologist with training at British, French, and American schools; he was later the editor (1967–1969) of the influential Cape Editions series of literary, political, and anthropological texts. Tarn's most recently published volume of poetry is *A Nowhere for Vallejo* (Random House), while Snyder continues to work on further sections of *Mountains and Rivers*, among other poetic/religious/ecological projects. (Acknowledgement for research aid on the interview to the Rutgers University Research Council. —N. T.)

Project: Compatibility & Mutual Relevance, Anthropology/Literature. Co-ordinated project: Amerindian Poetry.
Previous ref.: 4/12–13/1970 Notre Dame Literary Festival: File UK101GS.
Loc.: 30 Jefferson Road, Princeton, N.J. 4/12/1971, 19h.-24.30h.

(From discussions on "Young America" and its greening, or not, (File UK103GS), into:)
Gary Snyder: Don't call this an interview, make it a conversation.

(Intention to write article; providential visit of Informant; "Well, it *is* an interview . . . in a sense it's anthropology. . . ." Pause, Kherdian on his concern with Amerindians in early teens. Did he ever meet any?)
GS: Yes, on this farm about twenty miles north of Seattle, when I was about twelve. An old Indian came around in a truck selling smoked salmon. We also saw many Indians at the Farmers' Market in Seattle. No, I don't remember talking to them. But I do remember clearly realizing at the age of about

five or six that these were the prior people. My parents said the old salmon-seller was here before them. I saw few other children and spent most of my time in the woods. When I asked questions about the landscape, plants, birds, etc. my parents couldn't answer. I thought perhaps they hadn't been there long enough. Then there were the Indian villages along Puget Sound. I became very conscious of the history of the American continent, the short-ness of occupation-time: the state of Washington was wild before 1860 or so. My sense of the Indian became very intense with this reading and the sense of what the White man had done to the land and to the Indians both came together very soon and aroused a sense of outrage.

(Realization that I sd. have had a tape-recorder. "You realize, I've got to reconstitute this conversation, er, interview, I've got to write Snyder." Feverish note-taking: hand no longer used to it. "What did your parents contribute to this orientation?")
GS: My father was a N.W. man, working on ships before he met my mother: as a coal-passer, then a purser. My mother had come up with her mother from Texas. She was working her way through college writing classes. She wrote a lot, got into journalism. She was the literary one, but they both pro-vided a background of political radicalism and non-conformism, sharpened by the Depression. A sense of detachment and a critical eye for your own culture may help you toward anthropology.

("There's going to be mile on mile of interpretation by and by. I think it's best to add to the facts. Who taught you anthropology? What excited you most about the courses and why?")
GS: I was onto this wilderness and anthropology thing very early. As a teenager, I subscribed to the journal of the Wilderness Society: *The Living Wilderness*. I'd write congressmen about danger from timber companies on public lands; danger from bounties on coyotes. I saw the treatment of Indians and this land exploitation as the same old rip-off. My parents made the identification with capitalism.

My parents broke up when I was about twelve, thirteen and somehow I was left alone in the city. Yes, Portland. I made a bunch of city-urchin adaptations to wild life. I kept my freedom by looking after myself, paying my own rent and so on. Worked as a copy boy on a newspaper from four to midnight: my mother had helped me. The newspaper men liked me and showed me the insides of the city: the courts, the jails, the city government; a nitty-gritty kind of education. Yes, a kind of sociology already. I'd gotten into high school and I knew I wanted to stay with it whatever else happened. Out of this tumultuous career, there were poems—a teacher showed them to a college friend; I got into Reed on my poetry alone. My first year I was a bad student. After that it was okay.

(Anthropology at Reed?)
GS: A one-man department: David French. He's still at Reed. He eventually became an ethnobotanist mainly and editor of the *American Journal of Ethnobotany*. His interest was in the Wasco and Wishram Indians on the Warm Springs reservation east of Mt. Hood. Took several courses over four years: "Intro to Ethnological Theory"; "Culture & Personality"; "Introduction to Linguistics"; "Physical Anthropology"; "Far Eastern Ethnology"; "American Ethnology." I enjoyed them.

(Remembering my own plethora of teachers and places, but had gone into it for religion, myth, weltanschauung: systems/what made them tick: from Griaule, Levy and Lévi-Strauss in Paris to Redfield in Chicago. "What was your main interest?")
GS: Mythology-folklore-linguistics. I did a tutorial reading course with French on this; he didn't teach it formally. Went through the Scandinavian classical material thoroughly, the Stith Thompson stuff on folklore classification, some Jessup North Pacific Expedition material, Boas on Tsmishian Mythology, Swanton. . . . No, not much Mesoamerican: I had a strong sense of the North West.

(Any conflict at this stage between Anthropological and Literary studies? cf.: easy to talk poetry & anthro. at Chicago in the same breath but back among the British Socio. Anths.: wow!)
GS: No: mythology and literature get along well. No conflict.

(Thesis? Is it available; has any one seen it?)
GS: Reed requires a B.A. thesis. Mine's called "Dimensions of a Myth." I like it: it's indicative of much of what happens in my poetry later whatever it's worth or not as anthropology. One Ph.D. candidate is looking at it. I have to give you a permit.

(Writes out permit on spot. "Did you ever do any field-work?")
GS: No, never formally. But I hung out a lot on the Warm Springs reservation collecting folktales pretty formally: noting, taping, typing. In the summers of '51 and '54. I also did some winter seasons as a student but didn't

use the material in the thesis. Then I worked as a logger (in '54) and got more information—it went into the "Berry Feast" piece. I hitched around and hung around and got onto very intimate terms with the Indians.

(Powerful reminiscences of a great time. Smile. We agree to cool some of the talk. Okay self-censorship. "Why did you put those reviews into *Earth House Hold?* They strike me as juvenilia, perhaps not worth reprinting?")
GS: Well, juvenilia yes, but they're not as superficial as they might appear. They were done while I was studying Chinese: no credits involved. For *Midwest Folklore.* The Clark piece is a put-down of course. I've never seen any bad reviews of it and yet it's a bad book. I really wanted to suggest that unexpurgated texts are needed rather than bowdlerized ones. But the Jaime de Angulo: well no one in Anthropology wrote a serious piece about A. But Jaime de Angulo you must realize was a great culture hero on the West Coast. He was a Spaniard with a Paris M.D., came to the South West, quit the army to live with Indians, moved to California. Self-taught linguist, a good one. He never had a regular appointment, he was just too wild. Burned a house down one night when drunk, rode about naked on a horse at Big Sur, member of the Native American Church, great friend of Jeffers—the only man Jeffers ever allowed to visit him day or night. No, I never met him or Jeffers. So at the end of World War II, Jaime de Angulo was one of the few people alive to jazz up California. These reviews have more meaning than you think in terms of the literary culture.

(Have to cool a wee bit more about J.de A's exploits. Ah the secret within the secret within the secret! "Well, this is bringing us to Indiana . . .")
GS: I wanted to go to Indiana to develop the study of oral literature, to study oral literature as style, as raconteur technique—yes, okay, narrative technique. In summer '51 I'd been on the reservation. Then in the fall of '51 I had this fellowship. I only stayed one semester.

(Where was everybody at certain times? NT at Chicago working up to the Maya. When was Charles Olson at Yucatan? And Black Mountain . . . I think Black Mountain starting just about when NT leaving for the Maya. Why was I never told? "Who did you work with at Indiana?")
GS: Well, Charles Voegelin, Thomas Sebeok, Fred Householder and a fine ethnomusicologist George Herzog. And Dell Hymes . . .

(Strong reaction. Ha! Saw DH at Sussex ASA about two, three years ago. Conference on Linguistics: I'd already quit. Asked DH about whom to contact to get material on the secret history of the anthropoets and he was full of suggestions. GS pleased about confluence.)

GS: Dell was at Reed, one year ahead of me and, of course, at Indiana one year ahead. He helped to get me to Indiana. He was my roommate for that semester. This putting of people in touch with each other: about four or five years ago, I put Stanley Diamond in touch with Jerry Rothenberg (I'd been corresponding with Jerry for about ten years) and it was Dell who had put Stanley in touch with me. And now we're all together on the editorial board of *Alcheringa* . . .

("This reminds me that in '51 there was this great Wenner Gren thing in N.Y. Lévi-Strauss was so surprised to see me in the corridors—I'd worked with him three years but we'd hardly exchanged as many words—that he took me for a drink along with Roman Jakobson. Do you remember this?")

GS: No, but come to think of it I now remember Sebeok talking to us about the great anthrolinguists conference at Indiana. That must have come before it?

(Up and down the East Coast after Yale and before Chicago: Kardiner in N.Y., Stirling at the Smithsonian, Steward and Kroeber at Columbia (Kroeber: "Young man, if you're going to Chicago, you'll need a thick scarf") . . . back in Yale: Murdock and Linton who could not help me get out from under Jefferson and American Democracy: Orientation! "Okay, we're getting to the crunch: why did you quit? We already both know this part by heart, I guess . . .")

GS: I decided to quit because it became evident that the things I wanted to do would be better done in poetry than in scholarship. The economic reasons for a scholarly career weren't incentive enough. At the magic-superstitious level, let's say the Muse is jealous. She won't tolerate you having several mistresses. A commitment is required. On the practical level—Dell and I talked about this a lot, Dell was going through the same kind of thing—well if you're going to do a good job it's got to be the whole time. I believe in scholarship if that's what you want but it has to be well done. A Ph.D. in anthropology is demanding. I did think about getting the Ph.D. and then quitting, but it seemed to me that the kind of effort one put into getting a Ph.D. was essentially repetitive . . . like proving some sort of point, almost like showing off.

It wasn't an easy decision. And I'm not sure I've found anyone to do what it was I wanted to do . . .

(When pressed on this a little—take Barthes' highly sophisticated S/Z for instance I'm teaching right now—admits graciously that maybe he has not quite kept up with increasing sophistication of narrative technique studies. NT disagrees a little with feelings about Ph.D. Things start getting repetitive after the Ph.D. These blank sheets in Rangoon the second time round and a big howl of "No" inside . . . "Did you ever feel also that the mental orientations were ultimately in conflict: you know, a certain kind of allegiance to 'objective' fact on the one hand going against the alchemist in you on the other?")

GS: Oh yes, very much that! And then the sense that in the world of folklore and mythology there's a . . . wisdom tradition if you like, half buried but that poets can dig it out and anthropologists can't, or aren't allowed to . . .

Three years out of the field, I think I realized that I didn't want to be the anthropologist but the informant. That's it: wanting to be a *subject* by which I mean being authentically what you are. I made it a rule in Japan not to elicit information that didn't come out naturally in my relationships with people. By really living with people you can enter into certain things . . . but then there's the difficulty of keeping quiet, of not betraying a trust. I was, yes, conscious of the "danger" of being an anthropologist; at the beginning, yes, I collected information, but in the world of Zen now, I'm an informant.

(NT: "Well like not being obliged to ask a certain type of *question* anymore, just being allowed to *be* with people—and not swamped by the culture coming at you 24 hours a day."

"On the other hand, it leaves one with a certain attitude to fact, right?" cf. Note to *The Beautiful Contradictions*: "For him—the anthropologist—scientific records serve as a formal constraint, as well as a point of departure, for the imagination and faithful topography may be very near to the concept of justice.")

GS: Yes, I continue to respect facts. To have your facts right is to allow yourself the latitude to be far out in other ways.

("Surrealism?")
GS: I admire it but I could never do it myself. Philip Lamantia, an old friend, is the leading Surrealist poet in America. I read him with great pleasure.

("How were other writers reacting to anthropology?")
GS: Whalen was a great reader. He was a veteran of World War II and had a better library than Reed College in certain subjects. He had a big collection

on Indian Philosophy. He read a lot of anthropology. Very remarkable man. Dell, Dell of course was more of a poet than an anthropologist, he was a very romantic, revolutionary poet, a good poet. Now he's gone the other way. Yes, Kerouac and Ginsberg were interested, but they weren't respecters of the fact, you know, like people who've been through this are respecters of the fact . . .

("And after Indiana?")
GS: I began to move towards Oriental studies. I had the sudden realization that anthropology was concerned with understanding human nature— but then why go to other people, why not study one's own nature? So . . . Zen. When I'd firmly decided that all this was to be done *as a poet*, then I went to Berkeley: 1953–55. I told the Head of Oriental Studies, Ed Schafer, with whom I still correspond, that I would never take a higher degree. At that time Oriental Studies had precious few people, they were glad to get students.

I still tell young people, I make a pedagogical point of getting kids to learn about as many cultures as possible: anthropology replaces history in this respect.

(Ask about any kinship with Olson's Sumeria, Maya etc. I've noticed Olson never really comes up in Snyder's work . . .)
GS: I never came to Olson. I was rather put off by the *Mayan Letters*, the Romanticism and the lack of scholarly seriousness. Around 1953. I never trusted Olson as a scholar. Maybe it's an East Coast thing against a West Coast thing. Non-Americans think we're all the same, but West Coast is West Coast.

(Express surprise; instance Olson's useful work on Maya fisheries for a start—(meeting CO for the first time at Bled in 64 or so, taking him the first Cape contract, saying, on meeting, just finished the *Letters*/him: Well? Well? As a Mayanist? —But Charles, you spend the whole book telling Mayanists to go to hell!—Ah! . . . Well, never mind, what do you think of it, what do you think of it? Very excited . . .) and Dorn among the Shoshone?)
GS: I always felt that Olson was an apologist for Western Culture; the trip from Sumeria to Gloucester a sort of justification for White-America. I *do* dig Olson poetically. Well, not since the beginning have people gone dry shod from Europe to the US and people have gone dry shod from Asia to America. That makes a difference. Ships? Well, it's not as old as walking.

And *animals* walked before men. As for Dorn: he came late to the Shoshone and under Olson's aegis. He didn't really like living in Idaho.

Now Duncan is possibly my favorite poet, of now. Duncan is Gnostic whereas Olson was esoteric. You know: Duncan, Spicer, and Blaser were all students of the great Medievalist Kantorowicz at Berkeley. Spicer . . . Spicer as a matter of fact was part Indian; he *looked* like a Sioux. . . . I don't know what he was: I think Sioux or Cherokee. He didn't go into Indian things specifically but if you look at the Grail poems and *Billy the Kid,* you'll see it was there . . . And Rexroth now: one of the first poets to clearly invoke Amerindian songs.

(Can we go back into the past a bit? What about Fiedler's *The Return of the Vanishing American?*)
GS: Fiedler: yes, but cranky. Looking for faggots under every bush. I start from someone like Lawrence who said, "When you think the Indians are gone look out." And then there's that kick-off I'll use for the final version of *Mountains and Rivers*: "Where there ain't no Indians that's where you find them the thickest." Jim Bridger said that, greatest of the mountain men in the 1820s and 1830s.

("What I meant was" (this unerring sense of his for scholarly transmission) "do you have any sense of lineage?")
GS: Well, Jeffers is very important to me as the man who claimed for the values of nature against those of technology. And Whitman, a sort of nineteenth century positive Jeffers. Lawrence I've mentioned. Pound, an American trying to construct a myth out of the *lore* of Europe and Asia with varying degrees of success. Rexroth a neo-classicist with his base in Greek, American Indians, etc. A great reclaimer. Further back? I find it difficult to relate to past America because it's Christian. I find it easier to go to the Greek Anthology, the Romans, the medieval Chinese.

(No mention of the great Mesoamerican phenomenon: Maya/Mexican/ Inca?)
GS: No, too abstract for me. You see, it was closer for me to get to China because it LOOKS so much more like the North West Pacific Coast!

(Can't help expatiating on the glories of "my" Americas. Hold that only a few places up here can one see the grandeur of that Center: the great Kiva at Chaco Canyon, e.g., greater than the one at Aztec that he has seen. Summer of '70: goodbye to Rothenberg at Aztec, after beginning *Alcheringa I* in Santa Fe. . . .)

GS: It's the next order of business and my wife is as keen on it as I am, I want to learn Spanish and then, off to Mexico. Since India, I've felt I'd be okay in a place like Mexico.

("A few last shots . . . What about your syncretism?" (GS blank) "Well, in *Earth House Hold,* e.g., p. 57: "involuntary gassho and bow to the virgin" note how you capitalize Buddhist icons but not others usually. I'm referring to my notion that syncretism is mankind's lot: only the very privileged can afford purism")
GS: Syncretism: yes in theory; no in practice. Both Buddhists and Gnostics agree on this. My practice is now syncretistic but only after many years of orthodox practice in Rinzai Zen. My teacher now agrees to this search here for ways of living Zen in America. Padmasambhava is my model here: the great Buddhist acculturator who took Buddhism to Tibet. Making contact with local spirits, getting onto terms with them.

("Lévi-Strauss? You mention him in *Earth House Hold.* I wasn't quite sure how you were seeing him?")
GS: Fascinating, a genius, but a rationalist. The insights are circumscribed by the commitment to rationalism. The dimension provided in anthropology by someone like Castaneda is not open to Lévi-Strauss. What's useful in him is the stress on the intellectual power of the primitives. This is his major insight: yes, I agree it came late in his thinking . . . I have read everything that Lévi-Strauss has done in English.

(Notice signs of tiredness. Suggest we are drawing to a close . . .)
GS: Yes, that was good. It helped me put some order into my thoughts. Now you must reconstitute the conversation.

("I'll send it to you. You should check it out.")
GS: Yes, and now what do *you* think of all this?

Interview with Gary Snyder

Lee Bartlett / 1975

California Quarterly (Spring 1975), 43–50. Reprinted by permission.

This interview with Gary Snyder was taped at the poet's home in the foot-hills of the Sierra, December 8, 1974, by Lee Bartlett, who edited it into its present form.

Lee Bartlett: You've often talked about people today feeling the need to get back to some kind of roots—if not by building a house in the mountains as you've done, then by somehow getting away from the rush of the city. What do you think is behind this?

Gary Snyder: Well, many things are going on simultaneously. The big flow of Americans away from the farm and into the city occurred right after World War I. That's when rural areas lost people as urban areas gained them. It's a demographic fact that only in the seventies has there been a reversal of that trend. It's now true, apparently, that more people are moving out of urban areas, back to small towns and rural areas, than at any time since World War I. Now urban congestion, smog, crime in the streets and so forth, are the most often cited reasons for this; people find living conditions are actually much more pleasant in the country. The suburbs become too expensive with high taxes, and they're not altogether convenient. But another reason is, for young people especially, that there is a genuine re-birth of feeling for nature. The old attitude that the farm is for the birds and who wants to be a farmer, has subtly been altered to the point where people feel that to get back to the land and to deal with living creatures and plants is desirable. Now that's a response to the tremendous alienation that urban people feel. It's also probably a sane move because in the longer range pic-ture it looks very much as though the present American agricultural system, agribusiness, which is so dependent on the petro-chemical industry, chemi-cal fertilizers, and machinery, is just about to become a losing proposition.

It's literally a losing proposition in one sense. Michael Perelman, who is an agricultural economist at Chico State College, has worked these figures out: it takes ten BTUs of energy to produce one BTU of food by our present agricultural standards. Now that's a losing proposition; we're putting more in than we're getting out. Perelman wrote an essay which points out that our enormous productivity in agriculture is only made possible by the way we drain our fossil fuel reserves. As fossil fuel reserves go down and the price of oil goes up, American agriculture is obviously going to be in for a rough jolt. In fact, it's already getting a rough jolt—the price of food is going up and up because the price of oil is going up and up. The price of soybeans went up from ninety dollars a ton to four-thousand dollars a ton, which is like a key index because soy bean is a key protein. So the self-sufficient, diversified organic farm, which sounds romantic and is actually a hell of a lot of hard work, is nevertheless the wave of the future for those who like it, and it may be for those who don't like it too, because that will possibly end up being the only way we can grow food. The return to the land is a return to a stable and noble state of affairs. An overblown urban population was something that was made possible by the artificially low price of fossil fuels during the late nineteenth and early twentieth centuries.

LB: Do you think it's economically advisable for Americans to continue to expect to consume large quantities of meat?
GS: Absolutely not. That's quite clear. Again to cite figures, Americans eat two-hundred-and-fifty pounds of meat per year per person, Western Europeans eat one-hundred-and-seventy pounds per year, and the Japanese eat fifty pounds per year. I have these figures at hand because Allen Ginsberg and I were just last week reading through an article in the *New York Times* about famine and food, and we were astounded by these statistics. It's extremely inefficient to feed grains to cattle. It takes five pounds of grain protein to make one pound of cow protein, if I remember my figures correctly.

LB: And that's not taking into account all of the grazing space animals need.
GS: Exactly. Now I'm not a vegetarian, per se, because I would not want to argue that Eskimos should eat alfalfa sprouts. I think it depends on how you live, where you live, and what the carrying capacity of your local ecosystem is. I think that ultimately, ideally, in the most poetic and visionary terms, the best economy is the hunting and gathering economy. But since we're not going to have an economy like that for a long time, it's

evident that America has in front of it now an enormous responsibility to cut down its meat consumption and divert those grains, that corn and that soybean, to help feed people in other countries. Another figure from the *New York Times* article is that if twenty percent of the grain that is now fed to cattle in the United States went directly to human beings, and Americans then ate less meat and got their protein from grains, with no loss of nutrition to the American population, there would be enough food left to feed all the people in India during the coming famine. Just by a change in American eating habits. That's not even a deprivation, except that you're going to have to give up your hamburger. Isn't that a shocking figure? But it's an optimistic figure in a sense. You see some articles coming out right now by economists and agricultural experts saying that we can't afford to feed India, and they cite figures. Well, their figures are accurate, but they're based on Americans continuing to eat in the same patterns. If Americans broke their eating patterns, we could easily feed India, at least for a few more years, without really suffering ourselves. On the other hand, to be fair, the one thing that must be argued is that if anybody, the Soviet Union or the United States, continues to send food to India, there must be a powerful birth-control program initiated. Feeding people without a birth-control program in a country with a rising birth rate is, as they say, pouring sand down a rat hole, and sooner or later there will be more people who will starve. Two things have to take place in the world simultaneously—one is that a number of countries have to apply population control measures, and the other is that the people of the United States have to learn to eat lower on the food chain.

LB: Do ideas of this sort carry over into your work as a writer?
GS: Well, Tom Lyon and I were talking about writing an ecology-revolutionary-science-fiction-pornography to turn the world around.

LB: I mean you were using words like "poetic" and "economy" and "visionary" and "energy" all in the same breath a minute ago. Are those concepts really associated so intimately in your own mind?
GS: Of course. For instance, going back to when I was seventeen or eighteen, I've kept notebooks of essentials. That is to say, I don't write down my daily thoughts. I only write down things that are on the concrete or intuitive plane, because those are the things I want to remember, I want to make use of. That's a very energy-conserving practice, don't you think, very economical?

LB: William Everson said a few days ago that he's going through a dry spell as far as the writing of poetry is concerned. For the past year he's been working on a long prose essay, but he's been unable to write any poems. Is that also an energy problem?

GS: Well, I don't view it as a problem. I have periods of greater or lesser poetic creativity, but when I'm not necessarily being so creative poetically, I'm being creative on some other level. I'm a very energetic person. I'm always doing something—building a house, having a family, doing zazen, or cooking. I don't view those things as being really separate. I'm just as happy doing one as the other, actually. I told Ginsberg that doing carpentry is more fun that writing letters, and he said it was his big realization this summer that I was right. Doing carpentry is as much fun as writing poems.

LB: You make your life sound like a nicely balanced ecological system.

GS: And farming! Learning plants, too. I've been really getting into botany. McClure got me started on learning plants more. It's so exciting to get through that initial kind of brush-tangle of taxonomy and get into *seeing* plants.

LB: Is there that same connection between taxonomy and *seeing* in poetry?

GS: Well, for myself, being a poet means first of all understanding the nature of language itself—phonetics, phonemics, morphology, syntax—and then understanding the particular history of one's mother tongue and its particular structure. This is what people used to call the "genius" of the language, the ways in which that genius is changing, since all languages are in the process of change continually, which is reflected in the subtle and ongoing changes in daily speech. The kinds of rhythms, expressions, syntactic constructions that you find used in the speech of different groups of people, such as urban black people with their particular rhythms, or country people with their particular phrasing and rhythms. Looking at, hearing, all of those things, one is able first of all to follow William Carlos Williams' dicta of having respect for ordinary speech and having an ear for it. Then, in terms of poetic craft, one must not only have an ear for daily speech, but the particularly poetic sense of refining, purifying, and compressing daily speech into the kind of compact utterance that a poem becomes. So first of all, in my poetry my craft has a sense of compression, a sense of ellipsis, of leaving out the unnecessary, of sharpening the utterance down to a point where a very precise, very swift message is generated, an energy is transmitted. In doing that, I have paid particular attention to the Anglo-Saxon or Germanic derived aspects of the English language, and have made much use of mono-syllabic words, of compactness and directness of the Anglo-Saxon heritage in the English language, which I have cross-bred with my understanding and ear for Chinese poetry.

At one time I wrote the first drafts of my poems down in a phonemic alphabet, other than an ordinary English spelling, because I thought it helped me see better what the actual sounds were. Doing that becomes in part an exercise in clearing yourself from an preconceptions you might have about the language system based on our somewhat outmoded spelling system, and returning one's sense of poetry to the oral; so that another aspect of my poetry is that I think of it as an oral poetry, as very close to song, or in some cases, to chant. Of course, I've given quite a large number of poetry readings. I consider the poetry reading to be the actual mode of existence of the poem, the actual place where it comes into its final existence. So that the written poem in the book is like the score for the poem—it is actually in its full life when presented in a poetry reading, read by me or by someone else.

LB: You talk about poetry as oral tradition, and we were talking before about Rothenberg and the work he's been doing. A lot of poets have recently taken to the translation or re-working of American Indian songs and prayers. What about the whole idea of ethno-poetics?

GS: Well, the interest in ethno-poetics derives in part from a general feeling among American poets of the last ten or fifteen years that poetry is close to song and that the oral quality of it is very important. Consequently, a lot of people have turned to oral literary traditions to look at them again, seeing that these literatures are true literatures and that you don't necessarily need a writing system to have a tradition with a rich body of song. That's what led people like Rothenberg, George Quasha, and many others into a study of ethno-poetry. To do it seriously means that you also have to become something of a linguist—it's very closely tied to modern linguistics, which brings you back to understanding your own language again with more precision. One of the things I have fun doing with people is seeing if they can identify the vowels of the English language. Most people can't do it because they're programmed to think that the vowels are the letters A E I O U. But those are only the symbols used to represent the vowels, which are actually much larger in number—nine, maybe, or ten.

LB: Getting back to energy again. Have you read Buckminster Fuller's work?

GS: I really haven't read much Fuller. What are you thinking of?

LB: His discussion of knots as self-interfering patterns. He takes off on a discussion of energy, the poem as energy, and so forth, but—
GS: Knots as self-obstructing patterns?

LB: Self-interfering patterns, he calls them. He sees the poem, the body, the universe as knots, patterns of energies.
GS: I see what you mean. In energy-system terms, bodies are temporary energy traps in which energy is held briefly and can be deferred into other uses, other eco-systems, on the path of energy from the sun to the energy-sink in the universe. And so all living structures, and perhaps all material structures, are various augmentations and temporary constructions that energy takes on its way to the heat-sink. H. T. Odum says that language is a form of energy trap, and that particular kinds of communications which he calls tiny energies in precise forms released at the right moment amount to energy transfers that are much larger than their size would indicate—which is what poems are, from an ecological energy-systems man's point of view. Let me also say that this bears on something I said in the essay "On 'As for Poets,'" which I find charming. The Japanese word for song, like folk song, is "fuschi." Fuschi literally means "knot" in the grain of wood, a whorl in the grain. The bass tone of the universe stops for a few moments and does some complex things, and then it goes on again. This is like what Black Elk says—the Sioux idea of living creatures is that trees, buffalo, and men are temporary energy swirls, turbulence patterns. Like Buckminster Fuller's knots.

LB: That's a metaphysical concept. The trepidation of the spheres creates music and all people are spheres and all entities are spheres.
GS: Yes, that's an early intuitive recognition of energy as a quality of matter. But that's an old insight, you know, extremely old—probably a Paleolithic shaman's insight. You find that perception registered in so many ways in archaic and primitive lore. I would say that it is probably the most basic insight into the nature of things, and that our more common, recent Occidental view of the universe as consisting of fixed things is out of the main stream, a deviation from basic human perception. This would be an anthropologist's overall way of seeing things.

LB: For the past few years, the confessional genre has been big in American poetry—most of it seems to be an attempt to work out the poet's own neurosis. Your poetry, however, has never seemed to rely on a brooding, melancholy, self-conscious approach, though much of it is extremely personal.

GS: I wouldn't want to slight people who write those poems because their suffering is real, and they have sometimes generated very powerful poetry out of their suffering. Though, you know, that sort of suffering is only one dimension to human life. It's one not everybody has in his life, for one thing, and it can, on another level, be transcended. It's not part of my life because I don't suffer in that way. I'm a Buddhist, which is to say you take suffering and impermanence for granted, as a base fact of the universe, and then proceed on from there. It has to do with how you relate to your own ego, I suppose. That's not my mode of poetry. I don't know how I would describe my mode of poetry.

LB: Your poetry has always been engaged, in a political sense. Yet your newest collection, *Turtle Island,* seems more explicitly politically oriented than any other volume, except *The Fudo Trilogy.* As conditions in the world worsen, do you see your work become increasingly more politicized?

GS: Here we go back to suffering again. We're going to see an incredible increase in human suffering on the planet, not only human, but suffering for all life forms. Any feeling person, poet or otherwise, is going to be driven to confront these things. As I've said in some of my essays, I think it is historically, and maybe in the very nature of poetry itself, a major part of the poet's work to be a spokesman for nature, for life itself. To be a spokesman for the non-human aspects of life, other life forms, wilderness. That's why poets have been agents of the great Goddess through history, as Robert Graves so eloquently describes in the *The White Goddess.* It's said over and over again in different primitive contexts that the shaman is one-half in the human world, but one-half out of the human world. That he draws on visions, songs, powers gained from animals, trees, or from waterfalls for healing energy. So the shaman-poet's function has anciently been, in part, to integrate the whole biological world together rather than just to be a human spokesman, as political writers, historical writers, and philosophers are. It's a larger, broader function, just as the issues which confront us now are also broader, really horrendous, like the coming food and resource shortages on all fronts. I would hope that poets could be committed ecological warriors to help bring this consciousness on a direct, imaginative, intuitive level to people. To bring the information in statistics, in charts of rising and falling curves, home on a more concrete level. So *Turtle Island* poems may be for me just a beginning of the kind of energy I'll give to that kind of poetry.

An Interview with Gary Snyder

Jack Boozer and Bob Yaeger / 1977

Unmuzzled OX, IV, No. 3, 1977, 106–17. Reprinted by permission.

Unmuzzled OX: McClure says that to Camus the twentieth century is a period in which man is alienated from everything, and McClure compares him to Thoreau, a sensibility more integrated, more at home with his environment. The opposition seems to be one of European and American viewpoints. It reminds one of your viewpoint, that America is salvageable . . .
Gary Snyder: Of course it's salvageable. If you go trucking around a dump yard you can find all sorts of things. There's always something salvageable.

OX: Actually, it sounded as if what McClure was proposing was that the European intellectual community was necessarily more alienated. It hadn't any contact with the land for generations. The American community had, more recently, and so was closer to the roots. Doesn't that apply to West Coast writers?
GS: Well, now—*that's* interesting. Take a look at Bill Everson's new book, *Archetype West*. It's a study of poetry going back to Joaquin Miller, in Jungian terms, culminating in Jeffers and a post-Jeffers chapter on my generation. The point he makes there, and it has all kinds of implications for poetry, is that California poetry from its inception has tackled one of the major problems of Western culture: how does man relate to his environment? That's not the only question we all face, of course, but it's certainly one of the major questions. It's one that we have to think about a lot. Thoreau lays a groundwork for that thinking. Whitman does too, though he pays more attention to social interaction, to the idea of social and cultural destiny. But Jeffers, say, looks at the more naked interface of human and non-human. That is something that has concerned the Far Western writers pretty much. It is not provincial: it's relevant in answering the major

questions. All of us out there are in a sense working with that, which is interesting to know—but we are not doing much in other areas, like human relations. Poets in other places are doing that. They are two kinds of poetry. You can't discriminate between them as to value. Different jobs are being done. One of the jobs we do out in the Far West is describe environment because we are out next to the Pacific . . . lots of deserts, lots of mountains. They become one of the problems we chew on. If you live in New York City, you chew on a different set of problems.

OX: But that's permissible.
GS: Sure. You have to chew on the problems you got.

OX: How do you view poets of human relations—confessional poets like Lowell and Berryman.
GS: I read Lowell's *Life Studies* in 1960, and I haven't read anything by him since. I liked that. We talked about it a lot . . . we turned it around a lot. And Berryman—I had a little correspondence with him. But, you know, like when Napoleon's soldiers marched back from Moscow, it is very painful to have to keep slogging by, past falling comrades, and not help them. And that's what I feel about Berryman: he fell, and there was just nothing we could do.

OX: Do you read when you're writing?
GS: I read all the time actually. But I don't read much poetry.

OX: What do you read?
GS: I read biology, history, anthropology, economics, everything except poetry and fiction.

OX: It's more interesting.
GS: It's more interesting.

OX: You don't need others' projections of the imagination? You're working with your own?
GS: Yeah, really. I do read poetry a little bit. People send me stuff and I flip through it. I hit things I really like once in a while . . . but I don't try to keep up. The thing I'm trying to work out as a poet is in no way limited to a specific literary or poetic aesthetic. It's visionary poetry, but it's pragmatic, too. You look constantly for facts, for what works, what makes things work.

OX: Is that why, as an undergraduate at Reed, you studied both literature and anthropology, and later did graduate work in anthropology and Oriental languages?

GS: Yeah. Once you decide to see the world in life terms, and that telling stories about the world is a good thing to do, then your interest is in finding out about the world—not going back and recycling literature over and over again.

OX: So you start with anthropology?

GS: And continue: biology, history, philosophy, whatever . . . I am curious about the way things work. If poems tell me how things work—fine. If economics tell me how things work—fine. You've got to find out how things work; there is no limit to that. You tinker. You save all the parts. And like Wendell Berry says at the end of his novel, *The Memory of Old Jack*: at the very last someone comes in and asks Jack where something is, and Old Jack says, "Hangin' up! Goddamn it! Hangin' up right where it ought to be!" Tools, parts of harness—hangin' up there. It's all right there.

OX: Yet in your poetry you mix so many mythologies together—Eastern and Western, Indian and Chinese and Japanese.

GS: I don't do that in a callous way. A lot of things have connections, culture to culture. Turtles are found all over the world—in the folklore. That's where they survive, in a kind of literary or literal continuation of types of nature. And it's time we did more with that. I like Joseph Campbell's work for just that reason. Campbell has laid out how the body of world folklore and mythology changes, how the varying changes store symbols and images that we all share. And it's international. It's the greatest international body of literary information that we have.

OX: What do you think of Jung?

GS: Jung's too vague.

OX: You mean he's not right?

GS: No, I'm not saying he's not right. But he's vague. He has a hard time dividing things up between hard facts and his speculations. But his speculations are very stimulating.

OX: I assume you don't consider his concept of archetypes speculation.

GS: The idea of archetypes is right. But that's not the whole answer. Jung or his followers were sometimes saying, or implying, that the only significance is the psychological significance. If you read hard anthropology, if you work with people, you see that they do not read or use myths only for psychological reasons; you see that they use them in an upfront political and social way, to talk about how they live their lives. And the play between universality and specificity is then really fascinating. That's what myth study is all about.

OX: You sound like a structuralist.

GS: Lévi-Strauss takes an approach which works towards another kind of universality, which is equally fascinating. But the Jungians *and* the structuralists are both tempted to ignore the specific in order to work on surface texture. That's why, for me, ethno-botany is so useful. Ethno-botany is always specific to a specific region, where people live their real lives. And how people live their real lives, in a real place, is an ineluctable part of the whole. The play between the two approaches is the real key to meaning. In other words, neither universality or specificity is thoroughly enlightening unto itself. You really ought to be considering both at the same time.

OX: Hence the mixing of mythologies in your poetry?

GS: Yeah, I'm really trying to demonstrate that in my poetry: how the two come together and how they fail to come together. The most personally exciting use of that insight came teaching on Indian reservations under an N.E.H. program. I was able to sit down and say, "Let's talk about the stories that your grandmothers and grandfathers told"—to kids who are going to be poets. I'd say, "You guys thought you were out of touch, pushed to the far end of some kind of geographical cul-de-sac where the rest of the world doesn't exist. But let me show you that the stories of your grandmothers and grandfathers are truly universal, part of the ground-level information that the whole world draws on." And then I'd show them the evidence for that. They discover that Occidental civilization is not something that rolls over them irresistibly. It shows them that they have all the information that lies behind Occidental civilization or Oriental civilization, that there's a shared body of knowledge.

OX: You're using "region" in two ways, then—one dealing with specific geography and culture, one with commonality of human experience. But isn't "provincialism," say, what occurs if both senses of "region" aren't realized or achieved?

GS: Yes, if the region is achieved at the expense of open communication. But that's a whole different question. Both types of situation can be found historically. The European Middle Ages is a case in point. The Middle Ages was an era of almost no centralization, yet, via the most caste-like occupational status of poets and entertainers, it had a great deal of mobility and communication across centralizing lines. Now that kind of thing is really an ideal balance, where centralization is not required for cosmopolitanism. India is another example. It's cosmopolitan by virtue of its metaphysics, the Hindu religion, which in typical polytheistic fashion is an outgrowth of observations on specific natural phenomena. So, like, they don't wipe out other religions, they just move on top of them. This is similar to what the Jesuits were trying to do in the sixteenth and seventeenth centuries.

OX: Aren't you really saying that there's a fundamental structure that human beings share not only with each other but with all living things, and that if we can get down to that basic structure, we will have a regionalism which is also an internationalism?

GS: Yeah. Rather than use the words "fundamental structure" I would use living system. I mean, shit, man, I was just walking along today and I looked at my hand, and it occurred to me again that this is all natural material—it's all okay. What the fuck are we, talking machines? Here we are, big chunks of protein moving around. It's such a funny thing that we have to *remind* ourselves about it, that the fingernails are like the claws of a hawk. How weird that we feel alienated from that.

OX: And poetry . . .?

GS: If I *really* wanted to be political, I would write a poem to convince people to connect with plants and animals on a subconscious level. Such things can be *evoked,* and I mean fully evoked: changes in consciousness are possible. Bly talks about changes from father-consciousness to mother-consciousness. Poets do that; that's what *real* politics is about. Of course, we don't get much done—little things over a thousand years.

OX: In the prose section of *Turtle Island* you say that man must alter the historic tendency toward urbanized civilization in exchange for an "ecologically sensitive harmony-oriented wild-minded scientific-spiritual culture."

GS: In part, that's a matter of community and region against nationwide networks. Over the last century the increasing centralization in the United States, and in other parts of the world, has caused us to lose our sense of being natives. As a population, we *were* beginning to become natives in this country about 1880–1890—my grandmother knew a lot about local mushrooms and put up wild blackberries. But now Americans move every three or four years, like ping-pong balls. That process may be on the edge of reversal with the new beginning of neighborhoods; and because the price of gasoline will rise too high, the mobility of American life will be slowed. Teachers should open the eyes of the children to all the useful jobs right there at home, so they won't feel bad about staying in, say, Iowa, and minding the farm. Professionalism is uprooted. Dentists and lawyers are dedicated only to their own networks; there's also a network of poets, and even a small network of canners—salmon canners. The trouble with networks, you see, is that you never meet anybody but those like yourself, and you always agree with each other. But in real communities there is diversity. The real art of living is living in communities. You have to learn to live with people who don't agree with you. Things really work out—they *have* to work out. You have to be ready to compromise. In the city, you get on the outs with somebody and you never see them again. You have infinite choice.

To put it another way: the cowboy used to be seen as the dominating image of American society. It's dying out now. Everyone today wants to be an executive. The accoutrement of the executive is power. Every manager waits his turn to run his office—like it was a little White House. "Learn to boss the big ones. Have a Caterpillar for your staff." We're fascinated by holding power in our hands—a Cat, a military jet, a truck. A vertical infrastructure fascinates Americans.

OX: How do you get out of the infrastructure, though? I was reading over some of the things you wrote about the Haight-Ashbury in San Francisco, about "new tribalism" and so forth, in *Earth House Hold.* Do drugs help get out of it? Obviously this also ties in with the spiritual vision so important to Indian cultures.
GS: You know it's true. For odd cultural and political reasons, it hasn't moved down as well as we thought.

OX: Why is that?
GS: It's a mystery, isn't it? Because you can learn from it, incredible learning. This is one of the great oddities of the past ten years: an enormous amount was learned from psychedelics, but it is something we don't talk about. We all know that it's true, but we are not willing to try and talk about it yet. And you know that it's going to swing around again. Whatever that

learning is will come back to us. It is in very initial ways important, but it is also mysterious, because we don't know how it relates to the human will.

OX: What is it, do you think, that psychedelics do? How do they help us break through to other levels?

GS: It seems like drugs take the structure out of information. One of the puzzles is that all primitive people who have any kind of psychedelic plants around them don't mind using them for visionary purposes—which everybody else has totally repressed. Have you read Wasson's book on the use of muscaria? But that's not really the question. The question is, why is the knowledge of this always repressed?

OX: Do you think it has something to do with the nature of the repression?

GS: Yes. And it has something to do with the danger.

OX: You mean that since we repress it so hard it must be really dangerous to face it?

GS: We don't know. We really don't understand it. I speculate on the nature of civilization: apparently the nature of civilization, whatever that is, requires that we repress the knowledge in order to organize people, to operate and accomplish things in another fashion. It is a completely different organization.

OX: I wanted to ask you a slightly more personal question—though it's also literary. You are clearly the Japhy Ryder character in Jack Kerouac's novel, *Dharma Bums*: an outdoorsman, lover, scholar of Eastern cultures, and mystic. How do you feel being Japhy Ryder in the account of a close friend like Kerouac?

GS: Well, I feel like the Kwakiutl do toward Franz Boas. They like Franz Boas; he's a really nice guy. They think, "He wrote about us, and we can read what he wrote about us. And it's kind of interesting and it's strange. Is that the way we look? No, we don't really do things quite that way, but in general it's all right. And how weird that somebody else should want to read about this. This is just what we do here at home . . ." You know, Jack was really kind of an anthropologist. He had a great eye and a great ear, and he really observed people well. He doesn't distort very much at all. The closest thing to a distortion in Jack's novels, I think, is that he plays down his role as "I," as participant. He acts like he's dumber and stupider than he really is. He uses himself as a straight man. Instead of making an ego-building character, he uses himself as the dumb-guy who asks the questions.

OX: Like the drunk who sits in the corner and just watches?

GS: Yeah. He does it really well. But he was a lot smarter than that.

OX: That's what I was getting at. Kerouac wasn't, in that sense, autobiographical. You don't use a lot of autobiographical detail in your poetry, at least not in the way that many people would say was autobiographical. Not like Lowell, for instance.

GS: Well, what most people mean by autobiography is that they want to hear a confession.

OX: That's exactly it. But when you talk about "Turtle Island," aren't you really talking about yourself?

GS: Sure, I'm talking about how I feel, and that's certainly my autobiography. You could, if you wanted, find all kinds of confessions in my poetry.

OX: Yes, but "kinds" is the emphasized word.

GS: "Kinds?" Okay. Confessional poetry is therapeutic. But it stems from, it is generated by, self-destructive habits that you have to excise from yourself. And I've had a lot of bad habits, though none of them has been that self-destructive. Just as a matter of historical, poetic aesthetics, I don't believe genius is a by-product of madness, although there's a whole string of poets since Rimbaud who've operated on that principle. I think that poetry strives for plain old garden-variety sanity, and that that sanity is nothing special, or it shouldn't be. But you even have to make a special point about it and say, "Well, this is sane." It's more interesting, valuable, to demonstrate what might be sane things to do than to confess, "I had some bad habits but now I'm doing sane things." I confess: "I'm perfectly sane." Who is going to pay any attention? You have to cut your wrists or something.

OX: Are you suggesting that it's easier to envision cutting your wrists than hoeing your garden?

GS: Yeah, I suppose there are a lot of people who, if they had only two alternatives, would think cutting their wrists was more interesting. Unfortunately a razor is somehow more attractive.

OX: Well, we were talking about autobiography. . . .

GS: Okay. I'll give you something autobiographical. That is that my mother has had a long history of mental problems. As I grew up most of my literary tendencies, capacities and ambitions were developed by her. And I had to work through the whole question of insanity and self-destructiveness as a child, watching her. It was a really difficult problem, watching and working through that. I had to come to my own definitions of sanity. And as a result, I have a certain aversion for making a big thing out of craziness.

OX: So for you autobiography is important insofar as it liberates you from that autobiography—in other words, from the *concern* for that autobiography as an ultimate end?

GS: Yeah, or liberates other people from similar kinds of things. Like Ginsberg confessing in the fifties: "I'm a Jew, I'm a homosexual, my mother was a communist, and I masturbate." That was liberating. He doesn't have to do that now.

OX: But you say your family started you writing poetry?

GS: We grew up very poor, like hobos in a sense, except it was the West. My mother had this extraordinary literary ambition. I'm not even sure where she got it. But she imagined herself as a potentially great writer.

OX: Did she read to you when you were young?

GS: Yeah, she read stories to me. I got to reading very early. But then it was like some validation of the literary life as a way to be, which I imbibed so thoroughly I never even felt conscious of it. If I had, it would have made a difference.

OX: What poets did your mother read to you?

GS: Edgar Allan Poe. I used to know "The Raven" by heart, and "Annabel Lee." Those poems are really good poems for kids because they are right up front where they ought to be, using the language, getting at all the mysteriousness of things.

An Interview with Gary Snyder

Peter Colson, Judith Schulevitz, Stacy Spencer, and Jim Tolley / 1979

Interlochen Review, (Spring 1979), 91–99. Reprinted by permission.

Student: Do you feel that your jobs and travels and encounters with other people have been particularly important to you as inspiration or material for your poetry?

Gary Snyder: "Material" and the idea of "getting material" is an insidious idea. The idea of "getting experiences to be a writer" is totally insidious. You have to realize that if you can't see your own life, what's in front of you, why should you go looking for something else? So never think that you should be traveling to get "material." That's an intellectually imperialist approach to creativity. It's a variety of capitalist ideas of production. You have to trust your inner light and your inner openness and capacity— and then perhaps travel. There's nothing wrong with traveling, but I would say in terms of experience (I've had much more experience than anybody needs), I wouldn't especially recommend it. I've read more books than anybody ought to read, too. There is a certain point beyond which it doesn't make any sense. As Confucius says, "The Inferior Man elaborates on his mistakes." The trick is to stop when enough's enough and move on or settle down or whatever it is that you're supposed to do. I did not travel randomly in search of experience; I have not had time to do that. I went to Japan with a particular purpose; to search for a good Zen teacher. I traveled nine months all over the Pacific in a tanker because I needed money, and I was getting paid, and so forth. There's always a reason for doing things. I've been pretty busy, in that sense.

S: How much did your studies in anthropology affect your values and your poetry?

GS: In terms of my own personal values, one of the things that I saw, very swiftly, was that there are many, many ways to solve the same problems all over the world, and it's very difficult to make a judgment as to whether or not a given group of people is doing things well or poorly. I did not and I would not now subscribe to the idea of total cultural relativism, which asserts that there is no way to tell if anybody is doing anything better than anybody else, that they're all too different and too unique, and it's all ultimately equal. I think that you can make judgments that are measured by the degree of coherence, style, harmony, clarity, beauty that a people have in their lives and also certain judgments into matters of whether they're careful or wasteful, kind or cruel, exploit each other or don't exploit each other—and I'm willing to make those value judgments. But the study of anthropology—which is really the total study of what the humanities should be—enlarges our whole understanding of what human beings are and what they've done and what they can do and to some extent what works and what doesn't work so well. Over a forty or fifty thousand year time span, there is no more interesting and large scale way of seeing human behavior than through the lens of the anthropologist. So it's one approach to human nature—it's the outside way, by studying out there what human beings have done through books and through field trips, and so forth. "What are we?" Okay? The other way is the way of meditation and the way of Zen, which is where you take *yourself* as subject for study and go at the question of what is human nature by asking, "What am I?" And the two together are a wonderful way to try to get at things. That's our occidental way of doing things, see. We want to do both [laugh] or I want to do both—go outside and go inside simultaneously. It was actually anthropology that led me to do Zen study. It was the question of objectivity really, the fundamental scientific question. Can an anthropologist be objective about another culture? Is it possible to even think about a sub-atomic particle without affecting the "nature" of the particle? The act of measuring affects the thing being measured. Realizing that and wanting to see if it were possible to approach naked mind, I went into Zen—to take all of the cultural and psychological clothes off.

S: Do you think that through your stays in Buddhist monasteries and your studies of Chinese and American Indian cultures that you may have acquired new perspectives or new points of view from which to perceive your own life?

GS: Well, Buddhist practices are more than just another point of view. They lead to an original, fundamental point of view, which is the heart of good poetry, of good anything—fundamental, original mind. However, "points of view" are also useful. Chinese culture, Japanese culture, Indian culture, American Indian culture and their poetries and their ways of dealing with their lives and their environments are all very instructive. But there's something that underlies them all, too, and that's what you deal with in Buddhist studies. In other words Buddhism is not the same as Chinese culture. It just happens that it uses the Chinese culture as a host organism to live within for awhile—and Japan. But the intention of Buddhist practice, or Zen practice, through meditation, is to go down into your mind to the place where it is truly universal and unconditioned and truly free. From that point you can see how it is that all these different kinds of trappings are put on and how you can take them off. And how you can freely play with them.

S: And then you can use this in your poetry.

GS: Ah, you don't exactly use it, because it can't be used, but it underlies it sometimes. You can't count on reaching those things by any deliberate means. So what I'm saying really is that practice of awareness and mindfulness and going into your consciousness and being aware of how it moves and what's in there can lead to a lot of solidity and understanding about daily life and personal psychological states of affairs. And occasionally it can even go much deeper than that as well. The power of poetry comes in through the gaps somehow.

S: Do you think your poetry has attained a greater clarity through the study of Zen?

GS: There was already a certain clarity in the earlier work. It's perhaps less abstract now, and less intellectual, and there are things I find still evolving in my most recent work that I can't quite put a name to. One is always practicing and always watching.

S: Is the cross between the East and the West for you natural?

GS: Well, being born and raised out on the West Coast, Asia certainly seems natural and close in a way that it doesn't perhaps to people on the Atlantic side. But it's not east or west that I'm concerned with. As I was saying earlier, Buddhism is not really Far Eastern culture, and vice versa. One is looking for what makes things work underneath, and the natural world is the natural world everywhere, and the birds and the whales move through it all independently of any national or cultural boundaries. So does myth, so does practice.

S: A wide range of eastern, and more exotic religions have in recent years acquired considerable followings in this country. Do you feel these religious movements are really beneficial?

GS: Well, there are things which are "trips," and there are things which liberate. Some things have great power, and draw on the power of archetype or the power of myth, and are very attractive. But the question is, do they make us "feel secure," or do they set us less free? Some of the religious enthusiasms that are sweeping around the United States today go to interesting places, but then they get stuck there, I think, and one must be careful not to fool oneself and settle for what it is one thinks one wants, instead of following the path of liberation that may take you where you don't even think you want to go.

S: In Zen one has to grasp the core and the mystery of things. The emphasis in western civilization, however, is on analysis and logic. Do you feel there is a basic conflict between East and West which makes integration of these modes of perception particularly difficult?

GS: Well, there needn't be, there needn't be. In actual fact, the rational-pragmatic-analytical mode is quite common everywhere on earth, and it enables people to get a lot of work done. Modern science has developed the possibilities to an amazing degree, and no one should have any quarrel with it. It deals with facts, demonstrably, and what you learn from it is fascinating and useful. It is not able to deal with the mind itself that has the facts, the mind that analyzes. That's the other side of things, the study of mind itself rather than the study of what mind does or can do. In a sense science is simply a manifestation of the natural world in the way that the mind can see it. To look at that which *looks* is another step, and there's no conflict between looking at that which looks while also looking. Although it's hard. As they say, it's like looking for an ox that you're riding on [laugh].

S: Much of your poetry deals with nature. I was wondering what you think the relationship between man and nature is? It seems to be a religion for some people. Why isn't it for all people?

GS: Well, I can't explain why it isn't for all people. If I knew, I'd use that knowledge to advantage [laugh]. But to answer your first question, what is the relationship of man to nature—it is very simple. We are part of it. It produced us. We are still part of it; whatever we are is a function of the nature of our nervous system and our vertebrate five-fingered, five-toed capacity. We're tied to a certain amount of primate history, and there's no way that we can't be part of that whole thing. It flows through us daily as air, as food, as water. It's really curious that human beings can imagine themselves as separate from any of it!

S: Is that why the natural experience is the basis for much of your poetry?
GS: It's just a matter of "here I am, here we are." To write a poem about nature is not to write a poem about something else; it's not to make a poem about something that's outside me. Mind and environment are one. So I don't make a distinction between writing a nature poem and writing a poem about my friends, and my family, or about politics. It's in the same fabric.

S: Is that essentially the meaning of interpenetration as you use it in, for example, "For All"?
GS: Yes. Interpenetration, as far as your imagination can carry it—in that not only do all things interpenetrate, but consciousness and matter interpenetrate, and the past and the present interpenetrate, and the future and the past interpenetrate and ten thousand things interpenetrate with one thing and one thing interpenetrates with ten thousand things simultaneously both in the past and in the future. That's the scope of it; it goes in all dimensions.

S: Do these concepts have technical applications in your poetry? *Myths and Texts,* for example, is a very long and complexly organized work. Does the concept of interpenetration apply there?
GS: *Myths & Texts* to a great extent planned itself after I had hit on certain key positions that the rest manifested in terms of structure. In the same way, I'm working on "Mountains and Rivers Without End," which is a long poem, analogous perhaps in some ways to *Myths & Texts.* It's a structuring that I discover as I discover relationships between the poems and relationships between certain intentions I have for dealing with things. It's obviously not the kind of organization that you can predict or project on something. That is possibly in the nature of the kind of interpenetration we're talking about, the kind of interpenetration that is expressed by metaphor, and eludes the simple linear way of organizing things that is done by rationality alone.

S: Does that apply as well to the juxtapositioning of apparently disparate elements in *Myths & Texts?*

GS: Well, that's also Pound's ideographic method—which works. A great deal more can be said by placing things in proper juxtaposition than by trying to describe the connections between them. That's why John McPhee's book, *Oranges*, is so interesting. A book all about oranges. If it were issued as a US Government Department of Agriculture publication in normal, rational, bureaucratic style, it would be organized in an entirely different way—1, 2, a, b, c, 1, 2. . . . All about oranges. And it would be crashingly dull. McPhee's juxtapositioning of the information is poetic and unpredictable and has an inner organizing principle, which is mind principle—or whatever you want to call it—that makes it fascinating and memorable.

S: You were talking earlier today about music in poetry and about American folk songs. Do you think there is a movement toward a highly sophisticated poetry/song, something that would be accepted as a serious art form rather than as "pop"?

GS: I think that's possible. What I'd really like to see, as that happens, is the separation between audience and performer eliminated as much as possible, and more people singing songs themselves—make their own music. I really don't want to talk about this in terms of "pop," of people appearing on television or at very huge audiences and being very popular—I mean that'd be all right, I suppose. But what is really necessary is that we all learn to play musical instruments and sing and do it at home with our families and our friends. Make your own music, make your own culture. Make your own culture. Don't rely on somebody else to make culture for you.

S: What about the cultural inheritance you have accumulated over the years, which you would not have if you had simply made your own culture?

GS: You always make your own culture with the help of teachers. The point is not to be a spectator, but to be a participant. Art should be a participatory activity, not a spectator activity, as far as possible—which does not contradict the possibility of there being a few unique great artists that everyone recognizes as such. We have far too much spectatorship now in all these things.

S: Do you think a specifically American consciousness is developing?

GS: Sure, it's developing all the time. Paradoxically, as we get more cosmopolitan—drink more wine, eat more pizza, etc.—we're also becoming more genuinely American . . . The surfacing of Black consciousness and Chicano consciousness and American Indian consciousness, and people asserting that a non-European heritage is as respectworthy as a purely European heritage—all of these things are contributing, *finally*, to the emergence of an America, of a United States that begins to fulfill its interesting promise. In fact, it may not be useful even to talk about an American consciousness forever, but to look at Chicano culture, Black culture, American Indian culture in the twentieth century. And WASP culture if you like [laugh] as one of the components. Or Hopi-Zen-Jew culture, which is what we have out in northern California.

S: Do you think of this new consciousness as being, or becoming, somehow rooted in a specifically American landscape or territory?

GS: Well, yes, finally we have to live in territories; we have to live in natural regions; we have to live in terms of the space that's physical around us. Bioregionalism we call it. Turtle Island consciousness. The time is not too far off when it won't be possible to get so many foods imported long distances, and you'll become aware again of the fact that wherever you are within a range of two or three hundred miles, the sunshine that falls on the plants there is essentially what is supporting you—the firewood, the corn, the vegetables, the mushrooms. That's literally how human beings have to live in the long run. We'll have to be more like our grandparents, but we'll also be more cosmopolitan. And I think the possibilities of a lower-tech, solar-powered future are fascinating: a more decentralized, comprehensible technology, in which we don't give up electricity, but we don't use it as much, and in which agriculture, fisheries, forestry are really seen as our main industries. Making what we need by understanding and utilizing living things—the plants, the animals, the fish—and training them really well and really finding out how the whole system works is the real job of science in the future. It could be very beautiful. It could generate wonderful biologists, and marine biologists, and agronomists who really are sensitive and understand the processes and respect them. Communication via radio technology is easy; it doesn't take much electricity to run a radio. Computers do not take very much electricity. Those are highly efficient tools that use a very low level of energy input. That kind of sophistication is quite possible. I know that I'll be having electricity where I live in a matter of four or five years when Matsushita Electric finishes its research on bringing the price down on direct solar photovoltaic cells, so that we'll be able to afford a bank of solar cells on the roof that will charge a 12-volt battery system and give us DC current lighting in our house. And we'll never have to buy a drum of kerosene again. Now I call that progress! [laugh] That's decentralizing. You're no longer reliant on a system that brings oil all the way from Saudi

Arabia but getting the energy from your sun right on your roof and via a highly sophisticated technology. Understanding that that's possible makes it actually worthwhile thinking about the future.

S: Do so you think that as we become more aware of being Americans, we will become more aware of the American landscape and respect it more?

GS: As we become less and less Americans, we'll become more aware of the Turtle Island landscape and respect it more [laugh]. Which is a way of rephrasing what you said to show you how I feel about it exactly. My friends in New Hampshire, for example, found that fuel oil is really expensive, so they're burning a lot of firewood. A lot of people in New Hampshire are heating with wood now. As you start to burn firewood you become aware of the trees and the forest, what species are there, what species burn well, how long will these woods last if we burn them too much, let's thin the woods, but be careful, etc. And as you come back to living in terms of your local ground, you really do see it then. And if you realize that you're going to be living there for the next thousand years, then you're going to be truly careful with it.

S: The only problem I find with that vision is that there seem to be just too many people to really make it work.

GS: Well, eventually populations will curl down. We should really plan for that by holding a zero or negative birthrate and letting population drop. Nobody has to be, you know, eliminated or anything. It's just planning to let the population go down for a century. Now, if people could understand that and not be scared by it . . . I have no idea why it bothers people to think of population dropping. Obviously, population dropping means a lot more space not only for human beings, but also for wildlife and diversity, and makes the planet an easier place to live for everything—everyone and everything. It's nonviolent and harmless to simply let the population go down, and not to get upset when you have a declining birthrate. But international politics militates against that, because every country is afraid to lose population if the other guys are growing. There are really tricky problems. Still, the vision is workable.

S: Your concern for the future is very obvious. What kind of effect would you like your poetry to have on the future?

GS: The effect of making people feel that such a vision is possible and to allay anxiety. And to remind us that even though the monolithic forces of contemporary industrial, technological, capitalist, and communist societies seem almost insuperably powerful, to bear in mind that we are not small egos pitting ourselves against this huge structure. Hopefully we are the power of the nature of the universe itself pitting itself against these structures. And they are really very fragile.

An Interview with Gary Snyder

Denise Low and Robin Tawney / 1980

Cottonwood Review, no. 22 (Spring 1980), 47–56. Reprinted by permission.

Denise Low: I was reading the massive interview with you in the *Ohio Review*, and rereading that I began to see how much your poetry embodies some basic anthropological perspectives. Do you consciously use anthropology in your writings?

Gary Snyder: Well, let's get away from the word anthropology, which is okay for starters, but what anthropology means to me is a broad view of the human condition, a broad view of and acquaintance with certain necessary information as to what man has been up to and what has taken place on this planet with our species for the last thirty-five, forty, fifty thousand years. This is not an exotic kind of information. Eventually it will become part of the lore that school children learn in our lifetime, by the third or fourth grade. It is only a special kind of information now because it hasn't been important to our view of ourselves. So it's a beginning and one that tries to move into pluralism and pluralities of cultures and diversities of value systems, cultural activity, etc., and to forge on ahead to find what peculiar rules of mind and behavior perhaps bind together and allow us to find some kind of wholeness. Anthropology as science, of course, is concerned with those rules. And I like to think of that information sometimes in terms of my own life, my own vehicle. There are two kinds of Buddhism, Hinayana and Mahayana. Hinayana is the Buddhism of individuals who are striving toward enlightenment, and Mahayana is the Buddhism of those who commit themselves to a vision of everybody becoming enlightened together. That's the anthropological vision I envision.

Low: That's another question I have: how does the wide cultural view tie in with Buddhism? I hadn't realized that larger social concern of Mahayana Buddhism. Hinayana is more commonly practiced, at least in Lawrence.

Snyder: The Hinayana psychology is widespread, even though people think they follow Mahayana. "Maha" means great; "yana" means vehicle: the great vehicle. It's the big ship that everybody can get on. The Mahayana spirit is an essential spirit for these times as we realize the need to embrace the whole diversity of the community while not losing individual characteristics and specificities of places and things. It's another way of speaking of planetary vision, or what the ecological vision suggests to us.

Low: So you're thinking of people having, in their approaches to life and in their ways of perceiving their lives, that whole history of thirty-five to fifty thousand years?
Snyder: I think that, for starts, that's where poets can get to work.

Low: Do you think this is a peculiarly American concept in poetry as opposed to British?
Snyder: It may be, at this time, something that appeals to the American mentality because of the oddness of the American experience in the sense of the quality of being a little forward in time, perhaps. This is to say, some of our experience is the experience that some other cultures will have shortly after we do. We live in a culturally disintegrated, highly industrialized society. We experience things that they aspire to, which is nothing to be proud of, but it gives our poetics a certain validity. There are hippies in Japan now that look like our hippies from ten years ago. So it's an artist's or poet's work, I think, to be the digesters of information.

Low: Back to the anthropology, or the "broad view of the human condition"; does that perspective give any general statements about human needs?
Snyder: Well, they used to think they would like to find the laws of cultural dynamics as though it were a natural science. There are things to be discovered as to how things work. I don't know how much that will teach us in terms of being wise. I think it helps. I have great respect for the structuralists and their research. They are looking for patterns, the way things work.

Low: Have you discovered any rules?
Snyder: Maybe I have, but I haven't figured it out yet. I'm not ready to articulate them. Now, to articulate them, I might have located some things, theoretically, say; I might have located some things and put them in poetry. But the articulation of them in official academic language remains to be done. I

haven't seen that yet or know how to do it. There may well be some things that cannot be stated.

Robin Tawney: You mentioned children learning all of this information very early on in their educational careers. How do you see trying to get this into a political reality?

Snyder: What I'm talking about is not and could not be a political reality. Politics cannot make culture, just like the Supreme Court can only make decisions that the majority of the people give assent to in the abstract. In the abstract, legal motions on the highest level are still dependent on assent, and what the people think is dependent on culture. So we work with the deep level of mind rather than with legislation to work toward a kind of transformation. It's a much slower process. It takes centuries.

Tawney: You work on a government's awareness through the California Arts Council. How does that help?

Snyder: It doesn't.

Low: It doesn't even work on the lower level of consciousness?

Snyder: Just barely, insofar as you encourage, by whom you aid and abet, the artists who might be involved in the deeper level transformation. In that sense I suppose the California Council of the Arts has moved a few tiny stones in its support of cultural diversity and especially its respectful attention to cultural and artistic standards of Chicano people and other groups, and in doing so has increased the richness of the consciousness, cultural possibilities of the future. But for me, being on the California Arts Council was largely an education in our government, in how our bureaucracy works.

Tawney: So this was for self-defense?

Snyder: No, self-education.

Low: So you're saying that briefly, through the centuries, or little by little through the centuries, we can raise up the whole cultural consciousness toward something. How does that fit in with the position that most poets find themselves in today; that is, they have no audience?

Snyder: Well, most poets are not poets, if you want to count five thousand American poets, of which a large percentage have no clear sense of what they are doing and certainly no vision that is really a larger vision. So that's why I say maybe most aren't really poets. So if we hold it down to those who have a vision and who don't tend to stop what they're doing, do or die, maybe there's a hundred of those. They have audiences. And the audience is slowly and steadily growing. Not that the audience should be too huge, but we do have a whirlpool of poetry growing in the last few years. And audiences come into existence when poets think about audiences and write poems with audiences in mind, and go out and read their poems to audiences and participate in the real world and make decisions and choices and commitments to the world. And audiences have heard. It's as simple as that. It's like a mirror. I've written a paper on this called "Poetry in the World." It's about the public process of poetry since World War II. It will be published in *Field* magazine sometime this spring [1979].

Low: What is your opinion of the small presses?
Snyder: Fine. They're excellent, especially if the small presses try to stay small, recognize their smallness, and try to serve the regional need. When small presses all compete with each other on a national level, it's kind of a waste of energy. We talk about regionalism and decentralization in politics and ecology. We should also understand this applies to culture. The decentralization of poetry and culture is as necessary as the decentralization of energy and bureaucracy, which means that little magazines should be responsive and responsible to their region. They should illuminate that region rather than aspiring to some kind of nationwide light that they will never achieve.

Low: Do you publish mostly in your region of northern California?
Snyder: In terms of magazine publications? My book publisher is New Directions, which is nationwide, so in that regard I don't practice what I preach. But, on the other hand, there is a level at which some poems do have a larger audience and my poems do have a national audience. When I publish new poems I publish them regionally, in the regional magazines. That's where I float them.

Low: What is the journal you just coedited with Ferlinghetti, McClure, and Meltzer last fall [1978]? Was it a reprint of "A Visionary and Revolutionary Review" of the sixties?
Snyder: Well, the cover is a reprint, but the journal itself is all new material. *Journal for the Protection of All Beings.* That's Stewart Brand's *Co-Evolution Quarterly,* a special fall issue.

Low: So that's the kind of regionalism you like to participate in?

Snyder: Well, that's not really regional because *Co-Evolution Quarterly* is a nationwide publication, although it is definitely West Coast and it reflects the northern California consciousness. Northern California is the center of the emerging meeting of poetry, biology, ecology, economics, and science. So *Co-Evolution Quarterly* reflects these. Another regional magazine I publish in is called *Kuksu*, subtitled, "A Journal of Backcountry Writing" [Nevada City, California].

Tawney: Is this vision unique to this time, or do you feel it is something you've discovered because of your contact with the East?

Snyder: Some people have discovered it by their own paths, have come to a view of biology or their own politics or their own ethnic politics. It's a place where a lot of interests intersect because it really holds the possibility of holding a large vision of the planet without losing its variety. The "global" vision of the planet, which is held by or peddled by the salesmen of the multinational corporations, they'll say "one world." Yes, and what they mean is one world which is all the same, in which the same government is the nation, and every little country has a role in it, and every nation is on a fossil fuel tit. So we try to distinguish between globalism and planetarian thinking, just as a matter of terminology. Planetary thinking is also one mouth, but it's a world in which biological solutions rather than technological solutions are respected and in which the ethnic and biological diversity and variety of the planet is respected for, if nothing else, scientific reasons, not to mention historical, compassionate reasons. And so that is a decentralist, appropriate technological, ecologically oriented vision of the planetary life instead of the industrial, de-evolution, one-world central government vision of the planet. It is very important to distinguish between the two, because the globalists would masquerade sometimes as though they were planetary.

Low: This is the whole "global village" concept, which is not really planetary?

Snyder: Yes, it's the trilateral commission. The trilateral commission is the three major industrial sectors of the village of the United States combined to promote fossil fuels, to mainline it—humanely and efficiently, right? They'll sell it to you by saying, "We can't let people starve." Of course we don't want people to starve.

Low: What is your answer to that?

Snyder: My answer to that is for a while, you might have increased food production, but you're riding it right to the edge. When it all collapses, when your soil fertility is wiped out, when your third world countries that have been injecting fossil fuel fertilizers cannot afford it on the balance of payments, and you can no longer afford to ship it to them free. And the answer is that we go back to, and step forward into, biologically sensitive, lower technological, higher labor intensive agricultural systems that permit people to be locally self-sufficient and not depend on expensive resources brought in from outside. And if anything needs to be rectified, it's land holding taxation and interest rate problems. You see, take India: Two solutions to the problems of the Indian farmer. The American solution is, give them pumps, tractors, chemical fertilizer and improved seed strain. They'll start growing more food.

Low: Isn't that what they are trying to get for China now?
Snyder: That is what China, stupidly, is asking for. So what happens is that after a while, they don't know how to maintain the pumps, they don't know how to maintain the tractors, they can't afford the fossil fuel fertilizer and the new strains of seeds deplete their soils and grow out of season. So that's one answer.

The other answer that comes in is simply the Chinese system; is, well, the top tier of the problem is we are over taxed, the interest rate is too high, so let's have some political changes for starters. Okay, so you free holders of land; you don't have debt or a tax burden. Now, without that, you can have only a social burden. Let's see if you can improve the agricultural use of the tools you have and make them more sophisticated, using tools that they already have, or if it takes new tools, using tools that can be maintained there. And in some cases the solution is not any of those. In some cases the solution has to do with overpopulation: eliminating, say, goats, reforesting forests. Slowly we must plan this.

Tawney: What is needed is a unique combination of individual production and self-sufficiency in an original way with the intent that it be unified in a planetary way.
Snyder: That's what it is; that's what the intention is. And that is the way people used to live. So, without talking about going backwards, we do it by work. People are always saying, you're trying to go back to the Stone Age. David Brower, who is head of Friends of the Earth, was once accused of that by a reporter: "Well, Mr. Brower, you should go back to the Stone Age." Brower said, "Well, I'd be satisfied with the twenties." The population of the world was only half what it is now.

Low: The other thing I wonder about, though, is what do you think about people like me, with electric typewriters? I read your interview in the *Ohio*

Review, along these lines, and went home and looked at my dishwasher and thought, Gary Snyder would not like this.

Snyder: Well, I don't know about electric typewriters—I get along fine with them. There is a question of appropriateness there. There are some things that only electricity can do. Only electricity can do this [taps tape recorder]: this is very appropriate. It's light, and it does a good job, and its energy cost is minimal. An electric typewriter is probably kind of a luxury. A dishwasher is a luxury if you are not working. If you are a working person, if both of you are working, then you can understand using it. Dishwashers really should be children. Children are dish washers. If you raise your children right—this may not apply in your case, but I see many families who are too goddamned lazy to raise their children to work. So the children are standing around with their dumb faces hanging out while the dishwasher is running. Now what way to do things is that? You've got all these suburban households where the kids feel useless. They feel of no value to the economic system. They have no role to play. What kind of self-esteem and dignity are you going to get out of having no role to play when you're ten or twelve years old? When Black Elk was twelve years old he shot a white man with a Colt revolver. He knew what he was doing. He was playing a role in his cultural life. And in former society, boys and girls knew that there is work to be done, and they love it. They get skills and they get pride. So if you have a situation in which a machine is replacing a child, how dumb. That's a double loss. On the other hand, a vacuum cleaner is a great tool, because there is nothing that will do what a vacuum cleaner can do, so that's a place where electricity is appropriate.

There is a basic laziness in the suburban life in the education of kids. It's work to raise kids to do the things. You have to pay attention, keep after them; although once they learn it, they'll do it. And a lot of people are so damn lazy they'll find machinery to do the work of the children. And that gets transmitted from generation to generation. That's really corrupt.

Tawney: I assume that began after the depression. Parents wanted to give their children what they didn't have. Parents of people my age just picked that up from theirs. It's become an automatic cycle.
Snyder: The intention is often too kind.

Low: Doesn't this go back to the breakup of the household as an economic unit? The father goes out to work and wants the woman home without an important economic role for prestige?

Snyder: Well, that's suburban life. Obviously farm families can't live like this. And it's middle class because up until World War I and after, women of the working class still worked in factories, participated in strikes, were socialists. It is really important and interesting to develop a concept of what household economy is, and how dignity and productiveness is possible both within the house and outside of the house. There is a good book on it, called *Household Economy*. It's really talking about how households and economies have similar approaches, seriously. It also really comes to the point that is obviously valid that the housewife is not playing a minor role at all. It is an extremely important role. That work can be measured in dollars and cents if you want to, if you want to talk about amounts of social security, how to do that. But beyond that, children have to work. It's alienation, just another variety of alienation that people have these machine operated, super-clean houses—which they go away from on weekends for recreation—surrounded by a well-kept lawn on which and in which nothing happens. Now how would you transform that? An Asian model, a future model: here is the vision of the future, twenty years from now.

Each suburban house will have a fence around it, and part of it will be a high wall, part of it will be a low animal fence. Where the lawn is today will be a vegetable garden. It will be a very finely kept vegetable garden. Maybe that part won't be fenced; it depends on what kinds of animals are kept. But the back yard part or one corner of it will be fenced with a high fence rather than just open to the world. And that will be a private outdoor living space, because people will be outdoors as well as indoors. And there will be a greenhouse. And the greenhouse will be oriented toward the south, will have heating and hot water recycling systems, and will grow almost all the vegetables you need the year round. Part of the property, if it's large enough, will be left to grow wood. And you'll see children back there, working in the garden, maybe with a fish pond, working in the greenhouse, splitting firewood (because more of the cooking and heating will be done by wood), and generally having a great time. There may be a few goats, maybe a horse or a cow, but the children are doing some of the work.

And every little suburban household will be like this. Every one of those suburban households quite possibly could be supplying almost all of its own food. Schools will be smaller and will be moved back into the different suburban localities, so the kids will all be within bicycle or walking distance of the school. There will be smaller work bases, factories, and industries locally that the men and women can walk or ride to. And there'll be community centers and churches that really serve as community centers and churches, and at which there'll be great dinners, pot lucks, dances, get-togethers every weekend because people aren't interested in or cannot afford to go long distances away, so they will turn back to their towns. And there will be poetry readings and drama and dance presentations. And it will all be within walking distance.

That's the post-fossil fuel world. Scary, isn't it?

Tawney: It sounds pretty nice.
Snyder: Yes, I know.

Low: But you're also saying we won't have to give up communications, like telephones, or all transportation . . .
Snyder: I doubt that we'll have to give up telephones, but transportation and telephones are two different kettles of fish. So you do your energy cost accounting. How much energy does it take to make a phone call? How much energy does it take to fly to New York? So you can talk on the phone to New York and do a little of business without having to fly there, as a lot of people are beginning to realize.

Tawney: It seems that telephones would be one of the things that would allow the decentralization of power.
Snyder: That's a point that McLuhan made ten years ago, that electrical and electronic communications really speed the cycle of decentralization. That's really true. Computer technology is the most cost-efficient in terms of energy than anything else going. More work gets done for less energy by the computer than anything.

So we're not talking about giving up everything. Where I live we don't have telephones or electricity, but people all keep in touch with each other with C.B. radios. The amount of electricity required to talk fifteen or twenty miles across a canyon or across a forest to another household seemingly is zero. You just have to charge your car battery twice a year. And yet the information that goes back and forth saves hundreds of miles of driving. That kind of technology, more and more sophisticated, will be part of the future. But still, you've got to grow your food. There's no simple way for that.

Low: But that's a pleasure.
Snyder: It's a pleasure; that's the way to see it. How better for your kids to grow up to learn about biology, soil chemistry, all those things they might learn in school but probably won't, and would learn right in their

own back yard. Entomology, ecology—entomology is the first thing they'd learn, and chemistry.

Tawney: I'm concerned about how the population is going to be tapered down. It seems that if decentralization occurs, and we are put back in an agrarian setting, that there is that added incentive to have a larger-than-two-child family for necessary purposes. I guess I am thinking in terms of the way the setting is in Lawrence, where the husband works in town and then goes home to the farm, which would not be the case.

Snyder: The farmers have to do that. They have to do that partly because they don't get paid well for the food they produce.

Low: Back to more literary topics, who are some poets you follow?

Snyder: Jim Heynen, I think he's back in the state of Washington. He has several books out, and he's got a new book coming out of what you might call real "poem stories." They are somewhere between prose and poetry and just marvelous stories.

Howard Norman has poems based on kinds of ways that Native Americans gave names to their kids.

Low: Harley Elliott has a notebook of real Native American names, like "The Guy Who Talks Too Much," "The One Who Passes Too Much Gas," everything from joke names to sacred names. And at a reading he will go through the notebook, John Cage style, flip the pages and read off names.

Snyder: Norman's poems are based on stories that people told him. Actually, every name has a story, how that person got their name. The names are interesting, like "Taps a Frog."

Low: How do you, and why do you, tap a frog?

Snyder: The first thing about this person, he is blind. When he came down the creek, with his stick he would tap, tap, tap. As he tapped his way, the frogs would jump in. Hearing the frogs jump in, he knew where the water was.

Tawney: That's called working with the system.

Low: But he's in trouble in the winter.

Snyder: You know how fast it freezes in Montana sometimes. Sometimes they have fast freezes where it freezes up so fast that frogs try to jump in and get caught half way in the ice. So people have businesses up there of harvesting frog legs. You just cut those legs off just to the right length and bundle them up solid.

Low: This isn't a tall tale?
Snyder: Yes, it is. I heard that from a friend from Wyoming.

Gary Snyder, the well-known poet and essayist, visited the University of Kansas from February 20 to February 24, 1979. During his stay he participated in numerous activities. He met with Japanese Studies classes, an introduction to literature class, and the advanced poetry seminar. He held individual conferences with student writers. For the Geography Department he spoke to the Human Survival Projects class. And at the Spencer Museum of Art, he presented a paper, "Landscape Poetry and Chinese Ecology." Off campus Snyder read and discussed his work at Haskell Indian Junior College. With a visiting Russian poet, he was interviewed by the town newspaper. He participated in a sunrise meditation service with a Lawrence Buddhist group. And he presented the Nelson Gallery of Art in Kansas City with four poems based on Japanese paintings in their collection.

The interview took place February 21, 1979.

Gary Snyder: A Centerless Universe: An Interview

Paul Christensen / 1981

Affinities 1, No. 1, 1981. Reprinted by permission.

Paul Christensen: I'd like to begin by saying that a number of signals are beginning to surface in American criticism, American thought, American poetry that we are at the end of the open road. We have begun to exhaust a land mass that was supposed, at least mythologically, to be inexhaustible; we thought we could waste and pilfer and plunder it at will. Now we are beginning to hear the conscience of a whole other attitude towards the environment that our lives depend upon, and clearly central to it is one of the great lyric voices of our time, Gary Snyder. So without further ado, I will say welcome Gary Snyder, it's good to have you here.

Gary Snyder: It's nice to be here, Paul. This is my third visit to Austin and I feel right at home in this landscape, in this biome. Not only because of the fact that my mother was born and raised over in Palestine [Texas], but because the kind of semi-arid, live oak and cedar territory you have here is not all that different from California, where I live. It has some similarities in feeling and climate. It is interesting to sense a continuity of territory down the West Coast that sort of sneaks across the deserts of Arizona and New Mexico and pops up again in Texas.

PC: What things specifically are you talking about?

GS: Well, all these live oaks around. Of course, in the rolling hills with the live oaks and early spring, mid-spring grass turning to brown grass later is California. We don't have the cedars there but we have Monterrey Cypress on the coast and equivalent plants which get by in this kind of marginally rainy climate. I would guess it's about the same as a lot of averages in Southern California.

PC: Yes, it's about the same.

GS: It's a challenge for Anglos to learn how to live in that kind of climate. Anglos, North European, Western European Anglos are still just barely beginning to learn how to build their houses, how to plant their gardens, what clothes to wear, how to move around in a Californian climate. I bet it is the same here.

PC: We were talking about that last night, Dave Riedel and I, that a house that might have been designed for New England, just because of the way technology replicates things, is built in every other region and terrain, simply because it's a building plan and it's easy to transfer it to the next contractor. But whoever is living down there on the Mississippi Delta is sweltering and is very unhappy. That whole idea of giving into the environment and building in accordance with it is still something that has to be learned.

GS: Nobody even thought of it for the longest time. We have a lot of work ahead of us. For centuries in learning appropriate styles to the place.

PC: Well, you are our best example. You were discussing last night at your reading that you have two kitchens, an indoor kitchen for the winter, an outdoor kitchen for the summer, and you spend fully six months in the summer kitchen, right?

GS: Right, six months of the year we cook outside and live to a great extent outside.

PC: What kind of house have you built for yourself? How would you describe it?

GS: My architecture—well, you know it fits what we set ourselves to when we came back from Japan and decided to build on this little piece of marginal brushy land up in the mountains that I had managed to get hold of back in the sixties when land in California was cheap. We said let's crossbreed the Spanish Californian, the Japanese farmhouse, and the native American house—that would seem right for this area. And we were relatively successful in doing that. What I did was take the old Neolithic and also Mandan Indian framing pattern of four central posts with a perimeter of posts and plates around the top of the four central posts, say sixteen feet off the ground, and then resting round pole rafters radially from the central box or frame to the outer box or frame leaving a hole in the center. And that's the old Neolithic smoke-house hole. It allows for a fire pit in the center and a way for the smoke to go up. That is actually found in ancient Europe, neolithic Europe and in ancient Japan.

PC: Is this the principle where you heat with an open fire?

GS: That's a way to heat the whole house fast and to have an open campfire in the middle of the house. You don't have any furniture—that's the Japanese part, no furniture, sit on the floor. So you can sit around an open campfire indoors. Very satisfactory.

PC: Also, there are no bedrooms, in effect, in a Japanese house—there are rolls that are kept in a chest or box.

GS: Or a built-in storage cabinet along one wall. Yes, we unfold our bedding for our different beds.

PC: Well, one of the things that strikes me in describing your life style is that you have made a connection which would be difficult for many poets to do, and that is to be at once lyrical from your own nature and to also be an activist of your own vision in many ways, both practically in the building of a house and the way that you live and in your involvement in a number of ecological issues and concerns. I understand from Paul Foreman that you were invited to the Stockholm Conference on the Environment in the early 1970s.

GS: In 1972, the U.N. Conference. I went with a number of people as uninvited participants. Sort of a counter group to critique and to raise issues that weren't being raised by the official Conference on the Environment.

PC: Was that mostly for scientists and social planners?

GS: Yes, global engineers. The star performer perhaps was Margaret Mead in the official conference, who did quite well. And elegant people like Barbara Tuchman, and other British upper-class ecology people with a Gandhian background—folks like that. And then the Chinese delegation to the '72 Stockholm Conference on the Environment. Predictably enough, for that time, they said there was/is no environmental problem, there is only capitalism for a problem and denied that air pollution would ever be a problem in China because they said we can make use of all our waste products and turn them into treasure. Since then the Chinese have probably discovered that it isn't all that easy. But this is an interesting little point in American cultural history, the number of us, including Michael McClure, the poet and playwright, and a number of American Indian leaders, Hopi, Navaho, Mohawk, all of us were sent there. Actually our expenses were paid for by the Point Foundation, and Point Foundation is the foundation that was formed with the profits from *Whole Earth Catalogue*. Stewart Brand's own little foundation to handle profits from the *Whole Earth Catalogue*.

PC: There are really two large centers of interest in your life: one, of course, is the perfecting of the craft of poetry, which you have been laboring at for twenty-five-thirty years; and on the other side is this growing concern with the state of the planet for human life as well as for all other forms of life. Are the two one in your mind? Is it in being a poet you have a sensitivity and an access to experience that goes outside institutional life or immediate social life? Is it in the act of the poem that you integrate yourself with a large world, or is it something that one struggles with beyond the poetry and tries to bring the poetry to that concern?

GS: Well, I would like to argue that at its most fundamental level any creative endeavor is a self-transcending act. Consequently, it reaches out in the large scale to the recognition of interconnection, interdependence, and compassion. Outside not only the self but the immediate family, the immediate group, the human race, and even outside of maybe the condition of living beings to embrace at its greatest expanse what Robinson Jeffers called the eternal sunrise on the rocks. (There's a poem where Jeffers said: "If all the life on the planet is destroyed it will still be beautiful. Eternal sunrise on the rocks.") And then, recognizing that the act of creativity is self-transcending. It does open us to scales beyond our personal concerns. That fact in a sense I think was almost formalized in primitive and archaic cultures in their recognition of the Shaman artist, singer, healer, as a being who brought a voice from the outside. We must recognize that most of us most of the time are living inevitably in a network of small concerns—our personal agenda—our day-to-day social agenda, and that it takes somebody who can step out of that agenda and come back and speak for hawks or speak for babies or speak for springtime, and continually reinfuse the social matrix with a vision that goes beyond self-interest. However, it is also true that in civilized times we have a great body of highly civilized poetry which does not necessarily touch on anything like a planetary or cosmic scale, or even show much concern for the nonhuman.

PC: This is what I was concerned with in my question.

GS: There is a poetry of human affairs: in Catullus, in a sense Pound. Although Pound breaks out of it sometimes with his own odd pantheism. Much of English and European poetry is a poetry of human affairs. The model for breaking out of ego-centered affairs in occidental poetry is love, it's romance, it's the formality of the troubadour and your lover, the woman, becomes nature, becomes the cosmos and you discover yourself in her. Rather than discover yourself in all that she might be just in that physical lover body relationship. It's curious, because we are breaking out of that now, too.

Paul Foreman: In your own work, would you say that the unfolding of the Chinese tradition was really important in that sense to that part of your natural scale and human—

GS: Yes, Chinese poetry has been very important to me, and to practically everybody who wrote poetry in the last few decades. It is able to accomplish the recognition of human affairs in poetry, frailties, wine, family, friendships, parting, and at the same time handle the large scale of nature simultaneously. It's an amazing achievement when you think that in general, in occidental poetry, there's nature poetry and there's poetry of human affairs. And they don't mix much. In Chinese poetry they weave it together, which I suppose is just another evidence that at its very best Chinese culture is more holistic, more organic than the occidental model.

PC: Would you describe your own early work as being concerned much more, almost exclusively, with yourself in nature—in the contemplation of nature, in a response to nature, but often depicting yourself in isolation from humanity?

GS: Well, in my early books, you see the poetry that I managed to write when I was working in mountain jobs. It came out of the context of being in isolation and working in the mountains. I was twenty-five, twenty-six when I started writing the poetry that's in my books now, wondering about the fact that I had gone through three years of graduate school and had dropped out—I kept saying to myself "What am I going to do?" So it's in that context that I began these poems which are indeed of myself in the mountains and trying to figure out where I am. In the mountains and also in my own civilization.

PC: Of course, I only have the record of what you have chosen to keep, but it would seem that you were not motivated to try to describe the camaraderie of working in the logging camps with others—the human affairs of that situation.

GS: Only marginally, when I could get some texts of the guys who were in those logging camps come in and out a little bit. Yea. Well you know the camaraderie is captured elsewhere, look in *Six Sections from Mountains and Rivers Without End.* As an artist I don't try to do what other people can do just as well as I can. I really thought about all of the funny anecdotes and jokes and stories of logging camp life, and I said, "Boy, that would make a good short story." But I never got around to it. Because somebody somewhere is going to do it, anyway. Sure enough Ken Kesey came along and did a good Oregon logging novel, so I didn't have to do it.

PC: Is there a special evolution in your work, though? It would seem to me that what I was trying to get to originally was to suggest that instinctively you were becoming that respondent to different specific phenomena in nature, not generality. It is always the rocks, we are here. No one loves the rocks, but we are here, we do hear these things. It would seem to me that you were growing in a certain direction which became partly argumentative with the reader. You seemed, in mid-career, not content merely with your capacity to enliven a particular experience with a natural phenomenon, any longer. It would seem that you wished to bring something else to your poetry, perhaps a more articulated, argumentative vision of what needs to be done.

GS: Actually, I think that I went through that phase. I'm not sure what phase I'm at, right now. *Turtle Island* (which is already five years old) is the book in which a number of somewhat argumentative poems surface, and in the late sixties and early seventies I felt most compelled to develop an articulate political statement in my poetry, even though there is political statement all the way back into the collection of poems called *Myths & Texts,* which evokes the IWW anarchist heritage of the West Coast worker, among other things. So, I have done that—the argument—I don't know if I'm going to be doing a further argument, at least on the same level. Because again, I don't have to. Other people are doing it better than I am now.

PC: Okay, I'm interested in that. You had given it as full a statement, I think, as you could in *Earth House Hold,* and then with *Turtle Island* you even address the reader directly, almost as if the book is a reading of the poems and then a commentary.

GS: Right. It's bald, it's shameless the way I did that in *Turtle Island.*

PC: Yea, but I see the urgency of it. You say it's a bald effort, but obviously the urgency was uppermost in your mind at that point.

GS: Exactly, and that's why I took the risk of laying my poems out and then saying, look, these are political—they are designed to challenge you and the whole society. And I think that was the use of it.

PC: Is there a way to capture the political argument of these years—late sixties up to and including *Turtle Island*, '75. Is there a way to capture it conceptually? What precisely was your concern at this time?

GS: Speaking for myself and some of my compadres, that political ecological direction was post-Marxian, decentralist, environmentalist, expansion of the concerns of liberation, justice, cooperation in such a way that it also recognized and included the necessity of honoring and nourishing older cultural models that worked, like the band or the family, like the importance of transmitted information, like the importance of certain kinds of tradition. And so I think I and a number of us have taken a turn in which we are profoundly conservative and profoundly radical at the same time—looking back to the early days of civilization as well as ahead. And I think all of these are rather new in a sense. They are certainly away from the more simple liberal model of the mid-sixties.

PC: You haven't changed your position in one way since 1961, in your address to the Patterson Society, when you described yourself as having the most archaic values.

GS: See, I didn't know what I was saying when I said that. Everything I have been doing since I have been trying to figure out if what I said was right, and if so what would I do?

PC: You must be sympathetic then to Olson's description of himself as an "archeologist of morning"—trying to get back to an utterly primal sense of how life should be.

GS: That's a lovely phrase. And it's a phrase that cuts both ways because morning is with us every day; it's not in the past. Here's a poem that captures my position of that era: "Revolution in the Revolution in the Revolution," remembering that there was that book that was circulating around in the late sixties. Who wrote that? [Régis Debray] He was a well-known revolutionary figure at that time and was referring to one of Mao's pamphlets on revolutionary guerilla warfare. [Poem follows]

Now that is a poem that could bear some commentary and explication, but for people who are acquainted with the general structure and language of Marxist thought, it is transparent in how I have played with certain things and restructured it. If the capitalists and imperialists, if civilization, or if abstract rational intellect are not to be conceived as mutually exclusive, it could easily be said, "When or on the occasion that, in the case that the capitalist imperialists are the exploiters, the party isn't communist, but if you see that it is civilization that is the exploiter . . ." However, if one side of it is deceived and the abstract rational intellect is the exploiter then . . . So it is a multiple level of strategies.

PC: That does summarize it.
GS: It's not complete.

PC: This position implies a coherent adversary. Do you have a sense of its beginning and end in your mind?
GS: The adversary?

PC: Yes. The thing against which the poets are all intending to state their own position. What happened to the occidental? What motivates him to continue to go wrong?
GS: Well, that's bad habit. That's habit energy. So much habit energy, that even if you might want to make things grow better, the habit energy keeps rolling. That's certainly a characteristic of the way things go anyway.

PC: You mentioned in the poem the dictatorship of the unconscious. Is that in a way pointing to causes as well?
GS: Well, the dictatorship of the unconscious there would be parallel to the Communist notion of the dictatorship of the proletariat, and the idea that you must pass through, that the evolving socialist society must pass through a phase which is undemocratic and in which the proletariat is calling the shots. Theoretically once that has been thoroughly achieved, and the means of production are entirely in the hands of the workers and the workers are doing all the production and they are very happy about it and it's all working, then comes the withering away of the state and true Communism. What I call true commun*ionism.* If the abstract rational intellect is the exploiter, the masses are the unconscious. Which is to say, if we decide to go after the dominance of one part of our nature, and maybe even one hemisphere of our brain over our psychic life, and indeed over our daily life, then what we run the risk of possibly is the dictatorship of the unconscious, in which the irrational rides over all our concerns. And we have seen the dictatorship of the unconscious running around California off and on in some quarters for several years now and it is not necessarily pretty always when it happens.

PC: So we also see one of the great patterns in the twentieth century in American economic life, the centralization of means of production and of control.

GS: Of course.

PC: Is that again in some way a misdirected unconscious energy? Why I ask is because so much of your lyric is a delight in peripheries. It is delight in the incidental, not in the centralization of anything.

GS: That's true, but then I don't believe that there is any center. I'm a Buddhist. Which is to say, it is my perception that the universe is equally real at every corner, and at every part, and that there is no one place which is the center. There is no one place it is created from. The parts all create each other mutually. It may be in some ways analogous to the concepts of modern field theory, I don't know. It doesn't depend on that—it doesn't depend on validification from modern science. It validifies itself from inside, from practices of study in meditation that have been tested for centuries. But in any case whether it's validified this way or that way, we see the relevance and the supreme importance of a model of the universe which does not depend on a single authentic center—that renders all the other parts subsidiary and client to it. And it makes everything else second rate and somewhat vaguely inauthentic. This on the political and psychological level has been the negative accomplishment of civilization, which in the language of Stanley Diamond, an anthropologist, the history of civilization has been the consistent, steady takeover and destruction of local kinship-based groups who have had their own sense of center. And their capture and employment by the metropole to be producers for the services of those who live in the capital.

PC: So it's one center taking over another.

GS: It's the concept of big center for the sake of a few taking over a mosaic of self-governing independent centers who work together for each other and who exploit no one.

PC: Yes, and those centers are not vicious or pernicious the way the grand center would be.

GS: No, they might gossip about each other and beat each other on the head once in a while, but they also intermarry, and the degree of conflict or exploitation is minimal and relatively playful. So the expansion of the metropole has also been the expansion of the destruction of the biosphere, the withering away of the green edge of life everywhere on the planet, till it all begins to look like a burning newspaper and you can see the flame moving back on it. This indeed is the adversary—it is maybe not even productive to say how did it start, where did we go wrong, at this point. We simply should put the fire out, and then try to figure out later how it got started. Because that really is what is critical to us—is to put that fire out and I confess, I ask myself every day as a human being, not as a poet, what could I be doing better than what I am doing? This is the question I find myself asking right now.

PF: Gary, I remember way back the first time I heard you at Berkeley about '68 or '69 when you said the one thing that we as poets must do is listen more closely to the mother earth, and I get that consciousness just sitting here listening to you—that we as poets have our limited role in speaking to the world, but that the world is constantly speaking through us and using us to heal ourselves.

GS: When we are at our best I think that's what we're doing, and we also, in that sense, have to be humble in the recognition that when we do that it doesn't necessarily produce an immediate impact or results, and so, of course, we are all tempted once in a while to get up in front of the ten thousand student audience at some rally and speak out in passionate prose to say the message in a way that will agitate the kids to get up and do something. But then we have also seen that that lasts for maybe six weeks and then it fades and so we have to be humble and patient—saying what our song has to say, letting the song come out and thinking that, hoping that, it will work into the mind and accomplish some tiny but real change over the years. And the patience is required because we don't have much time and yet we can't speed it up, either. We have to do the best work we can and hope that it gets there in time. The only alternative is activist politics. I don't think you can easily do the kind of delicate sensitive listening that you and I are talking about, and at the same time be in activist politics. Maybe some people can, but I don't feel I can do it. So I stay quiet and do my work, but I still ask myself, am I doing enough?

PC: Is it because there are too many intermediaries for the political activist? All that he says gets filtered through one medium after another before it finally gets down to the large, large audience.

GS: It is a question of medium too. The political activist speaks to rational abstract intellect through rational abstract intellect.

PC: But the song doesn't.
GS: But the song doesn't. So you are delivering the right message, but between the wrong carriers. You know, it's like telling the FBI what you want to do, and the FBI may very well subvert your message on that account, and say I don't want this to get down there where they'll understand it.

PC: Can we turn now to your poetics and techniques?
GS: Sure, let's do that.

PC: All right, the earliest poems are very open, and they have a kind of prospective line to them; it's a very free open kind of poetry. I hear a rhythm as a subtext running through these, but I understand from listening to you and from reading about you over the last several years that you have a stronger sense of returning to a more formal kind of measure. Is this true?
GS: Well, I might, theoretically, but I don't see it actually manifested in my poetry. The rhythms in my poetry, the music in my poetry, I can speak about only in the faintest way—I recognize that in the early poems, like *Riprap*, there is a strong and quite visible influence from the monosyllabism of Chinese poetry. And I kind of crossbred that with the rereading of Anglo-Saxon poetry and its monosyllabic stressed line, and an appreciation and a little bit of study of a few poets in the English language like Robert Frost, who developed that kind of crisp clipped poetic language. So that became a way of writing for a while, and I would call that the formal Chinese influence. But going back into one more round of folksong and oral literature in my thirties, and then reading the vernacular devotional poetry of India and the very lush Sanskrit poetry also, and listening to Vedic chanting—the chanting of the Vedas by young Brahmans in India (which is a daily exercise). Every afternoon young boys chant the Veda, the Vedic service. The rolling and fluid and sinuous music of Indian poetry I think brings an influence into the poems in *Regarding Wave*, that are actually a little like devotional hymns—they are more Indian than they are Chinese.

PC: There is an incantatory quality about them in *Regarding Wave*.
GS: I'll give you two examples of radically different modes of poetry in my own work. I understand the difference between them which is more than

I always do between poems. A poem from *Riprap*, "Above Pate Valley." [follows]

Now that's in the Sierra Nevada high country working as a trail crew laborer, and it's a Chinese poem, "Ten Thousand Years." It's the evocation of both nature and history, of both nature and human events, and the recognition of a people who were there before. The formalities of it are fluently Chinese.

PC: I hear that rhythm through the way that you've performed the poem—you have these rhythmic fragments almost—it's almost as if you have a rhythmic decentralization in that poem. There is no set measure, is there?

GS: There is a consistency, I think, in it, though, a consistent running through of stress patterns, probably. It might be decentralized but it's not formless, but then decentralization, we should hasten to say to anyone who asks, is not formless. Anarchism is not a political philosophy of formlessness; modern poetry is not formless.

PC: I am intrigued because in a way I hear something that reminds me of Robert Creeley.

GS: Well, Creeley is another worker in the same mode, as I should have mentioned. But Creeley and I came to this independently. I recognized Robert's interest in those very fine lines and the strengths of monosyllabic Anglo Saxon vocabulary.

PC: Which makes the voice halt and dart.

GS: Nice language, it's like a fish in a pool. Anyway, it's one mode of poetics I would call faintly Chinese. Now here's one from *Regarding Wave* called "Burning Island" that has its locus down on one of those islands on the East China Sea. This is a celebratory poem prior to my own marriage, which also would be a good Indian subject.

PC: This is a pre-epithalamion as opposed to a post—

GS: Pre-epithalamion—my own pre-epithalamion. I wrote it myself. But I am reading this for as much the way the movement of the poem goes. ["Burning Island" follows]

PC: What's the difference in the rhythmic structure? It has a different impact on me.

GS: Well, it's longer, for one thing. The breath is longer.

PC: The lines all seem to be much more enjambed; there's elisions between the separate words. You don't stress your voice, you do separate those notes. It all has a wave motion.

GS: Well, that's what this book is called—*Regarding Wave.*

PC: So, literally a more fluid thing has come into it.

GS: And *Riprap* is the word that means little bits of rock. So you know the poem titles are really speaking to the form, to the poetics.

PC: You started then writing *Mountains and Rivers Without End* which are, if anything, larger constellations of language. Are they also in that wave pattern?

GS: No, I don't think so. I think *Mountains and Rivers* is more analogous to a long epic. It is like poetic narrative, almost, and thereby looser. Thereby more prosy sometimes. To be imagined more as chanted or sung in a narrative way.

PC: These are not songs.

GS: They are not songs, although they may have songs within it. There are probably songs within the poems. I haven't really worked that out to my own satisfaction, yet. I am probably going to structure that and clarify more of what is narrative and what's lyric song within it.

PC: "Bubbs Creek Haircut" is an example of that—it is where you are intercutting almost in a cinematic way. All the time scheme is rearranged freely, and then of course you shock your reader by being cranked down from the chair—that's "your Bubbs Creek haircut, boy." You remind us, you shock us with that time frame, almost like a time experiment. In a way I get the sense (and I'm an Olsonian, I'm too much of an Olsonian), but I remember Olson separating two areas of poetic or even of language expression—mountain time being discontinuous and jagged; river time being continuous and flowing. I almost wonder if you are not playing intuitively with those two conceptions.

GS: Sure, but I never heard Olson say that or read Olson say that, but, that's charming. I like that very much. And it's not unlike the Chinese use of mountains and rivers themselves: mountains and rivers or mountains and waters is the Chinese compound word for landscape. And there are some very charming little old Zen sayings about that.

PC: And there's our Christian metaphor of drawing water from the rock. In a way, trying to find the convergence between these two separations of change and time, I would guess.

GS: The Zen master would give it to you like this: he'd say, "The rock flows, the river stays still." How do you deal with that? I talked to a class in the *I Ching* yesterday at the campus (of the University of Texas in Austin) and talked about nature in China at some length. At one point in the discussion of the evolution of Chinese landscape painting, I mentioned how I learned to sing mountain ranges and actually have done it on a number of occasions. All you have to do is pick a good place where you can see a long mountain horizon. I have sung the whole Panamint Range from Desert Valley, and I have sung the major part of the Southern Sierra Nevada from standing on top of the White Mountains, which gives you a good scope of it. The way you sing it is very simple—you start at one end and you get your pitch and establish the pitch from where the grade is, then you sing up and down and up and down—you sing the whole mountain range. Then you go back and do it again, and you get it down. Then you begin to sing variations on it if you want. Variations on the Panamint Range.

PC: A final question. David Kherdian has made much of the sense of a San Francisco Renaissance. Do you take it to be that or was it something more— a whole generation coming of age at that moment with its own peculiar sensibility and sense of problems that created a camaraderie and fellowship in the arts in the fifties, which became characteristic of the poetry of the second half of the century? Is it just that or was it an accidental convergence of people in San Francisco?

GS: Well, it's both. Certainly there is a whole generation of people who in a sense constitute the first post-war generation, that are standing on their own creative feet, who were ready in the middle of the fifties to turn away from anything that the fifties represented. They were all over the country, no doubt. But San Francisco served as one of the several folky habitats, places of gathering, meeting places, a good place to meet. And in part it served as a good place to meet—I have my theory about this—because of the relaxed Mediterranean style of San Francisco culture and the strong emplantedness there of a non-Stalinist anarchist intelligentsia. New York was wracked at the same time by the gnashing of teeth and the feelings of guilt of ex-Stalinists who went conservative, and the whole radical and critical undertaking of looking at our society and our civilization anew was stymied on the East Coast by people who were still swirling around in the morass of who-was-a-Trotskyite and who-was-a-Stalinist when, and now-I-am-going-to-join-the-Catholic Church. The intellectual blinders of that whole generation in New York, San Francisco was free of with its much stronger libertarian tradition.

Gary Snyder: On Biocentric Wisdom

Charlene Spretnak / 1987

Creation 3, no. 1 (March/April 1987), 8–11. Reprinted by permission.

Gary Snyder, whose poem on eating introduces this issue, is one of America's pre-eminent poetic voices on nature, culture and spirituality. He was born in San Francisco in 1930 and raised on a dairy farm in Washington state. A camper and mountaineer from an early age, he graduated from Reed College in Oregon and then studied Oriental languages at the University of California, Berkeley. His poetry initially received acclaim during the Beat era of the late fifties. He studied Zen Buddhist meditation for several years in Japan before settling, with his wife Masa, in the Sierra Nevada foothills of California, where they have homesteaded and raised two sons.

Snyder is author of five volumes of essays and eight collections of poetry, including *Turtle Island,* which was awarded the Pulitzer Prize in 1975. He is a cultural historian, a member of Earth First! and an active Chan Buddhist. Among his best-known essays is "Good, Wild, Sacred," which has been widely reprinted.

He was interviewed on ecological wisdom for *Creation* by Charlene Spretnak, coauthor of *Green Politics: The Global Promise* and author of *The Spiritual Dimension of Green Politics* (both from Bear & Co.).

Creation: What do you consider to be the main sources of biocentric, or ecological wisdom in America today?

Gary Snyder: First of all, I think there's a basic level of insight and wisdom in all cultures and all places, which I like to call "grandmother wisdom" or "grandmother ethics," which is what grandmothers always teach little kids. That includes such things as "Don't leave tools in the rain"; "Don't be mean to the cat"; "Eat all the food on your plate"; "Fold your clothes up"; "Have good manners"; and so forth. That's basically the same as the Ten Commandments or the Buddhist precepts. And so the great ethical systems of the world religions don't impress me very much. They neither invented them, nor did they add anything new in them. Or what they *did* add—like "Thou shall have no other gods before me," was irrelevant. Vernacular culture, wherever you find it, is a source of wisdom and sanity. So we have that for starters. We have vernacular culture—in the farmsteads of Kansas or the back alleys of nineteenth-century Brooklyn.

In addition, from the eighteenth-century Enlightenment onward we had a profound expansion of interest in the natural world, which originally took the form of rural gentry "taking the weather" and writing down taxonomies corresponding with Linnaeus in Sweden and with each other. That non-theological, non-mythological Enlightenment spirit of detached and interested observation is what became our natural history and ecology on the scientific level. Jefferson or William Bartram looked at the world with an open-ended fresh eye, which is a great plus. It's the foundation that lies behind the accuracy of Thoreau's observations and the fact that Thoreau's *Collected Journals* have one whole volume of botanical index, indexing all of the plants that Thoreau speaks about specifically throughout his lifetime of journal-writing, because those guys were all into specifics as well as generalities. They were all bird-watchers and plant-watchers. And you can't do much for nature, or in favor of nature, if it's only an abstraction. You have to know the specifics. So this is a step in the right direction.

The rationalism of the Enlightenment is a step that was then flushed out and filled out and given soul by the Romantic movement, which trusted the individual sensibility and amounted to a kind of a revival of polytheism, of paganism in a kind of diluted way, on many different levels, as we all know. To continue, the Transcendentalists—the line of John Muir, the line of Emerson and Thoreau, passing over on the side through Whitman, and passing directly to John Muir—continues with the presence of the Sierra Club in national politics today. It's a direct inheritance of Transcendentalism, which in turn is based on the marriage of Romanticism, Unitarianism, and the Enlightenment. So we have a counter-tradition without having to go back into subcultures and heresies and all that great stuff that's earlier, which I also like.

We have an eighteenth-and post-eighteenth-century tradition that is expressed in the sizeable literature of the American nature essay—by John Van Dyke, John Muir, John Burroughs, all the way up to Edward Abbey and people like myself included in some way, I suppose—which cuts back and forth among accurate scientific observation, cultural reform, the ethical imagining and extension of values to all life, including political moves and the whole fabric of what amounts to American environmentalism. Stephen Fox, in one of the recent books about Muir, *The American Conservation Movement: John Muir and His Legacy* makes the point that the movement is, in sense, off to the side of the mainstream of Occidental and American culture. From over a century ago it has spoken consistently of the value of the non-human, of the beauty of continental North America, of appreciation of specific plants, animals, trees, and systems, and in many ways and at many times it has stated totally biocentric positions, as John Muir often did. That whole thing emerged from within Western culture. It was not really touched off by much contact with Asia or the primitive, but it comes out of one of the subsidiary streams, I guess, of the possibilities of Occidental culture, and it has a power that is not merely literary or abstractly scientific. Fox says it amounts to a new religion that has not yet even been called a religion—because the energy and the sprit that people give to it is from a deeper place than just natural history or science class commitment. Our tiny wilderness areas, which are only two percent of the US land mass, are our cathedrals—to North America, to Gaia, to that great wilderness area that is the universe.

I've been watching that side of things ever since I was a kid. I was a member of the Wilderness Society when I was seventeen and joined the Mazamas and then joined the Sierra Club later. I was involved with various active environmental and mountaineering groups and was writing letters to Congressmen and evolving and refining my thinking all along, but some of the very first things I read that touched me off were by John Muir, on the one hand, and Native American stuff on the other. It took me a long time to sort of bring them all together. Then I also got into the Oriental stuff, as well. But I'm impressed by the fact that we can see a line of clear insight and sanity that is there right within the West, and that's where David Brower comes from. Or Dave Foreman. Or Aldo Leopold. Or Mary Austin, a very insightful nature essayist who wrote several books in the 1920s. Or a number of other really fine, sensitive minds that are speaking about these things.

Creation: What do you think are the major dynamics thwarting the realization of our biocentric wisdom?
Snyder: The other dynamic is that combination of entrenched ruling elites based in cities with vast trading networks and economic systems that are structured so as to be based on a profit motive only, to the exclusion of other concerns, with an obligation to maximize profits in the short run, without regard to long-run implications. It's that huge dynamic that we recognize as

Occidental materialism and its current forms of expansive industrial socialism or expansive industrial capitalism, both of which I take to be a Protestant
heresy. They're both heretical, and they both come out of Protestantism,
in my notion: trying to realize the Kingdom of God on earth in a material
way. It's the utmost in spiritual materialism. And the Protestant element
in it is that you can still see the self-denying quality of American affluence.
American affluence does not enjoy itself. You have to live in Japan to see
what happens when people enjoy themselves and don't have an inward self-
denying habit. So that's an interesting paradox, too (laughter).

Creation: Your practical sense of biocentric wisdom seems to be centered
mostly on the ideas of bioregionalism.
Snyder: Bioregionalism is a fancy term for staying put and learning what's
going on. It's a way of seeing. You don't gain biocentric insight too well by
doing it in the abstract, by traveling long distances and reading certain
books. You do it better by going for local walks and paying attention to the
daily fabric of the natural world wherever you are, right on the street in
the town you live in, and becoming tuned into that. It's great to go off on
a wilderness trip to some distant river and run it, in some totally different
bioregion where you don't know any of the birds. That's exciting. But the
real fun is in deepening your self on all levels *where you are.* Realizing that
it starts at home is the beginning and is, in every sense, biocentric. Home-
centric, ecocentric, begins in your belly, begins in your lungs, begins in your
genitals, begins in your ears. Start out by realizing that you are your own
closest animal (laughter).

Creation: How do you encourage people to think about living in place?
Snyder: One little exercise as far as just getting people to imagine what a
place is and to see a place with their mind's eye more vividly is to ask them
to think of how they would describe how to locate the house or apartment
they live in without using the name of any state or county or street, any
human-made recent construction, but to describe how to find their place
in terms of natural land forms and natural watersheds. It really gets people
thinking. That's a nice start. Then they often ask, "Well, how do you do bioregionalism?" And the answer to that is take a vow not to move. Stay where
you are. Having decided to stay where you are, which doesn't mean you can't
go away on trips, imagine all the things that you can and should and want to
do to make living where you live more pleasant for yourself and your friends
between now and when you die. Where do you want to be buried locally

(laughter)? The whole mind-set changes. If you think, "I'm going to be here the rest of my life," then you get serious.

Creation: As you are an ardent defender of localism and bioregionalism, I'm wondering if you acknowledge a potential dark side of localism—by which I mean these alarming news stories we've been reading about groups in farm communities that are very racist and anti-Semitic and fond of violence and have large caches of weapons. Some of them say they don't acknowledge any authority higher than the local sheriff. And they're apparently very widespread in the depressed farm areas of the Midwest and the northern Rockies. I remember hearing Wendell Berry say a couple of years ago that he feels there's been a brain drain out of a lot of rural communities such that the kind of people who would have said in the past, "You're not listening to *that* kind of hogwash, are you?" are no longer there. Also, in Kirkpatrick Sale's book on bioregionalism, *Dwellers in the Land,* he says rather obliquely that if we locate all morality at the local level, civil rights and everything, it's not going to be very pretty sometimes but that's the way people are, and it'll be more honest. I find that disturbing.

Snyder: First of all, it's a dark side that has to be acknowledged in the particular context of our culture today, which is a *fellaheenized* (the fellaheens were the landless peasants in the Ottoman Empire) alienated population that has not learned how to live in place, has lost that sense and doesn't have the customary or traditional ways to keep some things in check. When people have been living in a rootless, mobile, democratic-pluralistic society governed only by a legal code for decade after decade after decade, it is quite understandable that different enclaves that are single-minded about one thing or another will spring up. (In fact, that's one of the things that America was founded on: fanatical single-minded enclaves that had to leave Europe.) That's not quite a normal situation you're talking about, but it does raise these issues.

Rather than "localism," what we in the bioregional movement have endorsed is the long, careful reconstruction of sense of place, starting with knowledge of history, of human communities, starting with commitment to the place, starting with ecological and natural history studies—and, in a sense, culture-building, the reforming of cultural values and community sense of how things can work. And in recognizing the difference between communities and networks. Networks are single-minded fanatics who all agree. Communities are people who are very diverse. Some are crazy. Some are right-wingers; some are left-wingers. You know, in any natural community you have a variety of people, and not all of them are going to agree.

We're not endorsing in any simple way the idea of constituting nothing but local authority right off the top. It is an interesting question in the long run, though, in the matter of deconstructing nation states into smaller entities, as to what happens when you begin to have some slightly divergent views, slightly divergent moralities. The only thing that ever held India together at its best, since it was always politically extremely diverse, was religion. I guess what would be a moderating control, a kind of balancer for a bunch of deconstructed bioregional communities in some kind of theoretical future would be a shared value system, a shared practice, a shared morality (though morality can be local and universal at the same time), a shared mutuality of respect. And then let them fight a little bit too. Why not?

Rather than thinking about bioregionalism in any kind of literal political program mode, I always refer to it as a perspective and as a visionary set of metaphors. It's a counter-mythology. It's an imaginary shadow-government. It's a sensibility. It's a way of changing how you think—and it's forming a new society within the shell of the old.

An Interview with Gary Snyder: "Language is Wild"

Donald Johns / 1990

Writing on the Edge 2, no. 1 (Fall 1990), 100–112. Reprinted by permission.

Gary Snyder's first volume of poetry, *Myths & Texts,* appeared in 1959. Other poetry titles include *Riprap, The Back Country, Regarding Wave, Turtle Island* (which was awarded the Pulitzer Prize), *Axe Handles*, and *Left out in the Rain.* His prose volumes include *Earth House Hold* and *The Old Ways.* A new edition of *Riprap,* with an afterword by the author, has just been issued by North Point Press. North Point has also recently published *The Practice of the Wild,* a collection of essays Snyder tells us was shaped and informed in part by his teaching of the "Literature of Wilderness" course at the University of California, Davis. As Professor of English for the past several years, he has also taught poetry writing at Davis, and this spring he will teach a course on the San Francisco and West Coast Poetry Renaissance. The interview took place May 24, 1990, in Snyder's office on the Davis campus.

Writing on the Edge: Can you remember when you first began to write, your motivations?

Gary Snyder: I don't like to use the term *write* if I can avoid it, in a way, because it always has the implication of using a writing system and putting things down on paper. My notion of literature includes a lot that is prior to the use of writing systems. So I first began to compose songs and poems when I was four or five years old, and my mother was my tape recorder in this case, and she happened to write a couple of them down. The rest were, as is appropriate, lost. So, when I was older, I also started making things up, and I also began writing things. Starting from the time I was sixteen or seventeen, I began to consciously use writing instruments, compose things and save them. Primarily poetry, or what we could call poetry, all the way through, although my published body of work for the most part reflects nothing that was written before twenty-two or twenty-three.

WOE: I think I remember your saying that at a certain point you burned or threw out your early work.
Snyder: That was when I was in college.

WOE: What was the cut-off point between the stuff that you threw away, and the stuff you felt was keepable?
Snyder: My education. My college education and the standards of literary criticism that I was exposed to with my peers and my teachers convinced me that a large quantity of the stuff I had done when I was younger was of no value. I was in a kind of a house-cleaning mood, and so I burned it. Since literary standards are as ephemeral as clothing standards, or almost as ephemeral, it may have been I made a mistake, and some of that would have been interesting. So this is one of the dangers of education, that you take the idea that critical standards are maybe eternal, whereas obviously they are not.

WOE: I remember your saying somewhere that things seemed to fall into place when you were working on the trail systems, when you stopped thinking about literature while you were working.
Snyder: I don't remember exactly quite what that was, but perhaps you're referring to something I have spoken of elsewhere. The summer of '55 when I was working trail crew up in Yosemite back country was a curious year because I had finally quit graduate school, and was thinking of myself as having left the academy permanently. Also, I was thinking to give up, or quit thinking about, or quit worrying about poetry—and having in a sense emptied myself of those concerns and ambitions, that summer I started writing pretty good poetry. The poetry did come along with a period of just doing hard physical labor and being rather isolated, although that wasn't exactly what the poems were about. So those were the poems that make up a part of *Riprap*. I just recently wrote a little more concerning that occasion, on that pivotal little turn of my life, for the afterword of a new edition of *Riprap* that will be out this fall from North Point. I went back and rethought that.

WOE: Can you remember who taught you to write prose, or which teachers you remember being effective and how they went about it?

Snyder: There are two kinds of prose: professional prose and creative prose. Professional prose is what you are required to write for advancement in academic systems. It's the prose you use to write that artifact we call "The Paper": the undergraduate paper and the graduate paper and ultimately the dissertation. That is a culturally designed object with its own rules, which belong only to its own sphere and are of not much use outside of that sphere. That is to say, nobody will publish it, nobody will read it except within its own sphere. So it is a highly refined, very localized kind of writing. I learned to do that by the feedback I got from my professors when I wrote papers as an undergraduate at Reed College, and then of course by reading professional papers, reading dissertations and so forth.

Learning how to write creative prose was partly a matter of trial and error and accident, as it usually is, and came from reading prose that I felt was good, fairly standard stuff. Certain works provide you with models, and in my case, as in the case of many people, I'm sure, one of the earliest experiences for me of admiring a person writing prose in modern American English was reading Thoreau. I could name others, but that is one that particularly comes to mind.

WOE: What was it about Thoreau's prose that you admired or that struck you?

Snyder: The combination of intelligence, relatively dense information, and a witty and vernacular and relaxed tone. Then I read Montaigne's travel journals. A novelist whose work instructed me was E. M. Forster, and *Passage to India,* as a piece of novelistic prose, at that time, in my twenties.

WOE: Most of the literature in composition stresses the fact that experienced writers do a lot of revising. Do you revise your prose very much?

Snyder: Sure. I find myself putting my prose through two or three levels of screening and revising. I'll find revisions to make quite well down the line. Part of that is getting increasing clarity of thought and expression, and part of that is nifty little details of writing that come to you gradually, little additional clarities, or turns that are actually what make the prose really interesting, some of the things that you see at the very last minute.

WOE: Do you keep a journal or notebook?

Snyder: I've kept a journal since I was eighteen years old.

WOE: How do you use it? What part does it play in material that you eventually publish?

Snyder: It plays a certain part. It serves as a kind of reference pool of information. I don't try to write a literary journal. I write hastily, on whatever occasion I get the chance, and I use it as a place to put information. As it turns out, sometimes the first drafts of poems are in there. Sometimes the passages that might be used later in prose works are in there. But a lot of it is simply like a reference tool: who I saw, where I was, what the first impressions of certain things were, what was going through my mind and so forth. Not an elegantly done literary journal.

WOE: Do you have students keep journals?
Snyder: I have done that, particularly in my "Literature of the Wilderness" course. I had students keep journals, partly because in the broader picture a lot of wilderness and nature writing out there in the world is journals: Lewis and Clark's journals, Cook's journals, all kinds of early travelers and adventurers that are providing us with information about the planet from the standpoint at least of the Euro-American imperialist invaders who were also keeping journals about it. Now finding out how the people that saw the invasion from the other side of the fence reacted to it is another exercise; I try to do both.

WOE: Do you give the students any prompts for journal writing?
Snyder: In the case of this particular course, in which I've used journals for three or four years in a row now, I ask them to keep a running account of one or another aspect of the natural world as they see it passing through spring—April, May, and mid-June—in the city of Davis. In other words, to be a nature observer, and to keep track of some observations of some natural object. People have used a tree in their front yard, Putah Creek, their cat, their baby, the weather, the sky, the crops in the fields, the bird-life passing through, and their boyfriend or girlfriend—all of these have been taken as natural objects to observe and write about through the ten weeks of the course.

WOE: At Berkeley in the 1960s you taught both the poetry workshop and some composition?
Snyder: I taught composition courses at Berkeley when I was hired as a Lecturer there for the fall of '64 and the spring of '65. I was visiting in this country for a year, back from Japan. After that was finished, I returned to Japan and continued my work over there.

WOE: What approach did you take in composition courses?

Snyder: I assigned a couple of good books. The ones I recall were Thoreau's *Walden* and W. J. Cash's book, called *The Mind of the South*, which is a good nonfiction prose work by a Southerner on the life and mentality as he saw it at that time of white Southerners. We read those, discussed them for content and for writing both, and out of that I assigned essays, and talked about the nature of good prose: very simple.

WOE: Comparing the students then to those you work with now, do you notice any significant differences in worldview or store of knowledge, that sort of thing?

Snyder: Those students were trembling on the edge of the sixties. The year that I taught at Berkeley was also the year of the Free Speech Movement. My poetry writing class actually continued all through the Free Speech Movement because the students in that class, although they were totally sympathetic with it, also were committed to keeping up working on their poetry.

The worldview at that time in its details was undoubtedly somewhat different. I think that the fundamental aspirations of people at that age are probably the same in every period of time, regardless of the details. Obviously, there is an impulse towards getting out and becoming autonomous, and an impulse to critique or resist authority, and also a contradictory desire to enter into a mainstream that will provide them with a way to make a living. I think it's perennial.

I would say that the students I had in 1964 and 1965 at UC Berkeley were far better read than the students I have now, the undergraduate students. Another feature that has changed is that a certain proportion of undergraduate students now are older students. We had no older students then; it was one age group. I didn't have any single mothers who were trying to reenter the career world in their late thirties or something, which I see a number of now at Davis. The classes were more uniform in their outlook. It's quite different to be teaching undergraduates who have such different outlooks.

WOE: What kind of differences does it bring about in your approach to teaching them?

Snyder: Well, you have to be broader and more balanced than when you're dealing with one young person whose idea of family and work in the world is entirely in their imagination, and another person who's had two kids and been in the work world for fifteen years; they're going to write different kinds of poetry, they're going to come to somebody's poem in a different way.

WOE: I wonder if you would talk just briefly about the strengths and weaknesses of student writing that you see, the expository writing.

Snyder: Good expository writing is obviously an important tool in one's personal advancement in this society, and so I will say nothing against it. I have nothing against it. I simply regard it, however, as a peculiar device and as a tool that is as peculiar as the style called "parallel prose" that was required of Chinese scholars that were taking the formal examinations to enter government service in the Sung dynasty: a highly artificial and a peculiar kind of prose style that was never used except within those circles. You can't say anything against it; they had to learn how to do it. It's the same way with formal expository writing.

Expository writing does have certain virtues: clarity, objectivity, accountability, and so forth. So, yes, students have to learn that. I have acknowledged that to high school students at Eskimo high schools north of the Arctic Circle, where we were ostensibly talking about how we maintain native cultural traditions. At the same time, I've said, you're going into an education in the white world that will require you to write certain ways. Don't fight it, just learn how to do it; it won't destroy your cultural values to learn how to do that. In fact, take western white culture as sort of like a second culture that you have to learn like you learn a second language. When you learn a second language you learn the grammar of that language and you use it as well as you can, and it's the same way with the customs of your second culture: use the customs, and use them as well as you can.

WOE: Are students in general doing well in expository writing?

Snyder: Not as well as I would hope them to.

WOE: Why do you think they have a problem with it, and what can we do?

Snyder: The answers I might suggest to that are no surprise to anyone. It goes back to the problems in the elementary schools and high schools—underfunding, overcrowding, teachers who are harassed and overworked as I know all too well since I have a number of very dear friends who are teaching in the high school systems. They teach much longer hours than anybody teaches in the university, and they have to deal with discipline problems as well, which you don't have in the university, and they get paid less, and don't have as much prestige in the community, either.

Now in the high school where my boys went, Nevada Union, there were some really tough and motivated teachers who were very clear about the necessity to be able to write good prose and gave them good exercises that pointed them in the direction of college level work. The teachers were able to intelligently respond to the rebellious attitudes of my own sons and their friends that said, "This is a dumb kind of writing. We'd rather write something much more creative that expresses the way we feel." They said fine, learn to do that as well, but this is perhaps not the time or place to learn to do that, and what I'm giving you is a tool. And so I think that's the way it has to be approached. Very unsentimentally.

Perhaps what also has to be said and this is not a hundred percent true, but I hope it's true, is that learning to write good expository prose will not destroy your creative potential. You can also go on and have a wild imagination. Or to put it in another metaphor, a cultivated plot of land is what expository prose is, that is to say mind and language cultivated for a specific yield—like we want to grow nothing but corn, we're going to do nothing but university papers, we're going to get all the weeds out. But right over the fence, on the other side, it grows wild, and so your creative mind can coexist, and does coexist actually, with the much smaller territory of your mind which is cultivated to yield a specific crop, to make you into an accountant or whatever. People have to trust in their big mind that way. The truth of the matter is cultivated mind is but a tiny part of consciousness, and the greater part of it, like the greater part of the planet, is wild, which is imagination and the unconscious, all of that.

WOE: Would you say that we have more than one collective unconscious, one that we share with the planet, with all living things, and another we share with people?

Snyder: On some level, yeah. It doesn't matter what you call it: the Buddhists call it "Big Mind." On some level we are obviously in the same reality zone as everything else.

WOE: The collective unconscious we normally talk about is the one we share with all preceding cultures, including the so-called pre-civilized cultures?

Snyder: Absolutely, and with all sentient beings. Buddhists call it "desire," *kama*. This is the realm of desire. Desire for us and desire for insects is the same mind. There's hunger out there on all levels.

WOE: Did you take much of an active role in educating your children personally, or working in the schools themselves and getting involved in curriculum?

Snyder: To some extent, not as much as I would have liked to. Like most parents, I was running around making a living, too, and I was fencing, and cutting firewood, and felling trees. It's just everybody's busy. In our school district at least we had the advantage of knowing a lot of the teachers personally as friends and could have really interesting discussions over a glass of beer about what was going on and keep in touch with things that way. What I did—and I'm sure many parents do—was to stress what I was just saying to my own kids. Master the required forms and your freedom will not actually be destroyed or impinged on. Your creativity is bigger than that.

WOE: Some people argue that creative writing courses might serve freshmen as well as expository writing courses, that the skills practiced and developed in there might transfer to other writing situations. Does that sound feasible?

Snyder: But still, we would hope that our expository prose writing is not without some literary merit. One of the disappointments of the modern world is that scientists and sociologists and anthropologists and so on all write so poorly. They write competently, but there's no spark in it. So there is a place for the imagination to enter in. The imagination entering in, so to speak, is in terms of metaphors, in terms of images. An expository prose that allows itself a strong colorful image, a vivid image from time to time, becomes instantly more interesting. So, rule of thumb: disciplined language, wild metaphors, and that will really make it a lot more interesting.

WOE: In an earlier interview, you talked about the teacher/pupil relationship—that of the poet and the person trying to write poetry—being somewhat analogous to the master/apprentice relationship. While that might work very well with a motivated student, what about what we could call an unmotivated student—a typical entering freshman who doesn't have a great knowledge of the world—how do we get such people involved? It seems that it would be hard to motivate students like this to see the value of Coyote, or to see the worldview represented in a poem like "The Dead by the Side of the Road," or to appreciate "no need to survive" wisdom.

Snyder: We must deal with a lot of people who aren't very clearly motivated, that's true. That's partly because the English department is a basket that receives a lot of students who can't make up their minds what they want to major in. So we find students who aren't quite sure why they're there. They think maybe they like to "read books" or something. It's not as though there is a clear competitive, intense, professional attitude such as you get with science students.

It need not be this way if there were a clearer understanding in the culture at large about what the humanistic project is all about. But in the current situation in which also the far more sizable rewards in terms of career are in the engineering, professional, and scientific fields, you have a very diverse set of intentions when you're dealing with the students who come into the English department. A big part of the challenge is to inspire those kids with values associated with the very nature of language and the nature of speculative thought. There isn't time to do that, and I regret that I am never able to get very far into that level, which is such a primary level, and so needed.

WOE: In our teaching philosophy, I see two broad schools of thought. One emphasizes the need for a better pedagogy, really understanding cognitive development, matching materials and assignments to each individual student's level of development. On the other hand, we have people calling for the return to basics and who would actually say that we would be better off just having students taught in large part by experts in their fields, not necessarily people who have been to the school of education and learned about cognitive development and so forth. I wonder to what extent being an expert practitioner in a given field qualifies one to teach novices in that field, as opposed to the other approach. How does your experience as a teacher and learner speak to this?

Snyder: I think probably in terms of writing, certainly in creative writing, that a student studying with an expert makes good sense. Especially if an attitude of apprenticeship can be inculcated. That's not always easy in that the expert, if you take the apprenticeship model really seriously, can teach working methods, can show habits, can show how and why judgements are made. But to do that you have to allow the expert to be the authority and to be authoritarian, and the model assumes that the student cannot ask for fairness, objectivity, or diversity in the presentation coming from the "expert," but will be willing to commit him or herself for a period of time simply to the way this one person works. I think that can be an excellent way to teach. But students are not prepared for that. What they are taught to expect is something broader and "more objective."

I find myself, in my own creative writing classes, not trying to enforce or run it on an apprenticeship level at all. A lot of the time I keep my own poetry and my own opinions somewhat back and try not to impose much on students, because I feel that they would resist that. In fact, the way it works is this: in the real world, someone has come to you and say "I want to study with you," not "I want to take your course." If they say "I want to study with you," then the two of you have agreed that they're going to study how you work, and you're going to share a lot with them. But if they want to take "The Course," then what they want is something more pedagogical, and so you prepare something more pedagogical.

WOE: What's the role of grading in teaching. Do you see it as a help, as a hindrance, as a necessary evil?
Snyder: I don't think it's an evil, and I don't think it's a hindrance. This is not a non-hierarchical world. Some people do better than other people. I think they need feedback, and grading is the way to give them feedback.

In creative writing, say a poetry workshop, work is very hard to grade. In a sense, nobody has written a poem worth an "A." I mean, what is an "A" poem? So you're grading for intention, you're grading for growth, you're grading for development, you're grading for other qualities than simply sheer accomplishment.

WOE: I know that you place a lot of importance on so-called pre-literate tradition, the oral tradition. In *Earth House Hold* you say poetry is not writing or books, and that's sort of what we were talking about earlier. There's research in composition and psychology suggesting that talking and writing stem from different organic sources and maybe represent different language functions. There seems an implication here that writing is necessary for a fully developed learning potential and a fully developed human potential.
Snyder: Without having read the literature, I can't imagine, I can't quite see how they would make that argument. To make such an argument would be to argue that 99% of our ancestors were dysfunctional, since writing has played such a tiny part in human history and human culture, over a large scale of time. We would have to dismiss 99% of human experience, if we said that writing was somehow essential. It's a rather bizarre thing to say because writing has been up until recently only the property, a skill, of the elite class in any given society, and only in a few societies.

Now in terms of modern literary productions, I would say sure, there is a difference between oral literature and written literature, particularly in prose. I would say that poetry maintains all the traces of orality, and in fact, the features that we value in poetry—the music—are oral features. Rhythm, song. Poetry is a variety of song; it derives from the song line.

The prose narrative, which in oral traditions has certain conventions of its own and tends to be repetitive or diffuse for its own reason, becomes more dense, more concentrated, when it's put into writing. I've noticed doing transcripts of my own talks and condensing them so that they turn into essays that they take up less space. The written prose is less, and also the sentences in oral presentation are much longer and more complex, and you don't close sentences off nearly so rapidly; you keep making new clauses. So there are some interesting differences, and we'd have to say that the conventions of writing are probably somewhat artificial conventions that do not reflect the natural syntax of the wild language. Language is wild.

WOE: I remember reading that when composing a poem you might go over it in your mind many times and that you do actually compose it in your head before you write it down. In a lyric poem like "Pine Tree Tops" what's the first impetus? Is it the image, the boots creaking, the footsteps?
Snyder: Oh, yeah, it comes directly out of envisioning something that actually happened and expanding it upward into the light of the night sky.

WOE: How about the line "the earth a flower" in "For Nothing"? Where did that image come from?
Snyder: That proceeds from a thought. The thought has to do with the nature of offerings and the fact that you offer flowers on the altar to the Buddha. That's one of the several offerings: flowers, tea, incense, and candle. I was thinking in those terms about the offerings on the altar, and then I was thinking, "What are flowers? In that combination of offerings, what is the role of flowers? What do they represent?" I realized that they represented biological life, all of biological life. Perhaps, in a sense, the physical universe, just as the candle is the offering of energy. So then I thought, well, this whole planet is just a flower being offered to the Buddha.

WOE: And the line "By a gulf where a raven flaps by once"—what's the source of that?
Snyder: I'll tell you what that is. That was trying to deal with emptiness. If earth is a flower being offered to the Buddha, it is a flower out of emptiness, it is a flower of the void. But to say "a flower of the void" is far too abstract. So the "gulf where a raven flaps by once" is putting a little detail on the nature of emptiness.

WOE: There's an outpouring of so-called nature writing, or people writing about nature, like John McPhee, Barry Lopez, Edward Hoagland, of course Edward Abbey. Do you read many of these writers?
Snyder: Yeah, I read them. I haven't read all of any of their works. I keep looking at them for what I think is really interesting. I don't think nature writing as such has yet accomplished its potential. I have an ideal nature writing in mind that I haven't quite seen yet. Barry Lopez is too wordy. Annie Dillard is too precious. Hoagland is very clear and precise. Wendell Berry is too preachy. McPhee gets redundant and overloads it with detail; it is too intellectual in a sense, too abstract a lot of the time. Abbey writes some great passages when he's up for it. A lot of the time he's just blustering.

WOE: Were you much affected by Aldo Leopold's *A Sand County Almanac*?
Snyder: There are some fine pieces in Aldo Leopold. Some of the small pieces are just beautiful. The question of how to let the non-human world resonate in the human imagination, that's the real challenge of the nature writer. Nobody yet has done it, except in bits and patches, which is like the essence, and then they go on doing other things for large stretches of time.

WOE: How had teaching affected you as a writer or a poet? What have you learned from teaching?
Snyder: Mostly what I learn from teaching is what the condition of my current society is. That's a complex question; there are many levels of answer to it. I see the university as an institution in transition that still imagines itself to be the inheritor and preserver of a set of valuable and detached humanistic values, whereas in fact it's become a key component in Euro-American industrial civilization. The university has not examined itself in this regard, has not examined the question as to whether or not this is a proper role for it to play, particularly in the light of the destructive direction in which industrial civilization seems to be going.

But at the same time, paradoxically, the university is the great repository of information and provides valuable riches in which all kinds of life forms can inconspicuously survive and do good work. It's fascinating, and I'm just looking at that and thinking about it. Maybe eventually I'll be able to write about it.

My own role in it is equally contradictory: I could certainly do the writing that I'm doing as a poet without being anywhere near a university. It contributes very little to what I do as a writer, except to sadden me, and make me a trifle more realistic as to what the larger mentality and value system of the society is. So in that sense it's good for me, it's a reality infusion.

WOE: What's your view on the controversy over the authenticity of some Native American biographies, *Black Elk Speaks,* for instance?

Snyder: Who knows what the truth of the matter is, or maybe somebody does know. Texts such as *Black Elk Speaks* have already played a role in our culture. They exist as texts regardless of the nature or the degree of their authenticity, which have played a cultural role not only for white people, but in a kind of feedback sense for Native American people.

As to the question of what a precivilized, preliterate culture is thinking and doing, that is a very tough exercise. I think it's a very valuable exercise, because my intuition and experience along those lines is that they are indeed fundamentally different from contemporary societies, and that there are some ways of seeing and being which are extremely interesting and very valuable. But you cannot make that happen, no matter how well intentioned, within the context of the way people live today. You actually have to sleep on the ground and walk twenty miles a day and gather wild plants before you can begin to talk about some of those things. So for all of us—contemporary Native Americans or contemporary white people—some of those things are really almost inaccessible to us, because we don't have the engagement in the details of the life. Authenticity in any case lies back a lot farther.

WOE: In "The Politics of Ethnopoetics" you granted the precision of the Marxist critique on most points. Which points of the critique, especially in the view of the collapse of the so-called Marxist states in Europe, can we use now—or which do you use in your approach to teaching writing or to viewing the world?

Snyder: What we're witnessing is not the collapse of the Marxist states but the collapse of the Leninist states. Marxism, as Marx envisioned it, could very easily have been social democracy, and this may yet be what we find. The collapse of the Leninist states does not imply automatically the collapse of Marxist thought. Those people are still going to work with his ideas for a long time, and we may end up with social democracies, as we have already in Sweden.

The critique stands, to my notion, although the conclusions to be drawn from that critique can vary according to how you see things: I start with a Marxist critique and end with anarchist conclusions and always have. As far as teaching goes, the most useful thing for me in recent years (that I can use a Marxist metaphor for) is that of extending our sense of vanguard and revolutionary classes to the non-human world. See my poem, "Revolution within the Revolution within the Revolution." Working at trying to break past the situation we have now, of various human constituencies competing for a piece of the pie, so that we come to a point of recognizing that the pie is much bigger, and that we are just part of that. I would like to see the issue of "diversity" taken to include the nonhuman.

WOE: Do you ever think of poetry in terms of dialectics?

Snyder: That word "dialectical" doesn't come to my mind that much, but "paradoxical," "contradictory," dealing with and resolving contradictions, acknowledging contradictions and playing them out is very much a part of my poetry. Trying to work with those things, and so it's a Buddhist dialectic in a way.

Basically, the dialectic in Buddhism is working between the absolute, actual irreducible groundedness of everything, and its simultaneous transience and emptiness. That's the paradox of existence: everything in a sense proceeds from the play between those two positions. That would be a Buddhist dialectic. Emptiness and concreteness, work and ideas. So that takes the form in my poetry as work and imagination. The physicality of work and the freedom of the imagination, the openness of the imagination. The totally conditioned quality of every move we make on the physical level, and the total openness of how our mind works.

Interview: Gary Snyder

Casey Walker / 1995

Wild Duck Review 1, no. 6 (September 1995), 4–6. Reprinted by permission.

Gary Snyder has lived in Nevada County and worked as an active member of the North San Juan Ridge community and Yuba Watershed region since 1969. A Pulitzer Prize-winning poet, Gary Snyder is currently a professor of English at UC Davis where he began the Nature and Culture program. His past books of poetry include: *No Nature: New and Selected Poems; The Practice of the Wild; Left Out in the Rain; New Poems 1947–1985; Passage Through India; Axe Handles; The Real Work; Interviews and Talks 1964–1979; He Who Hunted Birds in His Father's Village; Turtle Island; Regarding Wave; Earth House Hold; The Back Country; Myths and Texts; Riprap* and *Cold Mountain Poems.*

Of his new book, *A Place in Space,* due out in August 1995 by Counterpoint Press, Gary Snyder writes: "This collection draws on some forty years of thinking and writing. It can be considered a further exploration of what 'the practice of the wild' would be.

The ancient Buddhist precept 'Cause the least possible harm' and the implicit ecological call to 'Let nature flourish' join in reverence for human life and then go beyond that to include the rest of creation. These essays are Buddhist, poetic, and environmental calls to complex moral thought and action—metaphoric, oblique, and mythopoetic, but also I hope practical. Ethics and aesthetics are deeply intertwined. Art, beauty, and craft have always drawn on the self-organizing 'Wild' side of language and mind. Human ideas of place and space, our contemporary ideas about watersheds, become both model and metaphor. Our goal must be to see the interacting realms, learn where we are, and thereby develop a complex consciousness of planetary and ecological cosmopolitanism.

Meanwhile, be lean, compassionate, and ferocious, living in the self-disciplined elegance of 'wild mind.'"

The following conversation took place on July 28, 1995 with Casey Walker at Kitkitdizze, Gary Snyder's home.

Casey Walker: Would you briefly talk about the genesis of you new book, *A Place in Space?*

Gary Snyder: *A Place in Space* is a gathering of pieces that span almost forty years. I was looking back over a number of pieces from the past for the threads that show links and connections between territories that might commonly be thought of as disparate—Buddhist thought, ethical concerns, Asian poetics, occidental poetics, oral literature, and ideas of place and environment. A number of the essays in *A Place in Space* were written since *The Practice of the Wild.* About one third of the book is current thinking and about two thirds of the book weaves around earlier work I did.

CW: In the process of synthesizing nearly forty years of work, what changes did you find in your thinking?

GS: The gradual grounding of ideas in practice! Also, my earlier outdoor experience was in the remote wildernesses of the North Cascades and the High Sierra working as a Forest Service seasonal worker, on trail crew or fire lookout, and a lot of remote long distance backpacking and climbing. I've been gradually descending ever since I was in my thirties. I've been very slowly coming down from the high country. I settled in here on the San Juan Ridge at the three thousand foot level saying, "Well, here I am living in civilization at the three thousand foot level."

It's kind of an ironic thing. A lot of people when they got to San Juan Ridge thought they were in the wilderness. I moved down to the San Juan Ridge and thought I was in civilization—only a few miles from a paved road and they actually deliver mail there! It is biologically rich at this elevation, it isn't really civilization, there is a tremendous amount of biological wealth, plant diversity, and animal diversity. But I've come to appreciate the forested zones, and to work from forestry issues and soil and biodiversity issues that belong to this territory—the interface—between human industrial-economic use and wild nature. The really high country has no forest, so it's not up for grabs with logging.

And through my work at UC Davis and from my wife Carole's influence, I've finally been able to see the Great Central Valley—the Sacramento Valley—to see through the mirror of agriculture and suburbanization, and urbanization that is over it right now, and to see what a remarkable region it still is. You can look at the birdlife, riparian zones, little and big stands here and there of Valley Oaks. And then also to see how those amazing alluvial soils turned into some of the best peach orchards in the world in the hands of Sikhs from North West India, around Yuba City. This gradual shift in focus is what the last third of *A Place in Space,* under the title Watersheds, addresses. The watershed starts with the high sierra, with the peaks, and the snowfields and glaciers, and finds its way down to the slow-moving warm sloughs and deltas. It's all one watershed and it's all connected. So it is a kind of a metaphor for my learning the continuity. There's a pond here at Kitkitdizze that flows out down through the meadow when the stream's running, and it goes to San Francisco Bay.

CW: Would you elaborate upon your logic when you wrote, "To work on behalf of wild nature is to restore culture"?
GS: We do not work on behalf of nature in a vacuum, in a solitary way. It's a collaboration in which people are teaching each other things—showing each other mindscapes, sharing knowledge of plants and animals and knowledge of environmental history, and passing knowledge of practices and processes by doing them together. To actually do restoration work like we're doing with the Yuba Watershed Institute in certain parts of the 'Inimim forest, we gather in group work days. We had a group work day two weeks ago, thinning brush and clearing around the bases of some big pine trees that are going to be part of a prescribed burn this fall.

So to restore wild nature is to get together with your friends and learn things about nature as you *do it* together. Working together creates conviviality and knowledge and the sharing of information, and that is the beginning of having a culture. It's as simple as that.

CW: How do you see a restoration of wild nature and human culture coming about on a global level?
GS: Global politics are out of control, and nobody's in charge. We probably wouldn't want anybody to be in charge. But at the same time we need people to see what is going on. Thinking globally means understanding the terrible complexity and intricate, dangerous karma of history and politics right now. Projecting "Think Unity" or "Think Peace" is fun to put on the bumper of your car, but if you really want to think globally you've got to get serious about economics, history, and politics. They tweak your mind and it's hard work and you still won't be able to know for sure what you think can be done. At this point in history, particularly, we can see the collapse of the totalizing and idealistic, and, at the same time, completely disappointing hopes of twentieth-century socialism and the international socialist

movement in which many people placed a lot of hope for a good part of this century. That hope is no longer there. Instead, what we have is rampant nationalism or simply rampant corporate market capitalism running this way and that way all over the planet.

CW: So you look to the profundity of microshifts?

GS: I think that the microshift is that everybody is feeling very soberly right now that there maybe are no global solutions as such. Of course, it's always worthwhile to wish that everybody would be good, and to wish that people would think peace, and to visualize harmony, but probably we're going to have to start with peace and harmony in the small communities that we live in wherever we are without becoming isolated, or self-satisfied, or ingrown and withdrawn—and without becoming an ideal enclave that survives by isolating itself from interaction with its surroundings.

So I do think that local action is probably the most powerful place to start, and then to expand outward in larger circles if possible. The world is full of disparate cultures with different ideas about the way it should be, but if they feel a shared grounding in place and nature, perhaps they can work together. *Everybody* lives in a place.

CW: Will you speak to the ironies implicit in "human management of the wild" where the successes of the conservation movement often do more to advance issues of legal control and human use than to advance a hands-off respect for an autonomous wild?

GS: First, we have to accept that we live in a society where the government does compromise between individualism and communal purpose. I'm willing to make compromises with Land Use Management legislation. There used to be a time when I wanted to go out in the high country in the Sierra Nevada that I didn't have to get a wilderness permit to just go out and walk. I'm willing to accept the need for wilderness permits in the high country. Management is something that we just have to be grown up enough to do, *and,* in the same way, we need to make social decisions across society as a whole that we don't want certain species to become extinct, that we want to maintain bio-diversity, that we value certain qualities in the natural world and that we are willing to pay a little price for that in our society.

We're running into the contradictions we've created—governments and people are discovering that the price was a little higher than they thought and people are being forced to put themselves on the line saying, "Do I want this? Am I willing to sacrifice a little bit of myself for it?"

But, you're right in pointing out that the American conservation movement so far has been a series of successes in legislation and programs which are usually within federal agencies and are not internalized locally. It is also an outstanding history, here in America, compared to the rest of the world. Most of the rest of the world does not have many public lands, national parks, or programs in place for protecting biodiversity. Some other countries in the world that have a wild base to defend and build on and protect are simply not protecting it—they're selling it. They're selling it out to the Japanese or American corporations for large-scale, hit-and-run logging.

So our record is relatively good in the United States, and it has been because there were some powerful and well-spoken people who made a powerful effort and championed the establishment of National Parks and National Forests. But it was from the top down, for the most part.

CW: Now we go from the bottom up?
GS: Well, the time has come when we *have* to go from the bottom up. Having that top-down holding action, which is what it was, was probably necessary in a culture that did not have a common sense of place. Everybody was still here just to make their own fortune. But, as we get settled into North America, and come to take responsibility for it, we have to have a culture of nature and a culture of place in which the actual people, the actual society itself, values good air and good water, good fishing, and wild life. It should become a cultural value, rather than a government-imposed value. On the scale of the United States it's still possible.

CW: In an ideal world, would we primarily act as 'appreciators' of nature?
GS: No, we're more than just appreciators, we're an active part of nature and interacting with it all the time. We're big consumers, which isn't all bad. Every creature is a consumer of one sort or another. What is most interesting is to understand nature, to know it, to understand our role in it, and that its processes are our processes. It is not necessary to put nature on a pedestal and say it's untouchable, but it is necessary to find the right balance with it. This is where we should hope to be. Thus nature becomes a source for our art, our philosophy, and our thinking.

CW: In your essay, "Unnatural Writing," you argue that consciousness, mind, imagination, and *language* are wild. Will you speak to language being wild?
GS: To put it simply, language is extremely intellectually complex, but remarkably enough we do it without conscious intellectual mastery of it.

Most of us do not know the rules of grammar, and we do not *have* to know grammar to speak grammatically proper sentences. We do it constantly, effortlessly, all our lives. Nor do you have to studiously pack vocabulary away in your mind, you learn language as a child, almost effortlessly, in your interactions with others. So you have this remarkable capacity of language as a gift, as part of your biology. Of course, you can get better at it by effort, by reading, by learning new words, by exploring earlier styles of speech through literature, and you can certainly, with education, enlarge and broaden your sense of language, but these additions are marginal increases to what you've already mastered. These are micro-marginal increases, in statistical fact, although it's a striking increase when we see it in practice, the refinement. But, in terms of the synapses and the connections, the neurological system that is so complex, learning your own mother tongue is the most complex and large-scale intellectual undertaking in your whole life and you've finished doing it by the time you're five. Well, now, what does that sound like? It sounds like something that is almost self-creating, is self-maintaining, self-determining, goes by its own rules, has a complexity we can't intellectually describe, and is able to do its work without ever understanding it. That sounds like wild nature! That could be a definition of what the wild is. As the wild is at work in organic evolution and ecosystem dynamics, in coevolutionary interactions, the symbiotic interactions between different species that are mind boggling, if you actually get down and find out about them—how insects are right there at the right time to pollinate a plant and only one insect will pollinate that plant and it has to be on a certain day.

It is all very elegant. Just like language. So, I would like to suggest that even as historically we've prided ourselves as being creatures that language has set apart from nature, the truth is that language is perhaps one of the finest expressions of nature. It doesn't set us apart from nature.

CW: You wrote, "Nature's writing has the potential of becoming the most vital, radical, fluid, transgressive, pansexual, subductive, and morally challenging kind of writing on the scene. In becoming so, it may serve to help halt one of the most terrible things of our time, the destruction of species and their habitats, the elimination of some living beings forever."
GS: There's a really good book on nature in America that just came out by Lawrence Buell called *The Environmental Imagination.* He traces what the history of nature writing so far has been. A lot of it has been very well-intentioned, descriptive literature, through human eyes. It's been observational,

descriptive, appreciative, sensitive, but with limitations that the authors themselves really couldn't have seen. For example, seeing basically with human eyes, and we can't fault that, but as we become more informed by the threads of new science, we're apt to get into some radically different ways of looking at nature. That's what I think will be exciting about future nature writing. And also, of course, it does pose some very interesting moral challenges. The challenge of giving moral standing to non-human beings.

CW: As you interested then in a multi-vocality?

GS: I'd be interested in seeing that. How would you see or hear it? I would imagine that somebody that has spent enough time scuba diving, and spent enough time around, say, fish, or say spent enough time in the surf with sea mammals, and could make the exercise, the effort of the imagination, to begin to see the land from the edge of the sea, rather than the sea from the edge of the land, could do it. Big leaps of imagination. It would be very interesting to see how far people could move in that direction.

David Rains Wallace is working on some very interesting stuff both literary and scientific simultaneously. Or Gary Paul Nabhan, who also, has a science background, does work with plants, desert plants. His book *The Desert Smells Like Rain,* a North Point Press Book, is very knowledgeable and beautifully written. Gary is a strong writer and is the kind of person who can go to the edge of that territory. Or Dick Nelson who wrote of Alaska in *The Island Within,* and who gets close to deer, almost to a deer's standpoint. It's one thing to know that bears can smell a rotten carcass two miles away, and it's another thing to really imagine what it's like to walk around in the woods smelling things that well. There are exercises and imaginative stretches out there for somebody to do. Then, just the sexual lives of the different creatures . . . you know, our sense of sex and sexuality is so *limited* to the primate model and particularly the human primate model, and we go around in circles talking about sex and talking about the relationships between the sexes and gender roles, and so forth. It's very refreshing to blow that apart and see what sexuality is among other life forms.

CW: What do you mean by pansexual?

GS: Pansexual means across all the sexual lines. To feel sexual energy across lines would be to imagine for a moment the sexual attractiveness of a certain bird just as the male of that species or the female of that species would feel attracted to it. We're not touched by it biologically, but suppose you could be touched by it for a moment? What if you could say, "I could love that bird?" This is also a theme in mythology, where there is a lot of pan-sexuality. Later, after the Greeks, we began to distance ourselves from pan-sexuality and these myth-stories which held real meaning for the culture.

I'm throwing out some ideas of what could happen, if we relook at the mythological interactions and redignify them. Also, if we are to understand sexuality, we should see it as an extraordinary means of expression that is based in biology. Nature writing has a lot of potential if we break out of the present, rather genteel forms that it stays within, the tourist forms—"I've walked over the area and I saw this."

Also, during the eighteenth and nineteenth centuries and the early 20th century, the novel had a profound moral impact on the matter of develop-ing a moral conscience, a social conscience on all kinds of issues. We do not get that exactly, as a full-blown parallel, with the moral issues in nature—of course there were Muir and Thoreau—but one can imagine that there's a lot of potential here to be done in other flavors and other aspects and angles—as Ursula Le Guin does in *Buffalo Gals Won't You Come Out Tonight.*

CW: How do you work—are you primarily intuitive?

GS: Well not *completely,* no; one follows intuitive leads in doing intellectual research. The leads that send you there are intuitive, "Why am I looking this up?" You don't have to understand why. You just have to do it. I was driven to spend a lot of time going to Noh theater while I was in Japan. I knew intuitively that Noh drama had something to do with my work. I did the research and it finally came out in a real long poem that follows a Noh play. But why I did it, what was in Noh that I saw that made me want to do that, I don't know yet. But you don't need to know, the main thing is to do it. You don't know those things—you don't need to—it's a waste of energy to try to come up with a theoretical reason for why you do a certain thing. The artist works intuitively and very swiftly sometimes, and the reasons why can be left to others. I pursue study and writing without having a schema that explains why I am doing it or what the necessity of it is. I follow, as they say around some parts of Nevada County, "My bliss." We'll see if it works out or not.

CW: Do you trust that self-correcting language—stories, poetry—will nec-essarily rise?

GS: No, I don't. I don't think that just the promiscuous use of language alone will do anything. The difference is self-awareness. And silence. When silence occurs—in reflection, interior, imaginative exploration, self-aware-ness, self-knowledge—it is possibly more important. Then the strength of language, the power of language as used on literature, is the power that comes with silence. The reflection. Everything is palpable. It is refracted. It comes out of a place of self-awareness and intuitive knowledge.

So, no. I don't have much patience with language poets' theories that poetry is pure language and that pure language is manipulation. Language is a fascinating tool, there is no doubt about that. But, that tool does not necessarily solve the problems that it creates. Good art comes from an awareness of self that leads past ego, self-centeredness, and makes one appreciate larger connections and larger interactions and be sympathetic to the world. And then language comes alive. Because it is a vehicle of higher use. And, it takes less work (laugh). The good part. Then you get a splendid haiku, and it's all you need.

Dogen has a great saying, "We study the self to forget the self, and when you forget the self, you will become one with everything." Very straightforward. Want to forget yourself? Study yourself! Haiku are the poems of people who have forgotten themselves and have gone on to be with one with everything.

There are a lot of things one could argue around the territory of the imagination and the deeper mind in its relationship with culture.

CW: Do you see the Eastern use of language as more powerful in that regard than Western?
GS: We have some philosophical ideas expressed here and there in Occidental philosophy—a little bit in Spinoza, Leibniz, Hume and so forth—but you don't see the personal, meditative training and practice that shows you *how to do it* anywhere in the West. The theories have been stumbled on, the insights have been guessed at by many people, including Rilke, but none have understood the trail by which they got there. Whereas as the Buddhists have been very assiduously making the trail clear. That's the main job of Buddhism.

In literary terms, you find different positions in literary theory right now which are: first, what is the basis of our entire language system—this is the concern of the postmodernists; second, what is the psychological center—the concern of Jungians; and then, such as the writers like myself who find their territory between the two. Writers like me look into the territories of archetypal imagination, the mind, and also look into syntax and meta-linguistic questions about language structures. The meta-linguistic proposition is that if we speak an Indo-European language with a subject: object dichotomy, you will see the outer world as subject: object. That is really just a language form, but our philosophy reflects it. Some of the critical language philosophers say, "Western philosophy isn't philosophy, it is just grammar."

A Place in Space is a collection of many pieces responding to specific questions, problems and situations over the last twenty-five–thirty years, some of which were published and/or given as brief talks, but in every case, these were created out of a living situation as I lived it. I did not write these as part of a long-range plan or for some kind of intellectual masterwork. In some cases, they are putting out brushfires, and in other cases they're making chess moves to point out or make a position. So, many of these pieces are, to my mind, different moves on the same chessboard. And part of the strategy is to take the territory of poetry, environmental ethics, and Buddhism, and see a way to pull them all together. I did most of these pieces while taking time away from cutting firewood, from doing carpentry, many seasons of spring or summer when there were other things to do, and everybody thought I was nuts. They'd say, "Why are you writing those things to appear in odd places here and there? It's not going to get you a job and no one is going to pay you for it." I'd say, "I have to make these moves on the board. This is an invisible game that we're in, and we've got to try to create a new moral consensus so that we can move off of this board, and find a better game."

The Wild Mind of Gary Snyder

Trevor Carolan / 1996

Shambhala Sun 4, no. 5 (May 1996), 18–26. Reprinted by permission.

For the nineties, the celebrated Beat rebel advocates "wild mind," neighborhood values and watershed politics. "Wild mind," he says, "means elegantly self-disciplined, self-regulating. That's what wildness is. Nobody has a management plan for it."

Asked if he grows tired of talking about ecological stewardship, digging in, and coalition-building, the poet Gary Snyder responds with candor: "Am I tired of talking about it? I'm tired of *doing* it!" he roars. "But hey, you've *got* to keep doing it. That's part of politics, and politics is more interesting than winning and losing at the polls."

These days, there's an honest, conservative-sounding ring to the politics of the celebrated Beat rebel. Gary Snyder, though, has little in common with the right wingers who currently prevail throughout the western world.

"Conservatism has some very valid meanings," he says. "Of course, most of the people who call themselves conservative aren't that, because they're out to extract and use, to turn a profit. Curiously, eco and artist people and those who work with dharma practice are conservatives in the best sense of the word—we're trying to save a few things!"

"Care for the environment is like *noblesse oblige*," he maintains. "You don't do it because it has to be done. You do it because it's beautiful. That's the bodhisattva spirit. The bodhisattva is not anxious to do good, or feels obligation or anything like that. In Jodo-shin Buddhism, which my wife was raised in, the bodhisattva just says, 'I picked up the tab for everybody. Goodnight folks . . .'"

Five years ago, in a prodigious collection of essays called *The Practice of the Wild,* Gary Snyder introduced a pair of distinctive ideas to our vocabulary of ecological inquiry. Grounded in a lifetime of nature and wildernesss observation, Snyder offered the "etiquette of freedom" and "practice of the wild" as root prescriptions for the global crisis.

Informed by East-West poetics, land and wilderness issues, anthropology, benevolent Buddhism and Snyder's long years of familiarity with the bush and high mountain places, these principles point to the essential and life-sustaining relationship between place and psyche.

Such ideas have been at the heart of Snyder's work for the past forty years. When Jack Kerouac wrote of a new breed of counterculture hero in *The Dharma Bums*, it was a thinly veiled account of his adventures with Snyder in the mid-1950s. Kerouac's effervescent reprise of a West Coast dharma-warrior's dedication to "soil conservation, the Tennessee Valley Authority, astronomy, geology, Hsuan Tsang's travels, Chinese painting theory, reforestation, Oceanic ecology and food chains" remains emblematic of the terrain Snyder has explored in the course of his life.

One of our most active and productive poets, Gary Snyder has also been one of our most visible. Returning to California in 1969 after a decade abroad, spent mostly as a lay Zen Buddhist monk in Japan, he homesteaded in the Sierras and worked the lecture trail for sixteen years while raising a young family. By his own reckoning he has seen "practically every university in the United States."

As poet-essayist, Snyder's work has been uncannily well-timed, contributing to his reputation as a farseeing and weather-wise interpreter of cultural change. With his current collection of essays, *A Place in Space*, Snyder brings welcome news of what he's been thinking about in recent years. Organized around the themes of "Ethics, Aesthetics, and Watersheds," it opens with a discussion of Snyder's Beat Generation experience.

"It was simply a different time in the American economy," he explained when I spoke to him recently in Seattle. "It used to be that you came into a strange town, picked up work, found an apartment, stayed a while, then moved on. Effortless. All you had to have was a few basic skills and be willing to work. That's the kind of mobility you see celebrated by Kerouac in *On the Road.* For most Americans, it was taken for granted. It gave that insouciant quality to the young working men of North America who didn't have to go to college if they wanted to get a job.

I know this because in 1952 I was able to hitch-hike into San Francisco, stay at a friend's, and get a job within three days through the employment agency. With an entry level job, on an entry level wage, I found an apartment on Telegraph Hill that I could afford and I lived in the city for a year. Imagine trying to live in San Francisco or New York—any major city—on an entry level wage now? You can't do it. Furthermore, the jobs aren't that easy to get."

The freedom and openness of the post-war economy made it possible for people such as Snyder, Kerouac, Allen Ginsberg, Lew Welch, and others to disaffiliate from mainstream American dreams of respectability. And as Snyder writes, these "proletarian bohemians" chose even further disaffiliation, refusing to write "the sort of thing that middle-class Communist intellectuals think proletarian literature ought to be."

"In making choices like that, we were able to choose and learn other tricks for not being totally engaged with consumer culture," he says. "We learned how to live simply and were very good at it in my generation. That was what probably helped shape our sense of community. We not only knew each other, we depended on each other. We shared with each other."

"And there is a new simple-living movement coming back now, I understand," he notes, "where people are getting together, comparing notes about how to live on less money, how to share, living simply."

When Gary Snyder points something out, it generally warrants attention: his thinking has consistently been ahead of the cultural learning curve. Nowhere is his prescience more obvious than in "A Virus Runs Through It," an unpublished review of William Burroughs' 1962 *The Ticket That Exploded*.

Snyder regarded Burroughs' portrait of a society obsessed with addiction and consumerism, "whipped up by advertising," as an omen. He concluded that Burroughs' "evocation of the politics of addiction, mass madness, and virus panic, is all too prophetic."

"We were very aware of heroin addiction at that time," Snyder explains. "Kerouac, Ginsberg, Burroughs, Holmes and their circle in New York became fascinated with the metaphor of addiction in the light of heroin, smack. Marijuana was not an issue, but the intense addictive quality of heroin, and the good people who were getting drawn into it, and the romance some people had for it, was a useful framework for thinking about the nature of capitalist society and the addiction to fossil fuels in the industrial sector. It was obvious."

Many of Snyder's original arguments addressing pollution and our addiction to consumption have by now become mainstream: reduced fossil fuel dependence, recycling, responsible resource harvesting. Others remain works-in-progress: effective soil conservation, economics as a "small sub-branch of ecology," learning to "break the habit of acquiring unnecessary possessions," division by natural and cultural boundaries rather than arbitrary political boundaries.

As an ecological philosopher, Snyder's role has been to point out first the problems, and then the hard medicine that must be swallowed. Snyder has become synonymous with integrity—a good beginning place if your wilderness poetics honor "clean-running rivers; the presence of pelican and osprey and gray whale in our lives; salmon and trout in our streams; unmuddied language and good dreams."

"My sense of the West Coast," he says, "is that it runs from somewhere about the Big Sur River—the southern-most river that salmon run in—from there north to the Straits of Georgia and beyond, to Glacier Bay in southern Alaska. It is one territory in my mind. People all relate to each other across it; we share a lot of the same concerns and text and a lot of the same trees and birds."

Raised in the Pacific Northwest, Snyder grew up close to the anthropomorphic richness of the local Native American mythology, the rainforest totems of eagle, bear, raven and killer whale that continue to appear in school and community insignias as important elements of regional consciousness. It is unsurprising that they—and roustabout cousins like Coyote—have long been found at the core of Snyder's expansive vision. Literal-minded rationalists have had difficulty with Snyder's Buddhist-oriented eco-philosophy and poetics. His embrace of Native American lore only further ruffled orthodox literary imagination, and in the past his poetry was criticized as being thin, loose or scattered.

As Snyder readers know, the corrective to such interpretations of his work is more fresh air and exercise. Regarding Buddhism, his take is offered simply and efficiently. "The marks of Buddhist teaching," he writes in *A Place in Space*, "are impermanence, no-self, the inevitability of suffering and connectedness, emptiness, the vastness of mind, and a way to realization."

"It seems evident," he writes, offering insight into the dynamics of his admittedly complex world view, "that there are throughout the world certain social and religious forces that worked through history toward an ecologically and culturally enlightened state of affairs. Let these be encouraged: Gnostics, hip Marxists, Teilhard de Chardin Catholics, Druids, Taoists, Biologists, Witches, Yogins, Bhikkus, Quakers, Sufis, Tibetans, Zens, Shamans, Bushmen, American Indians, Polynesians, Anarchists, Alchemists, primitive cultures, communal and ashram movements, cooperative ventures."

"Idealistic, these?" he says when asked about such alternative "Third Force" social movements. "In some cases the vision can be mystical; it can be Blake. It crops up historically with William Penn and the Quakers trying to make the Quaker communities in Pennsylvania a righteous place to live—treating the native peoples properly in the process. It crops up in the utopian and communal experience of Thoreau's friends in New England.

"As utopian and impractical as it might seem, it comes through history as a little dream of spiritual elegance and economic simplicity, and collaboration and cooperating communally—all of those things together. It may be that it was the early Christian vision. Certainly it was one part of the early Buddhist vision. It turns up as a reflection of the integrity of tribal culture; as a reflection of the kind of energy that would try to hold together the best lessons of tribal cultures even within the overwhelming power and dynamics of civilization."

Any paradigm for a truly healthy culture, Gary Snyder argues, must begin with surmounting narrow personal identity and finding a commitment to place. Characteristically, he finds a way of remaking the now tired concept of "sense of place" into something fresh and vital. The rural model of place, he emphasizes, is no longer the only model for the healing of our culture.

"Lately I've been noticing how many more people who tend toward counterculture thinking are turning up at readings and book signings in the cities and the suburbs," he says. "They're everywhere. What I emphasize more and more is that a bioregional consciousness is equally powerful in a city or in the suburbs. Just as a watershed flows through each of these places, it also includes them."

"One of the models I use now is how an ecosystem resembles a mandala," he explains. "A big Tibetan mandala has many small figures as well as central figures, and each of them has a key role in the picture: they're all essential. The whole thing is an educational tool for understanding—that's where the ecosystem analogy comes in. Every creature, even the little worms and insects, has value. Everything is valuable—that's the measure of the system."

To Snyder, value also translates as responsibility. Within his approach to digging in and committing to a place is the acceptance of responsible stewardship. Snyder maintains that it is through this engaged sense of effort and practice-participating in what he salutes as "the tiresome but tangible work of school boards, county supervisors, local foresters, local politics"—that we find our real community, our real culture. "Ultimately, values go back to our real interactions with others," he says. "That's where we live, in our communities."

"You know, I want to say something else," he continues. "In the past months and years Carole, my wife, has been amazing. I do my teaching and my work with the Yuba Watershed Institute, but she's incredible; she puts out so much energy. One of the things that makes it possible for us and our neighbors to do all this is that the husbands and wives really are partners; they help out and trade off. They develop different areas of expertise and they help keep each other from burning out. It's a great part of being a family and having a marriage—becoming fellow warriors, side to side."

In 1968, Snyder stated flatly that, "The modern American family is the smallest and most barren family that has ever existed." Throughout the years his recommendations concerning new approaches to the idea of family and relationships have customarily had a pagan, tribal flavor. These days he calls it community.

"I'm learning, as we all do, what it takes to have an ongoing relationship with our children," he says. "I have two grown sons, two stepdaughters, a nephew who's twenty-seven, and all their friends whom I know. We're still helping each other out. There's a real cooperative spirit. There's a fatherly responsibility there, and a warm, cooperative sense of interaction, of family as extended family, one that moves imperceptibly toward community and a community-values sense.

"So I'm urging people not to get stuck with that current American catchphrase 'family values,' and not to throw it away either, but to translate it into community values. Neighborhood values are ecosystem values, because they include all the beings.

"What I suspect may emerge in the political spectrum is a new kind of conservative, one which is socially liberal, in the specific sense that it will be free of racial or religious prejudice. The bugaboo, that one really bad flaw of the right wing, except for the Libertarians, is its racist and anti-Semitic and anti-personal-liberty tone.

"A political spectrum that has respect for traditions, and at the same time is non-racist and tolerant about different cultures, is an interesting development. I'd be willing to bet that it's in the process of emerging, similar in a way to the European Green Parties that say, 'We're neither on the left nor the right; we're in front.'

One of the things I'm trying to do, and I believe it's the right way to work," he says, "is to be non-adversarial—to go about it as tai chi, as jiu-jitsu. To go with the direction of a local community issue, say, and change it slightly. We don't have to run head-on. We can say to the other party, 'You've got a lot of nice energy; let's see if we can run this way.'"

Yet as anyone involved in community activism learns, amicable resolutions are not always the result. "Sometimes you do have to go head to head on an issue," he agrees, "and that's kind of fun too. 'Showing up' is good practice."

Snyder remembers a fight some four years ago over open pit mining. "I was the lead person on this one, to get an initiative on the ballot that would ban open pit mining, or at least put a buffer zone around any open pit mine. The mining companies from out of town spent a lot of money and did some really intense, last minute, nasty style campaigning, so we lost at the polls.

"But not a single open pit mine has been tried in our county since then. We understand from our interactions with these people that we won their respect. They were smart enough to see that they may have won it at the polls, but we were ready to raise money and willing to fight. That's standing up."

With the growing importance of community coalition-building, Snyder says he is finding it increasingly useful to narrow down his ideas about bioregionalism, or his notion of a practice of the wild, to a shared neighborhood level.

"That's why I talk about watersheds," he explains. "Symbolically and literally they're the mandalas of our lives. They provide the very idea of the watershed's social enlargement, and quietly present an entry into the spiritual realm that nobody has to think of or recognize as being spiritual.

"The watershed is our only local Buddha mandala, one that gives us all, human and non-human, a territory to interact in. That is the beginning of dharma citizenship: not membership in a social or national sphere, but in a larger community citizenship. In other words, a sangha; a local dharma community. All of that is in there, like Dogen when he says, 'When you find your place, practice begins.'"

Thirteenth-century master Dogen Zenji is a classical Asian voice which Snyder has discussed frequently in recent years. "There are several levels of meaning in what Dogen says. There's the literal meaning, as in when you settle down somewhere. This means finding the right teaching, the right temple, the right village. Then you can get serious about your practice.

Underneath, there's another level of implication: you have to understand that there are such things as places. That's where Americans have yet to get to. They don't understand that there are places. So I quote Dogen and people say, 'What do you mean, you have to find your place? Anywhere is okay for dharma practice because it's spiritual.' Well, yes, but not just any place. It has to be a place that you've found yourself. It's never abstract, always concrete."

If embracing the responsibility for the place and the moment is his prescription, a key principle in this creative stewardship is waking up to "wild mind." He clarifies that "wild" in this context does not mean chaotic, excessive, or crazy.

"It means self-organizing," he says. "It means elegantly self-disciplined, self-regulating, self-maintained. That's what wilderness is. Nobody has to do the management plan for it. So I say to people, 'Let's trust in the self-disciplined elegance of wild mind.' Practically speaking, a life that is vowed to simplicity, appropriate boldness, good humor, gratitude, unstinting work and play, and lots of walking, brings us close to the actually existing world and its wholeness."

This is Gary Snyder's wild medicine. From the beginning, it has been devotion to this quality that has served as his bedrock of practice, his way of carving out a place of freedom in the wall of American culture. In his omission of the personal in favor of the path, he exemplifies the basics of the Zen tradition in which he was trained. The influx of trained Asian teachers of the Buddhadharma to the West in recent years has raised questions about whether the first homespun blossoming of Beat-flavored Buddhism in the fifties actually included the notion of practice. As one who was there and has paid his dues East and West, Snyder's response is heartening.

"In Buddhism and Hinduism, there are two streams: the more practice-oriented and the more devotional streams," he explains. "Technically speaking the two tendencies are called *bhakta* and *jnana*. *Bhakta* means devotional; *jnana* means wisdom/practice. Contemporary Hinduism, for example, is almost entirely devotional—the *bhakta* tradition.

"Catholicism is a devotional religion, too, and Jack Kerouac's Buddhism had the flavor of a devotional Buddhism. In Buddhism the idea that anybody can do practice is strongly present. In Catholicism practice is almost entirely thought of as entering an order or as becoming a lay novitiate of an order. So that explains Jack's devotional flavor. There's nothing wrong with devotional Buddhism. It is its own creative religious approach, and it's very much there in Tibetan Buddhism too.

"Our western Buddhism has been strongly shaped by late nineteenth and early twentieth century Asian intellectuals," he notes. "D. T. Suzuki was an intellectual strongly influenced by western thought. And the same is true of other early interpreters of Buddhism to the West.

"We came as westerners to Buddhism generally with an educated background," Snyder continues. "So we have tended to over-emphasize the intellectual and spiritual sides of it, with the model at hand of Zen, without realizing that a big part of the flavor of Buddhism, traditionally and historically, is devotional. This is not necessarily tied to doing a lot of practice, but is tied to having an altar in the house—putting flowers in front of it every day, burning incense in front of it every day, having the children bow and burn incense before it. The family may also observe certain Buddhist holy days such as the Buddha's birthday by visiting a temple together, and so forth.

"With that perspective in mind, it isn't so easy to say, 'Oh well, Jack Kerouac wasn't a real Buddhist.' He was a devotional Buddhist, and like many Asians do, he mixed up his Buddhism with several different religions. So, it's okay; there's nothing wrong with that. You can be a perfectly good Buddhist without necessarily doing a lot of exercises and sitting and yoga; you can be equally a good Buddhist by keeping flowers on your altar, or in winter, dry grass or cedar twigs.

"There's a big tendency right now in western Buddhism to psychologize it—to try and take the superstition, the magic, the irrationality out of it and make it into a kind of therapy. You see that a lot," he says. "Let me say that I'm grateful for the fact that I lived in Asia for so long and hung out with Asian Buddhists. I appreciate that Buddhism is a whole practice and isn't just limited to the lecture side of it; that it has stories and superstition and ritual and goofiness like that. I love that aspect of it more and more."

Snyder says that at sixty-five, he's "working like a demon." For the past ten years he has taught creative writing at the University of California, leading workshops and participating in the interdisciplinary "Nature and Culture" program. This year will also mark the arrival of his long-awaited sequence of forty-five poems called "Mountains and Rivers Without End," portions of which have appeared intermittently since Jack Kerouac first dropped word of it in *The Dharma Bums.*

"I realized I wasn't going to live forever and that I'd started a lot of parallel projects, with lots of interesting notes to each one, so it's be a pity not to put all that information to good use. Once 'Mountains and Rivers' is done I won't have to write anything further. Anything after that is for fun. Maybe I won't be a writer anymore. Maybe I'll clean out my barn."

Aging and health are not at issue with Snyder. He works at keeping in good condition and several months ago spent three weeks hiking in the Himalayas with a group of family and friends.

"We trekked up to base camp at Everest, went over eighteen thousand feet three times, and were seven days above sixteen thousand feet," he says with obvious relish. "Everybody was in pretty good shape and I only lost four pounds in a month, so I'm not thinking a whole lot about aging."

Snyder's recent journey provided him insights into the questions of karma and reincarnation, which eco-philosopher Joanna Macy believes may hold special relevance for North Americans. She argues that deeply ingrained American frontier values such as individualism, personal mobility, and independence may contribute to the idea that, "If this is our only one-time life, then we don't have to care about the planet."

"The concept of reincarnation in India can literally shape the way one lives in the world," Snyder notes, "and many Tibetans also believe in reincarnation quite literally. So in that frame of mind, the world becomes completely familiar. You sit down and realize that 'I've been men, women, animals; there are no forms that are alien to me.'

"That's why everyone in India looks like they're living in eternity. They walk along so relaxed, so confident, so unconcerned about their poverty or their illness, or whatever it is, even if they're beggars. It goes beyond just giving you a sense of concern for the planet; it goes so far as to say, 'Planets come and go.' It's pretty powerful stuff. It's also there in classical Buddhism where people say, 'I've had enough of experience.' That's where a lot of Buddhism in India starts—'I want out of the meat wheel of existence,' as Jack Kerouac says."

An ecosystem too, Snyder concludes, can be seen as "just a big metabolic wheel of energies being passed around and around. You can see it as a great dance, a great ceremony. You can feel either really at home with it, or step out of the circle."

"We are all indigenous," he reminds us. So it is appropriate that in relearning the lessons of fox and bluejay, or city crows and squirrels—"all members present at the assembly" that we are promised neither too little, nor too much for our perseverance. This poet, who for so many now reads like an old friend, invites us to make only sense. After all in recommitting to this continent place by place, he reckons, "We may not transform reality, but we may transform ourselves. And if we transform ourselves, we might just change the world a bit."

Living Landscape: An Interview with Gary Snyder

John P. O'Grady / 1998

Western American Literature 33, no. 3 (Fall 1998), 275–91. Reprinted by permission of Western American Literature and University of Nebraska Press.

In October 1997, I interviewed the poet Gary Snyder. The subject of our discussion was the influence of the American West and its literature has had on him and his work. Over the course of his long career, he has published more than two dozen books and has been awarded both the Pulitzer (1975) and the Bollingen (1997) Prizes, but his importance extends well beyond literature. "I wish to be a spokesman," he has said, "for a realm that is not usually represented either in intellectual chambers or in the chambers of government" (*Turtle Island* 106). Snyder is one of our culture's venerable teachers. Since 1986, he has been a professor at the University of California, Davis, where, in addition to conducting classes in writing and literature, he founded that institution's acclaimed Nature and Culture Program.

I first met Snyder at Davis in April 1986, during my first year of doctoral studies and his first year on the faculty. To introduce himself to the university community, he gave a reading and talked about the mountains of the West. In particular, he spoke about the Cascades, that snowy string of volcanic peaks that extends like a necklace along the Pacific Slope, from northern California to British Columbia. "Those unearthly glowing floating snowy summits are a promise to the spirit," he later wrote in *The Practice of the Wild* (117). Even when shrouded in clouds, the "Guardian Peaks" of the Columbia—now bearing the names Hood, Adams, and St. Helens, but formerly known as Wy'east, Klickitat, and Loowit—were always visible in his imagination. He came to know his home place intimately by climbing its mountains. He stood on the summit of his first major peak when he was fifteen years old, and from there he could see the next mountain. He resolved to climb it. From the top of that peak, he could see the next. And on it went, one climb leading to another, a life measured in mountains rather than years.

In the library of the Mazamas, a mountaineering organization in Portland, you can browse through the old summit registers, those ledge books that used to sit in heavy aluminum boxes at the top of each peak. Successful climbers would sign in on these pages. It was a record of achievement, as good as pinning your name to a cloud. In the register from Mount St. Helens on August 13, 1945, you will find the bold signature of a fifteen-year-old boy named Gary Snyder, who would one day write a line that, if now applied to this particular volcanic landscape, would seem an understatement: "Streams and mountains never stay the same" (*Mountains* 143).

John P. O'Grady: What do you remember about your first climb of Mount St. Helens?

Gary Snyder: I was first doing backpacking and then snow peak mountaineering. I really got my initiation into snow peak mountaineering in the summer of 1945, when I was fifteen, climbing from the YMCA camp at Spirit Lake. That was an old-style climbing party in which the guide was from Yamhill County, Oregon, an old gent who had climbed western snow peaks many, many times. He was the last person I ever saw who wore the garb of the earlier generation of Pacific Northwest climbers, namely, stagged-off logger's pants, caulked, twelve-inch logger's boots, and a black felt hat. Instead of an ice axe, he carried a long alpenstock, and he covered his face with white zinc ointment to prevent sunburn. You look at early photographs in a Mazama yearbook and that's the way everybody's dressed. It was great! (Laughs) I loved snow peak climbing from my first ascent there on Mount St Helens. The next year, '46, I signed up for a Mazama climb. I knew that the Mazamas led mountaineering trips every year. I did my first ascent of Mount Hood with the Mazamas, who were based in Portland. Having once or twice climbed a snow peak, you are eligible to apply for membership. I applied and was accepted, and one or two of my high school friends—all about the same age, sixteen—were accepted, making us the youngest people in the Mazamas at that time. That was the beginning of a youth group in the Mazamas, which was otherwise all middle-aged people. Then, shortly after, veterans back from the 10th Mountain Infantry came into the Mazamas. They had both war and mountaineering experience and were returning home to the Pacific Northwest. Those guys, I remember them well, became my generation's—the sixteen-year-olds—teachers in that era's state-of-the-art snow and rock climbing. So we all went out climbing together with these twenty-five-year-olds who were very sharp and did winter camping, skiing, winter ascents, and so forth. It was a very good time to learn mountaineering, and the Mazamas hosted it. It was a great organization, and it's still going.

JO'G: As one of the youngest people in the Mazamas, you published a piece in 1946 Mazama annual. Was that your earliest publication?
GS: Either that or the Lincoln High School [Portland, Oregon] newspaper. (Laughs) They were both published about the same time.

JO'G: That Mazama piece was prefaced with a laconic note from the editor that read, "This is a new point of view on mountain climbing" (56). It seemed as if he did not know what to make of this voice of a younger generation.
GS: That's what it was, alright! (Laughs)

JO'G: You once told me about a climb you did on Mount Rainier, where you ran into some problems with ice fall.
GS: It was a Mazama climb, and we had made the summit via the south-side route up the Wapowety Cleaver. We were in descent. It was cloudy and warm, which is the worst kind of mountaineering weather. Quite warm and cloudy up there, and sort of heavy. We had to descend through some seracs. At one point, we were below an ice fall on a steep icy slope that was smooth—it was below a system of seracs about two hundred feet wide. Our return route led across the ice chute to a rock ridge that was well above any surrounding glacier and seracs, and was a safe place. I was the leader on the last rope, and we were all wearing crampons. The rope ahead of us went across. We would have followed right behind them—we had been following just a few yards behind—but my crampon ties had loosened up, so I stopped the group to tighten my crampons, and I urged everyone else to tighten their crampon straps, which took us five or six minutes. During those five or six minutes, an avalanche of broken seracs swept down the slope that we would have been right in the middle of if we had kept going. It was quite astonishing to see where we would have been. Then it stopped and froze up in a big jumble. As for the party that was ahead of us, their route had taken them out of our sight. They were around the corner of a rock wall, so they had no idea how we were, except that they had seen this avalanche come down too. So we all took a big breath and looked at it, and then we looked up. I said, "Well, you know, there's no point in waiting here. There's less

chance that it'll avalanche again right now than if we wait a little longer." So we dashed across. We unroped, actually, and dashed across as individuals, with our ice axes and crampons. Close call!

JO'G: In *Earth House Hold,* you included your journal from a 1965 ascent of Glacier Peak with Allen Ginsberg.
GS: The only snow peak that we had to rope up on, I'm sure! (Laughs) He had done trail hikes, you know, up to mountains, but no, that's the only time he put on crampons and ropes and things.

JO'G: Many people have asked you about the writers who have influenced you. What about mountaineers who have been influential?
GS: You know, I'm about to attend a three-day celebration of Willi Unsoeld at Evergreen College. I'm giving the annual Willi Unsoeld lecture, which is going to be a poetry reading. I was looking at a video of Willi before he died, giving a talk called "Spiritual Values in Wilderness"—boy was he good! That guy was sharp!

JO'G: What will be the subject of your talk at Evergreen?
GS: I'm going to read from *Mountains and Rivers Without End* and talk about Willi's life as a teacher and mountaineer.

JO'G: Did you know him?
GS: Never knew him. He was only two years older than I, and he was from the Northwest. He was part of the same mountaineering culture that I grew up in, which is very romantic in a certain way.

JO'G: It's hard to be a mountaineer and not be a romantic.
GS: Well, yeah, okay. (Laughs) Except he got to *Sagarmatha,* Everest! When he was young, he and Tom Hornbein did the West Ridge traverse ascent. By the time I got to Everest, all I could do was stand around and look at base camp. (Laughs) But seriously, Unsoeld, who died in an avalanche on Mount Rainier and was a professor at Evergreen College, was a brilliant, creative, bold, radical mountain man. I bow to him.

JO'G: Turning now to the subject of western American literature, the writers most frequently cited as precursors to your own work are John Muir, Robinson Jeffers, and Kenneth Rexroth. What other western American writers would you say have influenced you?

GS: I was an extensive reader as a kid and lived on a farm. We made really good use of the Seattle Public Library. It was a standard Saturday trip to the university branch of the public library to pick up a new round of books for me. I took out ten or twelve every week. I read John Muir very early on and was suitably inspired. I was inspired about how light he went. And this thing about having just a tin cup and a dry crust of bread and some tea (Laughs)—I'm still not sure about that! (Laughs) I read the biography *John of the Mountains* [Linnie Marsh Wolfe, 1938] when it came out. I also read a number of lesser-known people: Stewart Edward White's novels about the Pacific Northwest and the West. Gad, I read everything. H.L. Davis, *The Winds of Morning,* a great novel about eastern Oregon. It catches the flavor of the twenties and thirties eastern Oregon sheep and ranch culture really nicely. I like it better than *Honey in the Horn,* which was Davis's most famous novel. Now get this (laughs): The Tugboat Annie series of stories, which were based in Puget Sound, came out serially in the *Saturday Evening Post* (Laughs). I also read some of the standard fare of western writers, including Zane Grey. Oh, and Oliver La Farge—the novel *Laughing Boy,* which was a very important novel to a lot of people and was quite a success in its own time. I'm sure it inspired D. H. Lawrence and a whole bunch of American Southwest lovers of that era, and brought a very sympathetic eye to Native Americans of the Southwest. It also has, as I recall, maybe the first account of a peyote vision, a peyote trip, in mainstream American literature—that's way back there. I was doing this just a year or two before I discovered D. H. Lawrence and Robinson Jeffers, prior to reading standard literary fare, but it's more like what a kid reads when he browses around.

JO'G: Do you regard your reading of Lawrence and Jeffers as somehow marking a transition in your development?

GS: Well, I became more self-consciously aware of quality and intellectual content in writing. Because of my connection with climbing and working with people in the logging industry, and a little bit of work in eastern Oregon around ranchers and loggers, I had been out on the ground long enough to know that these guys weren't real westerners (Laughs). There is a level of writing in American western writing which does come pretty close to the ground, although it isn't always considered high-quality writing.

JO'G: When you say "eastern Oregon," do you mean that country east of the Cascades?

GS: Well, yes, the dry country. Madras, Oregon, for example. I worked around Madras, which is in sight of the Cascades, but it's into the sagebrush. But at the same time, I was reading Native American stuff. My introduction to writing about Native Americans was very early, with Ernest Thompson Seton. Then I picked up all kinds of things, which I can't even keep track of. I had a kind of double vision of the West, seeing it simultaneously from the Native American angle and from the white settler angle, which I think is typical of many imaginative people of the West—they see both sides of the picture in their mind's eye. As far as my Native American interests went, oddly enough I didn't just stick to the West and the Pacific Northwest. As we were taught as school kids up in Seattle, there were the "Canoe Indians" and there were the "Horse Indians"—the Canoe Indians were on the west side of the mountains, and the Horse Indians were on the east side of the mountains—that's the way we were taught to distinguish the cultures in the third grade. I also became very interested in the Native American cultures of New England and the Ohio Valley: the Shawnee and the Delaware and the Iroquois. I read a great deal about the Eastern Woodland Indians and their different cultural manifestations—I had a lot of interest in that. I had also read James Fenimore Cooper. And I read some horrendous novels about people like Simon Girty. I just reread a fine, dispassionate book about Girty that brought all of that back to me. Girty was a troubling figure to me as a boy. He was a white renegade who joined the Indians after 1778 or '79 and fought with the Indians for the rest of his life. He was really demonized by the whites. According to the story, he delighted in watching whites being tortured—that was a heavy torture culture anyway. Trying to establish Girty's character in my own mind was a really interesting thing for me.

JO'G: Why was he troubling to you?
GS: He was troubling because I wanted to join the Indians, so to speak, in my mind, but I wasn't sure I wanted to cheer when people were being tortured (Laughs) as Girty supposedly did.

JO'G: In the genre of Indian captivity narratives, we find this motif of "going Indian." According to those who analyze these stories, there is a kind of projection going on there on the part of the Euro-Americans, an unconscious, deep-seated fear coming out. The most fearsome thing that could happen to a white person in these stories—even worse than being tortured— was for one to "go Indian," to become one of the "savages."

GS: Yes, I know that literature. Girty was at one time seen as virtually a demon; he was taken as an example of the worst case of what a white man can become. He moved to Canada, joined the British, and fought against the Americans on the side of the British in the Revolutionary War, because he said the British are better to the Indians than the Americans are (Laughs).

JO'G: In regard to this particular aspect of American culture—the deep ambivalence about Native Americans and those whites who become involved with them—do you see this trend continuing down through history to the present, or does it disappear?

GS: I'm sure that that goes on, but one would have to think about how these threads reveal themselves today. There's a big difference in the psychology of American culture in regard to Native Americans before the Civil War and after the Civil War. The experience of the East Coast and the Ohio Valley was one experience of Indians, and then the defeat of Tecumseh and the Euro-Americans winning the "Middle Ground," as they called it, was the end of a period in Native American relations. That was the defeat of the Indians east of the Mississippi, basically. There's a whole lore there, which we don't think about much out in the West. After the Civil War, the expansion into the Plains begins, and there's another whole chapter that starts with the Plains Indians. That's the chapter we're more acquainted with. The western Indian cultures—on the Plains and westward—were perhaps not as troubling to whites; the Plains Indians were not as demonized.

JO'G: The European encounter with Indians in California was different too—the Spanish coming from the opposite direction of the English and French, and much earlier.

GS: It's hard to figure out how the California Indian imagery plays, because apparently they were so decimated already by smallpox by the time the Yankees came, you don't get a clear picture of who they were in their own terms. When I was a youngster, what inspired me and influenced me greatly was the case of Chief Joseph. The history of Chief Joseph of the Nez Perce, and their attempt to be free, led right into my political radicalism. And the connection with Charles Erskine Scott Wood. He was a Portlander, an anarchist, an IWW follower after he resigned his commission in the cavalry. He's part of another chapter of American left-wing and West Coast left-wing life. There's a pamphlet on him in the Western Writers Series. He has published several books of poetry—one called *The Poet in the Desert*. He's a most remarkable American literary figure who started as a cavalry officer. He was present at the surrender of Chief Joseph and was so moved by the whole situation that he resigned his commission, moved to Portland, became a lawyer, and then became a supporter of the IWW and the socialist left. He later moved to Stanford, where his children and he—but mostly his children—became Stanford people and Berkeley people, living near the core of thirties left-wing activism in Stanford and Berkeley university circles. I know some of those people today—children of those children. One thing I should say: I am deeply imbued with a lot of western American political and literary lore—I grew up with it, through my mother who's a Texan who moved early to the Northwest, and my father, who's native to Washington. What with the reading and the stories and the work, I guess I qualify as a westerner! I grew up in the left-wing branch of the western culture. So labor history, strikes, IWW, early socialism, people like Charles Erskine Scott Wood and Joe Hill were part of—were in—our thoughts to a certain degree.

JO'G: That's a sort of subterranean current in the story of the West.
GS: Just a quick story: I worked with an Indian guy my age on a choker-setting crew in eastern Oregon in 1954. His name was Lyle LaFramboise. He was a Wasco—big, handsome, cheerful guy. I asked him one day, "Lyle, where did you get that French Name, LaFramboise?" And he said, "Don't you know? LaFramboise was one of the great voyagers who came down the Columbia." And it's true! He was a descendent of the great LaFramboise. You can read about it. (Laughs)

JO'G: Let's talk about the West Coast. You were born in San Francisco, a California native. The recently published *Updating the Literary West* [see Lyon et al.] devotes over 160 pages to California alone. In his introduction to the California section, Gerald Haslam writes, "Those who think California is 'West Coast, not West' simply don't know what they're talking about" (297). What is your take on California as a place and as a culture?
GS: California's relationship to the arid West, the West that we think of as west of the Rockies, is always an interesting question. It does and it does not relate. In a certain sense, California is Pacific and Spanish. California's culture comes around by sea to it, or up from Mexico, rather than across the Great Basin. My friend Drum Hadley, a cowboy poet, and sustainable rancher who used to really study this stuff, says that older-style California ranchers and cowboys had far more Mexican lore and Mexican-derived gear around the ranch than anyone did in Arizona and Texas. He says these early California ranchers were deeply Mexican (Spanish) influenced, and

he could see it in the kinds of knots they tied and in the way they did their rawhide braiding and in certain ways they handled horses. Drum says some of the knot systems go, via the Spanish, back to North Africa!

JO'G: An awful lot has been written about your work in relation to landscape and nature, but comparatively little about your relationship to West Coast cities. You were born in San Francisco and the raised in Seattle and Portland. To what degree would you say these cities are western?

GS: Well, again, the West Coast is and is not part of the West, depending on how you define it. It's not part of the "Dry West" or the "Rancher West." I believe that if you define part of the western story as direct resource use, men and women working very close to resource extraction—which I think is a fair way of looking at it—then the whole logging industry, and to some degree the mining industry, should be brought into it. But logging and mining have not created myths or stories like ranching did, and I'm not entirely sure why. If there's a romance of logging, it's more of the politics of the IWW days and the strikes—labor strife romance. They never tried—or if they did, it never worked—to organize cowboys, though the IWW was out organizing Montana miners and the loggers in the woods. Anyway, Portland and Seattle are one set of cities, San Francisco is another. San Francisco is a Mediterranean city, originally dominated by French, Portuguese, and Swiss-Italian settlers, all Catholic. Kenneth Rexroth was very articulate about this—he gave me my sense of San Francisco and Bay Area culture, and the old power elite of San Francisco, who were graduates of the Jesuit high school and the University of San Francisco. The Aliotos, for example. Really, I felt San Francisco to be like a cosmopolitan European city when I first came here. The Northwest—Seattle, when I was a kid—was a faintly Scandinavian town. And Portland not quite so Scandinavian, more like a transplanted Boston—it is more like a New England city. These are all interesting speculations. But I didn't live in Seattle. I lived out of Seattle on a farm, so Seattle was not really a city that I knew. I was never intimate with it. I was intimate with the countryside north of Seattle, the Puget Sound country and the woods, but not the town really, except to go in as far as the university district to the Goodwill and to the library. I went to college in Portland, and Portland is (in certain ways all of Pacific Northwest culture is) kind of uniquely liberal—and I'm not sure where it all comes from. But it includes the radical Swedes, Finns, and New England Unitarians, who became part of the early Portland scene.

JO'G: Did living in Portland have a decided influence on your work, your evolving sensibility?

GS: Not so much as my connection with the Cascades to the east and the Pacific to the west. You know, one of the things that would be said about me as a westerner would be that I placed myself regionally, really very early, by the landscapes. So the bioregional threads in my thinking actually go back a long ways. The ideas in my essay "The Rediscovery of Turtle Island" are actually very old ideas for me. I'd say that suggests another kind of westerner—the westerner who bonds with the place early on as a kid and for whom the place is the source of their loyalty, not the political system or the nation-state. But then that's not only western—that's the old ways.

JO'G: On the subject of bioregionalism, those same ideas that you had early on about one's relationship to place and identity have now entered into contemporary academic and political discussions. Where did all this discussion of bioregionalism come from? Where is it now? And where is it going?

GS: Oh, that's a huge topic! (Laughs) Of course, the term was borrowed from biogeographers to begin with. And we put a spin on it ourselves, which was social and cultural. But in a sense we were looking for any language that would help us clarify that there was a distinction between finding your membership in a natural place and locating your identity in terms of a social or political group. The landscape was my natural nation, and I could see that as having a validity and a permanence that would outlast the changing political structures. It enabled me to be critical of the United States without feeling that I wasn't at home in North America. They used to say "If you don't like it here, go back to Europe"—which is to assume that your identity is entirely given to you by being a member of the state and that you have no stake in the landscape. It's very revealing. I'm sure many people have discovered that, as a matter of their own sensibility, their loyalty is to the land, but they haven't easily found a way to articulate it in their lives. Then they become environmentalists or something, but they don't bring it into the foreground of their thinking. They don't understand that loyalty as an alternative political-cultural-personal strategy. I would suggest that the terminology comes way after what is actually a shift in sensibilities and that the feeling for the landscape has been present in some territories of American life from the beginning. It is simply penetrating deeper and deeper as the "newcomers" stay around longer. It's a nascent sensibility that, I think, marks the future of western writing, something we'll see more and more henceforth in various forms, whether it's called "regional" or "bioregional."

JO'G: This ties in with the essay by your wife, Carole Koda, which is entitled "Dancing in the Borderland: Finding Our Common Ground in North America," a piece she published in a little book along with essays by you and Wendell Berry. [This essay is reprinted in *Terra Nova* 3.4 (fall 1998).] She discusses how ethnic identity merges with place sensibility.

GS: Yes, Carole finds that the place provides more of her being than her ethnic background, although she honors it. That little essay is very interesting. It points a way beyond unreflective identity politics to the serious consideration of membership in North America. Now, here's one more little thing about the West: huge public lands. When I was still a teenager, I woke up to national forests. I grasped that much of the land around our place were national forests and took great comfort in its vastness. That may have been misplaced, looking at the history of the Forest Service since, but it gave me as a youngster—out of my backpacking and hitchhiking trips and so forth—a sense of a stake in the land. It brought me cheer to think that we had huge areas of open space and wild land and forests that belonged to all of us. That's part of the American western experience, whether people realize it or not. It's not just that there's open space there and that it's big, but that it's *public* land, the Commons. Now none of this would come out of anybody's interest in Asia! (Laughs) These are very American interests: that the Commons might still survive.

JO'G: *The Practice of the Wild* has been around for several years now. What's your feeling about the critical response to that book?

GS: The critical response has been a little disappointing, in that I have not yet seen—with one exception, which I'll come to—what I thought was a really reflective review of it. It's had lots of favorable reviews, with many good things to say. But there are some angles in *Practice* that people are still going to stumble onto yet. It's a complex text. It has not been picked up very much by the official environmental world, but it's been used steadily as a textbook all over the country, in many universities. I think that's what one of its uses is, a textbook. There is a dissertation now on it by a woman named Sharon Jaeger, who lives in Alaska. She got her Ph.D. from Johns Hopkins. It's called "Towards a Poetics of Embodiment: The Cognitive Rhetoric of Gary Snyder's *The Practice of the Wild*." So I'm charmed by that. There's a post-West, "western" book for you, *The Practice of the Wild*!

JO'G: Using *Practice* in my own classes, I have found that students consider it a very challenging text.

G: Yes, I guess that the demands it makes might be unfamiliar. There's an aspect there that is not part of mainstream intellectual life. We are just beginning to have a few "intellectuals" who are also nature literate.

JO'G: We need to be looking for Forest Service people who are reading *The Practice of the Wild.*

GS: You know, Forest Service people do read *The Practice of the Wild.* I get letters from some of them every once in a while.

JO'G: People coming up in the ranks!

GS: Yes! (Laughs)

JO'G: Has your involvement with the Yuba Watershed Institute over the last several years had a significant influence on your writing?

GS: Let's see. There are a couple of essays in *A Place in Space* that came directly out of working around here [on San Juan Ridge], "The Porous World" in particular. And actually (Laughs), they are some of my favorite little essays! It's hard to say. Right now we're scrabbling around in the ongoing problems of how to deal with the US Forest Service, which has infinite ways of avoiding being responsible, as we keep finding. How a community interacts with the public lands management policies, and how a community keeps the public lands employees focused, is the challenge of this. It is going to be a long, hard haul. To transform public lands management in America is going to take a lot of people who stay pretty much in place and who hold the public lands managers' feet to the campfire—you know, to make them realize that there are living people involved in the lands. That would be a whole book in itself, except I don't know if I'm the one who's going to write it. I'd have to say that the effect of all this political work may be more spiritual in my writing than visible in such an obvious way.

JO'G: Between *Turtle Island,* which seems to be the most overtly political of your bigger books, and the books you have published since, there seems to be a translation of the way political involvement manifests itself. It is interesting to read those critics who praised *Turtle Island,* but when it came to *Axe Handles,* they either did not know what to say or they said, "Well it's okay, but it's not up to the standard of *Turtle Island.*"

GS: There are a lot of people—and I grew up with them—for whom "political" means trying to affect public policy in obvious ways by political activism. Something of that does surface in *Turtle Island.* The approach of working, empowering, rooting in, and getting community consciousness established is much slower and is not nearly as obvious. The points in *Axe Handles,* a lot of them, are about what happens when you stay in a place in time. You go into various sensibilities about a place, and some people just aren't bright enough to see that that's political! (Laughs) Although in bioregional terms that *is* political. *Axe Handles* is a description, an account in many ways, of coming into the community and coming into the place in many subtle ways. From there, I took the idea of "Turtle Island" as a new narrative, which I write about in my essay ["The Rediscovery of Turtle Island"] in *A Place in Space.* Somebody wants to talk about new narratives for North America, okay, here's a new narrative. It's really thrown out there as a kind of challenge: to drop the United States and to drop America and to think in terms of Turtle Island, to think in terms of ten thousand years on the continent instead of five hundred years. Again, most political, educated, intellectual type people don't quite get it yet. That belongs to the next generation, I think.

JO'G: Turning to *No Nature.* Many readers say something like, "Well, here's a collection of selected poems, but we're just waiting for *Mountains and Rivers Without End.*" It seems to me that this is a unique book unto itself, with its own design and purpose.
GS: Oh, yes, it's deliberately selected. It's not as tight in quite the same way as *Mountains and Rivers* is, but it has its own coherence, that's true. That's the major part of my poetry right there!

JO'G: Your career at this point is bracketed by two major long poems: *Myths & Texts* early on and the recently published *Mountains and Rivers Without End.* To what degree is *Mountains and Rivers* a work in the tradition of western American literature?
GS: In a sense, what I've done is globalize the West. It began for me with working on lookouts and seeing the huge spaces that you see from high peaks, to the point that when I saw Chinese landscape paintings, I thought, "Now these people had a way of seeing that, of representing that kind of huge space." I wondered if there is a way of representing huge space in poetry. Reflecting on this challenge finally led me to launch into the project. It was the North Cascades from Sourdough Mountain and Crater Mountain lookouts for three months each—almost six months in two subsequent summers, being soaked in that—that really got me going on the idea of how

one can deal with space in a poem. You begin to see it in the poem when you get to "Bubbs Creek Haircut" and look around the Sierra Nevada. But then the poem meanders and convolutes in a lot of ways and ends in the space of the Great Basin. It starts and ends in the West, and is never far from it but uses the western landscape as a metaphor for the whole planet.

JO'G: Do you see what you are trying to do in *Mountains and Rivers* as being in any way similar to what Charles Olson talks about in *Call Me Ishmael,* where he opens with that passage on "SPACE" (11)?
GS: I took that to heart, and I think Olson was right. In a sense I'm taking up the suggestion that Olson offers there, seeing what can be done with it. But I also translate space from its physical sense to the spiritual sense of space as emptiness—spiritual transparency—in Mahayana Buddhist philosophy, and that's a significant element in *Mountains and Rivers* too, the play between formal landscapes and impermanence, emptiness, throughout the poem.

JO'G: The Mahayana notion of emptiness, *shunyata,* how would you explain what it means to people unfamiliar with this Buddhist term?
GS: Well, I wouldn't. If I wanted to talk about *shunyata* in *Mountains and Rivers,* I would have. What I've done there is give the concrete correlative in the poem, so I would say, "You want to get some sense of *shunyata,* read the poem." (Laughs) The poem cuts back and forth across the different levels of what that term might imply. Certain people will always pick up the term *shunyata* and just try to define it, but it's best defined in terms of images or metaphors—or experience.

JO'G: The Black Rock Desert?
GS: Yes. Or transparency, or space—you have to use an interconnection—space, transparency, solidity, irreducible solidity, total emptiness. (Laughs)

JO'G: In our discussion yesterday, you remarked about the western American landscape being transformed into a Buddhist landscape. What did you mean by that?
GS: (Laughs) Well, that's a little bit about what *Mountains and Rivers* tries to do. But I'd better say "cosmic landscape" or "mind landscape."

JO'G: Do you see other writers doing that at this point?
GS: Well, yes, Philip Whalen has done it all along. And so did Lew Welch. Look at Lew's lyric Klamath Rivers poems in that light! If we don't need to call it "Buddhist" but instead work at "process," we can see it in the work of

Jerry Martien, Michael McClure, and Jim Dodge—and then Tim McNulty, Michael Daley, and Sam Green, three Puget Sound poets.

JO'G: What might a Buddhist landscape be?
GS: That's a nice question. A Buddhist landscape would be a living landscape. It would not just be rocks and minerals and plants, etc. It wouldn't be an assemblage of things. It would be a spiritual ecosystem, and energy-flow model. It would be like a Chinese painting trying to present landscape—it would be matter in process. It would be landscape as, in the words of one Chinese landscape painter, "solidified Tao"—energy in its hard form rather than energy in its fluid form. Rocks and waters are complementaries to each other, not opposites, is one way to put it—which is part of the way Buddhism becomes translated into Chinese painting. Landscapes seen in that way are not the world of Cartesian thinking: material forms wearing out and running down in time. More as per modern physics, they are a remarkable flow which has many levels of simultaneous being. That would be a Buddhist/Taoist landscape: the land as the way in motion.

JO'G: Well, is there anything else you'd like to say about yourself as a western writer?
GS: Oh, I've said too much already! (Laughs)

Notes

1. Edwin R. Bingham, *Charles Erskine Scott Wood,* Western Writers Series #94 (Boise, Idaho: Boise State University, 1990)

Works Cited

Lyon, Thomas, et. al., ed. *Updating the Literary West.* Fort
    Worth: Texas Christian University Press, 1997.
Olson, Charles. *Call Me Ishmael.* Baltimore: Johns Hopkins University Press, 1997.
Snyder, Gary. *Mountains and Rivers without End.* Washington, D.C.: Counterpoint, 1996.
___.*The Practice of the Wild.* Berkeley: North Point Press, 1990.
___.*Turtle Island.* New York: New Directions, 1974.
___."A Young Mazama's Idea of a Mount Hood Climb." *Mazama* 28.13 (1946): 56.

A Conversation with Gary Snyder

Luke Breit / 2003

Tule Review, 4/1, Winter 2003, 3–4. Reprinted by permission.

When I was a young man reveling in my first discoveries of a new litera-ture: Norman Mailer's *The White Negro,* Lawrence Ferlinghetti's *A Coney Island of the Mind,* Allen Ginsberg's *Howl* and Jack Kerouac's *On the Road* and *Dharma Bums,* I fell in love with the idea that there could be heroes in literature foreign and distinct from the "I Like Ike" type heroes that Middle America sought in the fifties. It was a time when literature changed lives, sent countless young men and women crisscrossing America with their thumbs out, in their cars or even riding the rails, seeking meaning.

Of all the heroes in that new literature, none appealed to me more than a character named Japhy Ryder in Kerouac's *Dharma Bums.* Ryder lived in a small cottage in Berkeley, studied Zen, lived simply but, unlike many bur-geoning Zen students of the time, Ryder was also a backwoodsman, a logger and mountain climber, a weird amalgam of Zen monk and all-American stud.

It was years later, when I moved to San Francisco and got a job at City Lights Bookstore, that I discovered Japhy Ryder was in fact Gary Snyder but, by that time, I had lost something of my fascination for the Beats and had drawn closer to the poetry of James Wright, Robert Bly, Pablo Neruda, and Stanley Kunitz. It was, in fact, at a party for Kunitz after a reading of his at Stanford that I heard Robert Haas call Gary Snyder the greatest poet in America. A few years later, Snyder won the Pulitzer Prize (the greatest ben-efit of which, he once told me, was that he no longer had to be introduced as a "Beat" poet), and his importance was no longer relegated to one literary movement—even the establishment saw Snyder for the poetic genius he had become, and perhaps had always been.

In the mid-eighties, Patrick Grizzell and I were given the opportunity to interview Snyder for the old Poetry Center publication, *Poet News.* And as

I embarked on this new journey with the *Tule Review*, I thought it would be instructive to revisit our great local poet and see what he's up to. Needless to say, he's still up to very interesting things.

The first thing you notice is that he both does and does not look his age of seventy-three. While his face is deeply lined from both years and his life-long penchant for being out of doors, he looks like he could keep up with an in-shape thirty year old. And while it may or may not be that he has slowed some, his mind is sharp as a razor. The twinkle in his eye that Jack Kerouac noted some fifty years ago is still there. And the eyes go deep. Far in. And you note with some surprise that it's no wonder he is a poet of such incredible observation.

Luke Breit: How do you feel your work as a poet has changed and grown over a half-century of publishing your work?

Gary Snyder: It's not something I think about a great deal. I'm too close to it still. I'm too intent on the present moment to want to step back and analyze what my course has been. I'll leave that to the literary scholars. I've been aware for many years, though, that I write poems that fall into two categories. One are shorter poems and the other are the chunks of writing that I knew belonged in *Mountains and Rivers Without End*. It's a difference between lyric and the more dramatic direction. Then, since finishing *Mountains and Rivers Without End*, I've turned back to very brief poems.

LB: One of the things I've noted, looking back at your earlier work and more recent work, is a consistency in terms of your relationship to the poem. I see you—unlike many of your contemporaries—as standing somewhat outside the poem, even though you are clearly in it. But you are in it more as an observer than the person being impacted by what's going on or even just having an emotional response to it. One of the things I've always loved about your work is the spare way in which you evoke a scene in which, while you're in, you are not the center of.

GS: I guess you're right. I'm not sure what the reasons for that might be. I took some of that from my studies in Chinese and Japanese poetry and a long-standing aversion to foregrounding the author. I've always felt that the larger moment of the world is more interesting than what one individual might feel about it. There are times when I do the more personal take too, but I am a natural observer. I like to think I observe from within as just part of the whole thing.

LB: I think of your poem that I have loved over the years, "The Bath," and your relationships with your children and your wife throughout the scenes in that poem, and you are so clearly there and yet there is also the role of observer. I'm reminded a little of the French objectivists like Robbe-Grillet, that sort of delicious feeling of you being there but not imposing your ego on what it is that is taking place.

GS: Well, it's not just my story. I'm a storyteller in a sense. In that poem, "The Bath," I'm telling a story of what's going on. The reader can infer from that where I am in it just as well.

LB: I find it an interesting and novel approach.

GS: Thank you! But what's truly novel, or at least not all that common, in the world picture of poetics, is the individualistic, ego-based lyric poem (laughs). I'm reaching out here to many other traditions. The self-conscious lyric poem is in a minority category in the world.

LB: I was reading this morning your poem, "Finding the Space in the Heart." What that took me back to was some of the work of Li Po, these poems that take place over many generations and is woven into the short space of a poem.

GS: The Chinese do that so well. Su Shih is a master of it. It's humbling to see what the East Asian poets can do in four or eight lines. They had a great sense how to hold their personal sensibility up against large chunks of history.

LB: When you think about your relationship to poetry and to history and many cultures, where do you see yourself coming from in relation to western culture and poetic history? Do you have any affinity for movements such as Ezra Pound's *Des Imagistes*? One of the things about your work, especially the shorter, more lyrical work is that they have what Pound insisted on, no extraneous language, no unnecessary words. It seems to me that's something you take pretty seriously in your work:

GS: Well, my literary friends of the late forties and early fifties and I were quite aware of Pound's admonitions. They were part of our poetic education. I also enjoy the challenge of getting there by the least possible number of moves, what the mathematicians call "elegance." I started cutting the bullshit and the excess out of my language fairly early—maybe sometimes cut too much, even. But as I broadened my study of poetry over the years

and read from the gorgeous dramatic poetry of Sanskrit and other traditions of elaborate language, I realized there's a place for that too.

To say a little more about my poetic history—first came the instructions of
Pound and Yeats. Then a retrospective admiration for the scale and boldness
of Whitman, and an appreciation for the magic punch of William Blake. Then
two other poetries, not just Chinese but Native American songs, and American
folk music from both the African-American heritage and the Scotch-English
side. In younger days I played the guitar and knew a good number of folksongs
by heart. At some point I found the brief poems of the Greek anthology, I'm
thinking in particular of Sappho but there are many others too. Another great
underappreciated tradition is that of the *Eight Anthologies* from early Tamil.
A. K. Ramanujan translated some of it into English.

A very useful book came out last winter called *This Compost: Ecological
Imperatives in American Poetry* by Jed Rasula. He is putting forth the poetic
that I've been trying to construct in my mind and practice over the years. He
links Whitman and Pound and Olson to Clayton Eshleman, McClure and
many poets working with nature. He says these are all poetries that work
with "ecological imperatives" and are committed to process, particularly
in the direction put forward by Thoreau when he said, "Decayed literature
makes the richest of all soils." This puts Jerome Rothenberg's "ethno-poetics" in a much clearer light and it also makes Eshleman's fascination with
deep history and his investigation of thirty-thousand-year-old cave art more
cogent. It's grand to have Pound included in this lineage, but it's true that
Pound was, oddly enough, a devotee of the Goddess (in spite of all his other
bizarre ideas) and that he takes the ultimate source of economic value on
the planet to be the fertility of nature.

LB: So is this instructing your new work in some way?
GS: I'm not sure. Maybe it is mystifying my old work (laughs).

LB: When you talk about this incredible compost heap of these classical
and archaic literatures, it seems to me that there's a segue there between
what you're learning and discovering there and your long work in terms of
protecting the wild ecologically and your deep involvement with that whole
movement.
GS: Yes, I guess there is, it's a matter of taking the metaphor of compost
literally. That's what you can describe the surface of the earth as.

LB: Isn't that really what *Mountains and Rivers Without End* touches on,
the incredible and historical formation of the earth?

GS: And prehistorical. Correct. I hadn't even thought of that. And in a sense, people who think like this, myself included, are "conservative." We are the arch-conservatives.

LB: You're certainly not the far right, but you're the arch-conservatives.
GS: Yes, in terms of valuing the richness of what nature can be, and the nourishment it provides. So, this is an argument for protecting the remaining old growth forest, and for maintaining biological diversity and not losing species.

LB: One of the interesting things about knowing you and your work over the years is, unlike many who decide to live a simple, self-sufficient life outside the cities, how little you disparage people who happen to live in urban settings and try to make their homes there. In fact, I would argue that you are very encouraging to those people.
GS: That's where I've been helped by the non-dualistic Buddhist perspective. Why make a dichotomy between the right place and the wrong? Who wants to disparage a landscape? There are extreme cases. I wouldn't encourage anyone to live on top of a toxic waste dump. There are places where there is no hope and no future and no space. But we are blessed in the United States from one end to the other with public land and the opportunity to get out and see what the world is about. Thus we should not accept insults to the environment for the sake of the short term, but value the world more.

Here's an interesting case. I recently became aware of the East Shore Regional Park project on the San Francisco Bay. I had not realized that over the past decade there has been so much work done identifying and setting aside so many little patches of public space, some of it with biological and wildlife value, and finding ways for the public to have access to it. Right now below Berkeley and the freeway, I went walking around in Cesar Chavez Waterfront Park with Amy and Michael McClure. Suddenly you're in a different world—Berkeley has receded back, there are two-foot waves coming in, there are birds all over the place, the San Francisco skyline is visible through the distant fog. You know that things are still wild, right there. Public space is to public life what poetry is to the life of the mind. It gives you a place to let your mind and body breathe.

LB: Do you feel hopeful?
GS: Not really. I'll keep going in this direction and encourage people to hold the line and stay the course, to defend the spirit, mind, and nature. But the forces unleashed against it all are extraordinary. The largest accumulated

wealth the world has ever had, the most powerful people, the greatest military potential the world has ever seen, centralized in a few governments and corporations. Gandhi said, for greed, all of nature is insufficient.

Obviously, this way of doing business has got to break at some point, maybe when fossil fuels become truly expensive, or when some other problem cracks the fabric. But until that happens, it looks like we're on a train headed to go off a cliff. When it does happen, it's going to be messy. The behavior of the present administration in regard to Iraq is just a little preview of what the developed world powers will do when they get really crazy about oil. Just a preview.

So you can't be too optimistic. That's no reason not to be present in the present moment and grateful for what we have.

LB: In the context of how quickly we seem to moving toward that train wreck, does poetry make a difference? Does it matter? I thought the phenomenon of what happened when Sam Hamill formed Poets Against the War, that literally thousands of poems flooded in, all raising their voices against invading Iraq, was amazingly helpful.

GS: Interesting point. When the "war" was launched so many Americans felt shame and outrage in their heart and many of those who could write poems did, thanks to Sam.

LB: And at least for a second, it reached into the highest offices in the land.

GS: They were aware of it, that's for sure. Some might have been reached, but in this administration some are just unreachable. There's an interesting change that's been happening over the last six months: the media has been changing week by week, more and more paying attention to—and releasing—information that is critical of current policy.

LB: And when it wasn't in the mainstream media, the word was getting out on the Internet.

GS: For the first few months of this year, my best information came off the Internet, through those mailings that we all circulated. Information was being presented there that eventually even the mainstream media could not ignore.

LB: Gary, you've been retired from teaching (from UC Davis) for a little over a year now. How does that feel?

GS: I like being back in my old business of writer, lecturer, and backcountry woodcutter. An examiner of brushfields and old burns. I enjoy teaching, but it's a lot of work and I was falling behind in my own projects.

LB: So what are you working on now?

GS: Literary projects of the moment—mainly wrapping up a manuscript of poems that will go off to the publisher in February or March. It's the work I've done since completing *Mountains and Rivers Without End,* and it's very different. Then I'm also moving a skittish group of short essays toward the corral.

LB: How are you?

GS: I'm pretty good. I'm challenged by engaging in forestry issues here in Nevada County, which are just like some of the world's large issues made small. Being a bit small, sometimes you can get a handle on it. And when you work on small problems you get a better understanding about how big things work, so that's useful.

I do take heart from visiting some of the public places that have been established. There's some little protected marsh and wetlands right up against the Richfield oil refinery. The birds might do all right there. And in a sense, nature itself is less discriminating and less picky than we are. Fish and birds will do anything almost anywhere given half a chance. Mixed in with the most horrendous industrial development, you'll find nature at least trying to thrive. It may not always succeed, but there's a source of hope, right there.

LB: Seems to me there's a good analogy between what you're saying and the way poetry survives and thrives.

GS: Don't you think that's because poetry doesn't require big publishers? It's not within the financial loop of money making. I tell my poetry students, be grateful for that. You are not going to have to think about having a career in literature (laughs). And then you can go out and be a poet in the school or a poet in the watershed, completely free of this idea of immediate national fame.

Let me give you a short poem to end with, called "Not Gone Yet." Last December, right around the solstice, there'd been enough rain that I could safely begin to start burning brush piles. You get these big fires going but your work is not over, because as the fire burns down you have to keep throwing logs and limbs and twigs from the edges back towards the center to get them down to ash. So I was doing that, and this one ("Not Gone Yet") came to me:

How many times
        have I thrown you
                back on the fire

LB: That's great. And I love the poem that ends *The Gary Snyder Reader.*
GS: Ah, yes.

This present moment
that lives on

to become

long ago

Grasping the Natural: A Conversation with Gary Snyder

Anne Greenfield / 2005

Bellingham Review XXVII, No. 2, Issue 56 (September, 2005), 51–59. Reprinted by permission.

In the fall of 2004, I heard Gary Snyder read from his most recent collection of poems, *Danger on Peaks*. In a calm, steady tone, Snyder delivered his selection to what is likely the most attentive audience that Bellingham High School auditorium has ever boasted. His poetry is renowned for its ability to arrest and articulate specific moments in nature. The simplicity and clarity of Snyder's rendering almost masks the careful rhythm, which implicitly structures his voice. His work blends respect for the natural world with Zen Buddhist thought, achieving truly innovative modes of telling.

Snyder was born in San Francisco and grew up in the Pacific Northwest. Over the years he has undertaken many endeavors: he was a logger in his youth, he studied anthropology at Reed College, then Chinese language at Berkeley, and Buddhism while living in Japan. In the late 1950s, he was influential in the Beat Generation/San Francisco Movements (along with Ginsberg and Kerouac). Snyder is now the critically acclaimed author of sixteen collections of poetry and prose and was awarded numerous literary prizes, including a Guggenheim Fellowship (1968) and the Pulitzer Prize (1975). Until recently, he taught Creative Writing and Literature as a professor at UC Davis.

Snyder and I met on the morning following his reading in the lobby of the Fairhaven Inn in Bellingham. Before we commenced with the formality of the tape recorder, we discussed our common literary interests and he even offered me thoughtful insights for my upcoming move to China. Eventually, we turned to a more formal discussion of his experiences in the Pacific Northwest as well as his most recent collection of poems. As I suspected from his public demeanor during the reading, Sndyer proved a warm, intelligent conversationalist.

Anne Greenfield: You mention Bellingham in *Mountains and Rivers Without End* and, more recently, in *Danger on Peaks.* How did you come to know Bellingham and how has this relationship changed over time?

Gary Snyder: I was raised on a little dairy farm just north of Seattle, through the thirties and up early into WWII. The country between Seattle and the Canadian border was most dairy farming or logging in those days. We had a little dairy farm, so in our spare time when we wanted to go out and travel and look at things we would go look at dairy farms. That would bring us all the way up here once or twice to Bellingham, Sedro-Woolley, up the Skagit Valley, Mount Vernon, and back down. That's my first memory of Bellingham. Later, from the age of fifteen on, I started mountaineering. And one of those summers (I think 1946 or 1947) I came up with some Mazamas (a climbing group from Portland, Oregon) to climb Mount Baker. And I worked in the forest service, up the Skagit, in the summers of 1952 and 1953, when it was still the Mount Baker National Forest. I often came to Bellingham with friends, particularly one friend who I'm going to meet for dinner tonight: Jack Francis, who's lived in Bellingham all these years. I came through here with Allen Ginsberg in 1966 on my way to British Columbia.

So, Bellingham has been in my consciousness as part of the Ish Country (the Puget Sound region) and the culture of Maritime Northwest Pacific.

AG: Speaking of sense of place, much of your work is grounded in and speaks to location and specific places. In fact, your recent collection takes up the 1980 blast at Mount St. Helens. Have the recent eruptions there triggered anything new for you?

GS: Well more thoughts of the same. Pacific Rim Circle of fire: the chain of volcanic activity down the West Coast as far south as Mount Lassen, actually as far south as Mono Lake. The actual instability of the earth's crust and the fact that every volcano that exists on the West Coast is more apt to erupt again than any place that doesn't exist as a volcano already. Mount St. Helens—if you look at its history, which I did—erupts every few centuries. It has been erupting every few centuries for some time. Mount Rainier is quite capable of doing a major eruption at any time. So this is part of our life here. Except, being very short-lived creatures, human beings, and being new to the region—that is to say the present American population has only been here for a hundred and fifty years—we don't have much consciousness of it. I am exploring what that consciousness would tell us. So, having some recent events at Mount Saint Helens is hardly surprising. It's part of the story and the story goes on. Who knows what comes next?

AG: *Danger on the Peaks* has been deemed your "most personal collection yet." To what degree do you see your poems as autobiographical?

GS: I've never written autobiographical poetry as such. On the other hand, whatever one does in poetry has to be grounded in personal experience. But personal experience is not necessarily autobiographical experience because we are all vertebrate mammals. And we live in very much the same body and the very same mind. To be grounded in your body is not autobiographical. And to be aware of the world is our mutual heritage, but not everybody sees it immediately and clearly. Which is something that my own artistic inclination, plus my Buddhist practice, pushes me toward: mindfulness in the present moment.

AG: So there's a distinction in what you're saying between having an autobiography that's based on one's personal life and having a text that's grounded in the universal, the physical body.

GS: Well there's the personal-history-ego mind and then there's what I call deeper being, which we share with all other human beings and indeed a lot of other creatures. And there is our personal and immediate ego history, and then there is the deep history of our nature, which is in our genetic and physical body that makes us turn our head when somebody shouts, "Hey!" or feel fear or have an adrenaline rush or have a sudden moment of overwhelming lust. Whatever it is, that is our deep heritage, which is as much what our poetry and art should do as your personal story, which is not, maybe, always that interesting.

AG: I want to ask you about a rumor that I heard recently: that there may be a Gary Snyder biography in the works.

GS: That's not even a rumor, it's an actual truth. John Suiter, who did the book *Poets on the Peaks: Gary Snyder, Philip Whalen, and Jack Kerouac in the North Cascades,* has decided to go ahead and do a biography of me. He's got a contract and he's working on it right now. I've very pleased to have John working on it because he is such a good writer and researcher. And he lives in Boston so he brings something other than just a West Coast sensibility to it, which is interesting.

AG: Turning to *Danger on Peaks,* I found one of the most innovative and interesting aspects of this collection to be the blending of poetry and prose.

GS: Good point.

AG: I noticed that the prose often puts forward a fuller story, filling in the background information to the reader, whereas the poetic sections seem to zoom in on the rendering of specific moments. How do you view poetry and prose in terms of their functionality in a text?

GS: Well, let's take the section called "Dust in the Wind," that is specifically inspired by the Japanese form called haibun: a little block of storytelling plus a short poem. Think of it as storytelling and singing, which would be the older, oral literature model for what that is. And out there from ancient times there have been people who told stories and sang a little song. It's modeled on that. But when Bashō and his circle (the Japanese eighteenth century Haiku masters) took up doing not only haiku but doing the little prose block and then the haiku, they were looking very closely at what the finer aesthetics of it might be. I studied Bashō's haibun with that question in mind and then took it, in a way, in my own direction.

How you just described it, yourself, is accurate. But to say a little more, what I would like to be able to do, and I'm not always able to do it, is to make the short poem provide something that you weren't expecting, to give it one more twist or surprise with a direction that is not necessarily implied in the introductory story. It is, as you said, narrowing in on one point. It might be narrowing in on what didn't seem the most important point and finding another way into it. So that's what's enjoyable in it: that's what the challenge is in that. That is, to make something happen that takes it beyond what the intention of the story might seem to be.

Now there are some other prose/poetry mixes in the Bamiyan section: "After Bamiyan." It is more traditional: prose, with points made in poetry, then prose again, each informing the other. That's what I intended there. In some cases prose is called for, in some cases the poetic line is called for. The section called "Daily Life Poems" is treading a middle ground between poetry and prose and that is like a kind of poeticized storytelling, which is (to a considerable degree) personal. But personal should be personal in the sense that we can all share this. If it is privately personal, it's not interesting. "That's her problem," you would say. Too personal.

AG: Looking at your poem, "Blast Zone," I wonder about the way you take up issues of environmentalism in your writing. Do you find it difficult to balance an environmental/activist agenda with an artistic one?

GS: What do you see as the activist message in this poem?

AG: Well, the poem looks at nature's ability to take care of itself and compares that with other, more artificial groups trying to restore the area around

Mount St. Helens. So, I guess I see the poem as exploring that distinction between the artificial and the natural.

GS: Yes, and evenhandedly. That is to say, the planted zone, the boundary of the monument, is doing really well. The trees are bigger and I'm not knocking that. The area inside the blast zone, which they have not done any tree planting in, is also doing well in its own terms, at its own speed. Both are okay; that's what I would like people to come away with.

AG: And this message does come out in the text. In the poem following "Blast Zone," you say that both the natural and artificial sides will be instructive to watch for centuries to come.

GS: And at one point, of course, they'll be equal. In about two hundred years the trees will be the same size. Now, how the understory will look will be an interesting forester's study. It'll be more monocultural on the managed side, more diverse on the unmanaged side. In general, ecologists say that diversity is a good thing. But it's not a major difference in this case. So my underlying message, if anything, is, don't be too judgmental either way, watch what happens. What else can you do when you take major volcanic eruptions as part of life? And keep your cool.

AG: In "Atomic Dawn," your fifteen-year-old narrator as self descends from Mount St. Helens to the news that the United States has dropped atomic bombs on Hiroshima and Nagasaki. Your narrator then swears a vow: "By the purity and beauty of Mt. St. Helens, I will fight against this cruel destructive power and those who would seek to use it, for all my life." Here, it seems to be the greatness of Mount St. Helens that makes this vow a solemn one. At what point in your life did you begin to view nature as sacred?

GS: Well, I couldn't say exactly at what point. I grew up in an area of second growth forest, kind of scrubby, coming back. But I didn't know that there was anything wrong with that, I thought it was great. This was north of Seattle. That country between Seattle and Everett was clear-cut around the turn of the nineteenth century. You've seen the photographs of gigantic trees? It was gigantic trees all the way from Seattle to Everett, probably from Everett to Bellingham too. So, this is the history of the West Coast. Then it was all clear-cut. And Seattle, Los Angeles, San Francisco, all the cities up and down the West Coast were built with Pacific Northwest Douglas fir. A lot of lumber went to Asia too, although maybe not so much as now. Now, a tremendous amount of ponderosa pine goes to Japan and a certain amount of Douglas fir. So, another forest came back except for the little places where people developed dairy farms which were gradually enlarged. So, it was either second growth stump land or dairy farms.

I realized at a certain point in my childhood that something else had happened by the size of the stumps. And my parents said, "Oh yeah, well those were the big trees." But the beauty of the second growth forest, and its energy, its vitality, can get lots of credit.

Then, I sought out the Cascades. We got into the high country and realized, this is the source of it all. That is truly impressive. To see the mountains and to be in the mountains touches you. It's a good question: why does it? To see from a distance Mount Rainier or Mount Baker sitting there. It's vertical, it's high. You look at it and you say, "What kind of place is that? Can I go there? Should I go there? What would it be like if I went there?" It's a different world. Archetypally, spiritually, psychologically, the mountains are a different world. They're not subject to our usual economic uses. They fit another pattern. And so, they enter our dreams that way.

So, I was touched by the mountains and the high country too as a zone that does not fit into ordinary human preoccupations. That was part of what I was feeling as the purity and the specialness of Mount St. Helens. Just before the line you quoted, I describe what it was like to be on the summit of Mount St. Helens. Just one little paragraph of how remarkable it is when you're on top of the snow peak. And I say you are higher than you ever get in an airplane; it somehow is a higher place. And then when I looked down, there was nothing down there. I actually experienced that and you would too if you went up on Mount Baker, which you ought to do, climb Mount Baker. Get out there and experience what is.

AG: Well, I have done some hiking out on Baker. I haven't yet made it to the top.
GS: You don't have to go all the way up. Go out to Skagit and go up on Sourdough Mountain, there's a trail that will take you right up there. You have the most extraordinary viewpoint of a country full of glaciers and peaks you didn't know was there. One can't see it until you get up there. So, it is archetypally another world. That is what I'm echoing back from the age of fifteen when I say "by the purity and beauty of Mount St. Helens," ironically.

AG: I want to turn now to some of the teaching you have done. Until recently, you were teaching poetry at UC Davis. What is your relationship to academia currently? Do you see writing as a process that should be taught and learned formally?

GS: I never got a Ph.D. and I taught briefly at UC Berkeley. I taught one academic year at Berkeley during 1964–65. I was back in the United States from Japan and then returned to Japan. Later I was invited to come to UC Davis primarily to teach in the graduate creative writing program but also to teach a literary course or two. I taught half time for sixteen years and I always taught a creative writing workshopping class. I also taught several various interesting (to me) literary courses like a history of the mid-century San Francisco poetry Renaissance and the beginnings of the Beat generation—that was fun to teach. Another class I taught from time to time was on Chinese and Japanese poetry coming into English language translation and its effect on twentieth-century American literature. That is a topic you might consider. Going to China you're going to get exposed to East Asian culture and there is a really interesting territory on the effect of the translations from Chinese that started before WWI even. And then through the translations of Arthur Waley and Ezra Pound, which had enormous influence on English and American poetry.

One of our most striking local examples is Robert Sund, whose poetry is shot through with the influence of East Asia. So that's been my teaching life. Half-time, courses of my own description, courses of my own choice, and always working at finding a good way to teach poetry. I experimented a lot with that. I never was completely satisfied with it but I always felt it was worth doing. I do believe that you can teach something about poetry. As I always said to my students: it's not a program that will lead to a career, but it will give you a hunting license.

AG: So, you see it as a venue for practice and conversation more than a place for formal instruction.

GS: And exchanging ideas and mutual critiques so that it's useful. I say, if you don't want to go to college and take a course in creative writing, go live in downtown San Francisco or New York and just hang out. That's the alternative.

AG: I wonder about the craft of your writing. Your language choice in your poems comes across as so carefully and thoughtfully crafted. Is this a product of many drafts and revisions? Or are you more apt to get it right the first time around?

GS: I have my own demanding standards, which some people might disagree with but at least they are standards of some sort. If a poem fits those standards right away then I don't have to revise it. If it doesn't fit those standards I'll keep revising it. So it depends. Sometimes I'm lucky and the first draft is almost exactly what I want. But I'm willing to spend a lot of time with a poem, sometimes seven or eight years. I just keep looking at it until it comes around.

AG: Speaking of craft, your poem "How" is one for which timing is important to the resulting meaning:

How

small birds   flit
from bough
to bough to bough

toboughtoboughtobough

As you create a poem, do you find that you always have pencil and paper to see how it will look on the page? Or do you find that you can imagine the line breaks before you commit it to paper?
GS: Well, I think I composed that poem in my mind entirely. You know, it's so short. I probably was just watching the little brown birds in the underbrush. Bush dwelling small birds, watching the way they move within the shrubs and the smaller trees, repeating it to myself in a way. So, saying it aloud as I watched them do it: to bough, to bough, to bough-to bough-to bough. And then saying okay, maybe I'll write that down. So the first version was probably oral, saying it to myself.

AG: I want to turn to the sequencing of *Danger on Peaks* because the movement from beginning to end feels very purposeful. You begin with your experiences on Mount St. Helens in 1945, eventually moving to the recent events on September 11, 2001. Do you find that the meaning of a specific poem is likely to change heavily based on its positioning?
GS: I wouldn't say that the meaning of a poem changes. But, its resonance changes. Which is a common sense observation. Things are affected by their surroundings and so you want them to inform each other and that's a choice: how you cause them to inform each other, how they relate to each other.

AG: I also noticed this with the photographs on the front and back covers. Even the positioning of these pictures informed my reading of the text as a whole. The front cover of *Danger on Peaks* displays a picture of Mt. Saint Helens after the 1980 eruption. The back cover has a picture you took in 1945, which is, of course, pre-eruption.

GS: Well, everything there is deliberate and by using graphics that way I don't have to explain it. It's truly visual.

AG: Because you've been writing for many years, I'm curious about your literary influences. Do you find that these change over time or stay fairly static?

GS: One has one's initial artistic influences that get you started and for me they were people like Whitman and Pound and Williams and Yeats and I could name others. And then, your own peers, your own age-mates, later, and people that you're working with, become influences. And you share with each other. That would have been people like Allen Ginsberg and Lew Welch and Phil Whalen. And the influences might be from music and painting and architecture. Oddball things that come not just from literature. Or from reading nonfiction, science and so forth. An artist is always curious. An artist is like a crow always picking up bits of string from everywhere, which some people call stealing. But somebody said, "Artists borrow, great artists steal."

An Interview with Gary Snyder

De Anza College Students / 2006

Red Wheelbarrow Literary Magazine, Student Edition, 2006, 70–86. Reprinted by permission.

Villa Montalvo's Literary Event Series features readings and book-signings year-round and also sponsors occasional meetings with guest authors specifically for De Anza students. These ninety-minute Q & A sessions provide students with the opportunity to dialogue with some of the best known writers of our time.

Snyder, a continually groundbreaking American poet and Pulitzer Prize Winner, read from his latest poetry collection, *Danger on the Peaks*, at Montalvo on Thursday, April 13. Our students then interviewed Snyder the next morning having prepared by reading and discussing *Danger on the Peaks* as well as excerpts from *The Gary Snyder Reader* and Snyder's interview with Bill Moyers from *The Language of Life*.

Irene Lau: People always talk about a sense of belonging to their own country; however in your own poems, like "Control Burn" and "For All," I realize that you're trying to foster a sense of belonging to the bio-region. In my opinion, to have a sense of belonging to the country is to become loyal and patriotic so that together we can contribute to the prosperity in many aspects of the country. On the other hand, to have a sense of belonging to the bio-region is to live at peace and harmony with the natural world, instead of exploiting the natural resources that are native to the land. So, do you think that it's important that we belong to both the country and bio-region as well?

Gary Snyder: What a great question. You know that really gets to the heart of a lot of questions, a lot of issues really, right there, that I've been working with for many years. So I really appreciate that. And you phrased it so concisely, very economically. Sense of belonging to a country, in our times, is what we call nationalism, maybe patriotism sometimes, and it's a very, very tricky idea of identity, national identity for example. This is one of the major problems in the world today. If you look at it in historical perspective and anthropological perspective you realize that human societies and human groups evolved in different places, where in the beginning one's sense of identity was simply to "place." I am a person of this place and I am a person of this family or this clan. Maybe a little larger you might even say this village or this tribe. So all societies and all natural nations were originally bioregional. Bioregion is a useful, simple term that means bio: life, and a region: a natural region. It means a natural region that can be defined by natural criteria. It's odd that we have to even explain this because the world is covered with natural regions. What's the problem then? The problem is that the contemporary world is divided up into nations which often do not follow natural regions.

Irene Lau: What are some examples of disjunctions between nations and cultures/bioregions?
Gary Snyder: Originally cultures and societies developed in terms of their natural regions. Your Chinese natural regions with two great watersheds and a couple of smaller, river watersheds had nothing to do with other kinds of boundaries.

Over centuries, we end up with national boundaries, because of the way history has worked. You look at the history of Europe, and the boundaries of the nations of Europe have changed every twenty or forty years, ever since the fall of the Roman Empire. Some more, some less. Eastern Europe and Central Europe have had very shaky boundaries, constantly changing. Great Britain only emerged after the English finally whooped the Scotch and completed their invasion of Ireland. The Welsh, the Irish, and the Scots are still angry about it. Some things don't get resolved easily.

There's a population in the borderline mountains between France and Spain which is still trying to accomplish its own bioregion identity and not to be considered members of either France or of Spain: the Basques, except they actually call themselves the Euskaldunak. There are a lot of known cases like that if you look: remnant populations. The Kurds are another that have a national sense of themselves, a linguistic sense of themselves and so forth. But they don't have boundaries of a nation. A "people" originally lived in a place where genetically, familially, clan wise all together, they also more or less spoke the same language. Japan is one of the few places left on earth where everything is intact still. They all speak the Japanese language, with a few exceptions. They all have more or less the same genetic heritage.

And they all still live within the same basic boundaries, the Japanese islands. That's a rare case. And even there the truth is, the present Japanese population long ago was an invading population that drove out the earlier inhabitants we call the Ainu who were not of the East Asian race, and the Japanese pushed them way up to the far north, where there still are a few people living in Hokkaido. There are Ainu place names still all over Japan like Mount Fuji. Most Japanese people don't know that. The name Fuji is the name of the Ainu fire goddess. So there are a lot of things like that if you really dig into it. And then there's the Okinawan population. Okinawa is not the same language as Japanese. It's related to Japanese in the same way that Portuguese is related to Spanish; they are very close but can't understand each other.

Irene Lau: How do these overlaps and cultural mismatches relate back to the issue of bioregion—nature itself?

Gary Snyder: What's important is that we are aware of the natural features of the land we live in. If we forget that then we have forgotten some of the most important things there are. It doesn't matter what the name of your nation is or what its boundaries are, you can have any feeling you want toward that, you can be loyal to it or you can be critical of it depending on what it does and how you feel about it. But there's the other kind of patriotism which is loyalty to the country, the land itself. I am very critical of the politics of the United States of America. I am totally loyal to the North American continent. I am loyal to the Mississippi River and to the San Francisco Bay. It's important to make a distinction, even in your own mind, to say, "I can be critical of this society but I really truthfully want to see the land itself flourish." And that doesn't necessarily mean just been a hardcore environmentalist, saying, "I've got to preserve this and I've got to preserve that." It means that you think about agriculture, you think about forestry, you think about water resources and air resources and you want them to go well.

Now, the truth is, if agriculture, forests, and air and water reserves go well, it benefits the economy—if the economy takes proper care of them. If the economy does not, why then you have to speak on behalf of the forest, rather than your economic interest: "I don't think you're doing the forest a good turn here. And that in truth means that you are ripping off the children of the future. It's temporal exploitation. Your grandchildren will not have the resources available to them, that we have now, if we extract them all now." You have to think of the future.

Irene Lau: What are some ways you think of California's future in particular—in terms of both culture and environment?

Gary Snyder: Well, who does not think of the future? Modern people do not think of the future. Modern people are caught up in the four year election cycle, and this year's programming on TV, and often do not have a strong family consciousness. This is not to knock the American society—it has many wonderful features. I'm not talking about government or administration. The people themselves are a very interesting and mixed bunch, very diverse, with different languages now, but particularly we have Spanish and English strongly established in America. We might as well live with it—let's be bilingual, what's wrong with being bilingual? Everybody used to be bilingual, or trilingual, or quatrolingual. Where you are from, Irene, everybody is bilingual and probably trilingual, right? Most of the world's people speak two or three languages. It's just considered natural, and you have to do it. Everybody in Europe is trilingual. And if you want to get historical about it, a society that only speaks one language is very rare. California had about three hundred Native American languages—just California alone. So does that mean none of them could talk to each other? No. They are all bilingual or trilingual, and they all talked to each other. They could use sign language as well.

Bioregionalism is a little force that I've been part of, which is an educational undertaking to make people aware of where they live and what's in it. It's as simple as that. And to urge them to include that in their thinking and a little bit in their politics. As a poet I have spoken for the bioregion. I don't think of myself as a nature poet exactly but I've written nature poems. But my nature poems are precise to the question of what is there and what is being spoken of. What we call California—which is actually about three different places, rather than one place, if you go into bioregional divisions—has a couple of unique features. One is that it has a summertime drought. So that makes it into what is known as a Mediterranean climate. If you live here on the edge of the ocean, under the shadow of the coastal range you're not aware of that because you get the fog and the clouds coming over from the ocean during the summer time. This little coastal strip here is anomalous; it's not typical of the rest of the region. The rest of the region has a drought from May to November. Virtually no rain falls anywhere in the great Central Valley or the Sierra or in the interior mountain ranges. That dictates an entirely different kind of vegetation than you'll find anywhere in Europe, or even in New England and the Midwest. That's one of the bioregional characteristics of California; it's a summer drought climate. And all of the vegetation has responded to that point. Also, that totally saves the agriculture and the agricultural economy. Without the Sierra Nevada, which is the big snow collector up there, there would be no agriculture at all in the greater Central Valley. The greater Central Valley is a desert, it only gets about thirteen inches of rain a year.

Knowing how much rain a year you get is bioregional knowledge. When I go somewhere the first thing I ask the guy who picks me up at the airport, "How much rain do you get here a year?" Some of them know, some of them don't. Sacramento gets thirteen inches. Where I live, we get forty inches at three thousand feet. At seven thousand feet it gets eighty inches. So it's an elevation thing. The eighty inches fall as snow. The summer snow melt is what gives California agriculture, through irrigation. And it is favorable to Mediterranean agricultural practices. It's no accident that there are all these Italians and Swiss-Italians and Portuguese people growing grapes up there at the North end of San Francisco Bay. They knew what to do. It's no accident that there are all these Armenians that are making raisins down around Fresno, and so forth. All of these crops are specifically brought over by people who had crop knowledge from other places. It's a wonderful history actually; it's a really interesting history. Chinese-American farmers, Japanese-American farmers, people from Portugal, Spain, Italy, Greece— they did a whole lot of things all over California that you might forget about nowadays. They really shaped what the agriculture of this state could be. And I still think California agriculture is far more interesting than California information technology [laughs]—which you could do anywhere.

Okay, so you can be a patriot but you can also be a matriot [laughs]. Patriot from patriarchal, and matriot from matriarchal. So a matriot loves the motherland, and the motherland is the land.

Linderpal Dhillon: In your essay, "The Place, the Region, and the Commons," you have mentioned the importance of preserving our own environments and practicing a profound citizenship in both the natural and social worlds. How do you practice bioregionalism in your own life and art and to what end?

Gary Snyder: Your question continues from what Irene has been asking and I can answer that very easily, having already given the full preface [everyone laughs]. I live in a high forest fire zone, in the forest surround by trees for hundreds of miles. So one of my specifically bioregional activities is reducing forest fire hazard by cutting out the underbrush and thinning, which is what we all do up in the Sierra Nevada. I have chainsaws and various tools and I rope in neighbors and my sons, and my step-daughter, who is pretty good with a chain saw, and we go out and do that kind of work.

I also do the educational work. For example, when mountain lions and bears moved back into our country fifteen years ago (before that there weren't so many) and started scaring people, we held workshops on how to live with mountain lions and how to live with bears, and not get buried with them and not be too afraid. That's a little bioregionalism local exercise. In the discussion of native plants and invasive or introduced plants, there are some introduced plants that we don't want to have around; it is possible to encourage the use of native plants in various ways. These are all simple things to do but they're also quite educational. Those are some of the things I've been doing.

Sarah Joy Callahan: I was at the reading last night. I enjoyed it a lot. One thing you mentioned was how long it takes to write a poem. You said two to five minutes and then you're done. So what I want to know is after you've done that two to five minutes of just writing, how long does it take for you to revise a poem once that process begins?
Gary Snyder: You know some poems you finish right away. You write it, you look at it and say that's done.

Sarah Joy Callahan: But are there some poems that you never revised?
Gary Snyder: Yeah, there are a few. In fact I wrote one that I never revised just about three weeks ago. It's called "Fixing the System." It's very short so I'll recite it to you.

Fixing the System
    Under the topless, bottomless,
        empty blue sky
  hands and knees,
  looking down a little hole

  leaky gate-valve   drip drip

Some poems take a long time to finish, so I have a little system of putting them in folders and looking at them after a few weeks or months. Eventually, after a few years if I haven't been able to figure out what that poem or what that language does, or what to do with it, I throw it away. But I'll wait a while to see if I can finish it. So, it was kind of a joke to say it only takes three to five minutes to write a poem. Your mind is ready, that's the thing. The first part of it is just having an open mind and listening to interesting language, interesting images, little insights, little pictures. And then maybe write a little of that down and then keep it around and come back to it. So how do you know you're doing that well? It helps to have read a lot of poetry so that you don't reinvent the wheel. It would be really stupid to try and build a house without learning something about carpentry. So just know what other people have done. There've been some great poets out there, great singers, and writers. Just read a lot, because you're using language. The tool of poetry is language—the material of poetry is language. So be acquainted with what people do with the language, have done with the language. It's fascinating.

Scott Lipsig: How did Buddhism and meditation shape your role as a poet and what does it mean to you as a person? Moreover, what should it mean to others?

Gary Snyder: Well, I've been interested in Buddhism ever since I was a teenager, and what drew me to it first was its ethical position. I was very sensitive and favorable to the natural world when I was young growing up on this little farm north of Seattle, and was learning all I could about the work there and the wildlife. And it wasn't that I didn't do a little hunting or fishing—I did—but even when I did hunt, I really tried to think about what the right attitude is when you hunt, and how do you express your gratitude. I learned something about that from the Native American studies, too.

I developed from that an appreciation of Buddhist ethics, which are sensitive to all living beings, and to put it very simply and bluntly, the Ten Commandments says, "Thou shalt not kill." That applies only to human beings. The Buddhist and Hindu precept is called *Ahimsa* in Sanskrit; it means not harming, and it is generally interpreted to mean not killing, and it applies to all living beings. So when I learned that—I read it somewhere when I was fifteen or so—I said that made sense so what's wrong with those Christians and Jews and Muslims? Don't they realize there's the rest of nature in there, too? Not considering the rest of nature—I think that's kind of an incomplete ethics. I paid attention to whatever I could run across about Buddhism after that and have studied it all my life and appreciated it all my life. It's low-key and totally realistic in the sense that it says, "The nature of this world is impermanence. We live in impermanence. You and everyone else are going to die."

The Tibetans have a little thing called the Three Reminders: *death is real, it comes without warning, this body will be a corpse.* So, how do you work with that? That's part of the Buddhists' question. The thing is, they work with this idea of impermanence and being absolutely realistic about the inability to make long-term projects that will last, and to be good-hearted about it. Because in truth, when you can accept that and give up on trying to create purpose around yourself, you feel liberated. People I met in California and also in Asia that were practicing Buddhists were very sweet people with very deep cultural ideas. My wife, who is a terminal cancer case, has lived already three or four years longer than the doctors gave her and they are taking care of her now, and when she'll die we don't know. Next week? Or six months from now? It's really hard to guess. She handles that very beautifully because she's Japanese-American and grew up as a Buddhist in the San Joaquin Valley, and her upbringing just gave her this great trust in the world. She says, "I trust the universe to do what it's supposed to do with me. I'm not going to fight with it, I'm not going to say I'm fighting against cancer." She says, "I'm sharing my body with cancer." She says that's the way it's going to be. She is quite elegant how she handles that, and that is kind of the way those Buddhist teachings can help you.

Sabrina Din: In your piece in *Danger on Peaks* titled "After Bamiyan" you describe the destruction of the Bamiyan Buddha statues. It seems to me that they no longer had a chance to speak when they were destroyed. It feels like poetry is often a voice for the silenced. Through some of your poetry, are you speaking for them? What are they (and you) saying?
Gary Snyder: I guess I am, I hadn't thought of it that way, thank you. To write or to speak, or to tell the story of something, anything, is also to speak for it, and to tell the story so that that story is not lost and maybe becomes part of what the world thinks. I would say in one sense the great Buddha statues in the Bamiyan Valley don't need me to speak for them. They were so appreciated for so long, for so many centuries, so many travelers and writers saw them, so many pictures were taken and drawings were made. They were totally studied by art historians and cultural historians from all over the world, and they made a complete record of how many there were, how they were built, everything. Yet, there's still part of the story to be told, which was the story I told in my poem, about the way several people reacted to it. A Buddhist friend I thought reacted very frivolously to it. Christopher Hitchens, a neoconservative writer who used to be with *The Nation*, reacted in a strangely cantankerous way based on his ideological antireligious position. I made the connection in passing between the destruction of the Bamiyan statues and the World Trade Center, and I did that quite subtly. I

didn't make a big issue out of it, but it's worth to see those two side-by-side, so that's what I did. I never got to the Bamiyan, but I will go there, it is my hope to get there. I traveled a lot in India and a little bit in Afghanistan.

Theresa Because: I came across the term "the real work" in your poem named "I Went into the Maverick Bar." To you, doing the real work seems to be a natural gift for you as you said in the interview with Moyers; that the conviviality between you and the natural world is a gift to you from childhood. Clearly, many of us are not born with that gift. What could we do in our schools or educational philosophies to create more adults who understand what "the real work" is, against only doing work that brings about material gain, self-advancement, pleasure and convenience at the expense of higher values? I think we all agree that the youth are our foundation for a better tomorrow in this world. In your poetry, do you intend to reach out to the youth and create awareness? If so, what age do you feel is appropriate to introduce your ideas and how do you feel your work influences our youth?

Gary Snyder: I don't think about that type of thing much. Not quite like that, anyway. I do write poetry in what we would call Standard English. I choose to. We all have a choice; what level of language we write in. I tend to write toward the simplest and clearest language I can. It's not like I deliberately said, "What level of difficulty do I want to write in so that everyone can understand me?" but I like the possibilities of clarity that you find in the English language, and its directness, its kind of oneness that's possible there. I like to think that most ordinary people can mostly follow what I write, and that distinguishes it from some sets of contemporary poetry, which are grammatically and in terms of vocabulary more educated and more complex. I only use more educated language when that's my choice, but if there's a simple way to say something, I'll say it simply. I'm not thinking about generation or age level, though. I think I'm probably speaking to peers, more or less, although I've worked on tankers and in logging, so I know how to talk to everybody.

Theresea Because: Do you go back in and look at your poems in reflection and think how it could affect the youth?

Gary Snyder: Not too consciously. As somebody who's read a lot and done a lot, when I write something, I'll say, "Oh, that'll work. Oh, okay, this'll reach out there." I can tell that in some cases better than in other cases. Like when I wrote a thing called "The Smokey the Bear Sutra," changing Smokey the Bear into some kind of ancient stone-age Buddha figure, I said this is funny. It can be used to catch people off guard. But the forest service never has figured out what to do about it. Strictly speaking, they can sue me. I found out that they copyrighted Smokey the Bear. But one approaches these things first and foremost as an artist. My sense of responsibility is first to the product. To make whatever point has been given to me as good as I can make it. After I've done that I say, well, who's this for? And maybe it's not for everybody, but maybe some of them are for a lot of people. But you choose the art first. You're not writing like you're an ad copywriter, saying, "Will this reach a lot of people?" You don't do that.

Wai Chau: The earth is a precious gift for human beings, and as everyone knows we should all protect this little planet we have. But so often environmental protection can be difficult because of people's selfishness and the high cost; for example not everyone can afford a hybrid car or a solar house, and public transportation can be impractical on many occasions. So what do you suggest to help motivate everybody to help protect the environment? **Gary Snyder:** See, this is a political question. This is a question about, "What would I do if I ran the government?" You're asking me to suggest major public policy, and I have a few ideas about those things like everyone else, but as a poet it's not my responsibility to make public policy, unless I have an expertise toward that. What I can say is that sure, there's a lot of economic inequality in this society, and in many societies, and in other societies. What should we do? We should not forget Karl Marx. Marxism, Marxist thought, has a very sophisticated, developed basis of history. It may not provide solutions, or political solutions that we might like, but it is a very good critique of how history has been dominated by the struggle between poor people and rich people, and how these things are still with us; they have not been resolved. So Marxist economic historical thinking is one thing that should not be forgotten. It's not forgotten in Europe. It's not forgotten in Asia. But in the United States it's forbidden to talk about it, except in a few universities. So that would be one basic, simple thing.

Another basic, simple thing is, if you're interested in these things, learn about banking. Learn about the stock market. Understand how it works, not necessarily as a critic, just understand how it works. What goes on? These are what you might call the Despised Mysteries. I just finished doing my taxes. We are surrounded by networks of power and money, which we prefer not to know about. But those who do know about it, they clean up like gangbusters. They walk away with the store, which is a way of saying, if you learn about these things, you can be rich. So that's the other choice. Anybody taking any classes in accounting? Accounting is a good career.

[Emin Ismayilzada asks Snyder to read a poem— "Mid-August at Sourdough Mountain Lookout" —which he does]

Emin Ismayilzada: I am from Azerbaijan, and in our culture, we are taught to imagine. In your poems, like the one you just read, I can *see* what you are saying. What is the difference between saying and imagining? Does poetry help readers to see or to imagine?

Gary Snyder: As I understand it, Azerbaijan has a great tradition of oral narrative, singing, dancing, and chanting for hours. I love it. Central Asia has a great tradition still of storytelling, chanting, and poetry, just like Homer's *Iliad* or *Odyssey.* They were long, oral, metrical chanted texts, but not texts. Before writing, they were part of the oral tradition, and later committed to writing in the Greek language. There's a book on this subject called *The Singer of Tales* about the connection between ancient Greek epic poetry and the poetic traditions of Central Asia and the south Slavic countries as well. They were, of course, narratives and often grounded in mythology, very much works of the imagination. Poetry and creative writing, creative literature in general, draw on the imagination.

There are great imaginary points in the English language: William Blake's mythical long poems. John Milton's *Paradise Lost,* which is totally a work of the imagination, based on both Dante and the *Old Testament.* What we call the lyric poem was written to be sung accompanied by a lyre, a little string instrument, originally. These shorter poems, the lyric poems, are always written in direct observation, as the longer poems are really works of the imagination. You can roughly divide it that way. I've written both, in both forms. I was particularly influenced by Chinese poetry, which is short poems, and almost entirely based on observations of the natural world. Japanese poems are very much so also. They're little bits of the world, but they also have ideas in them: *"Tsuyu no ya wa/tsuyu no yo nagara/sarinagara"*—"This dew drop world/this impermanent world/is but another drop" [Issa]. It's just that and yet, still, it's something else. So that is observation, but it's still complex thinking. It's a complex philosophical proposition that really throws you back on yourself. So that's all just energy. For example, I wrote *Myths & Texts,* which is largely a work of the imagination. I wrote *Mountains and Rivers Without End,* which is a sequel to *Myths & Texts,* which is again a work of the imagination, but at other parts, they're more observation. I enjoy doing both. I think it's just great to write prose. I also write essays; I find it purely satisfying to write prose, and it's also very satisfying to write poetry. Writing a good sentence, any sentence, is very satisfying. So don't feel hampered by what is possible, just do whatever you feel like.

Dan Snyder: I'm in PR, as part of the great California tech machine, at a small company called Intel. I'm getting into writing, and I'm frustrated with my angst and my issues with technology and what it's doing to the world. It seems like in your work, you don't take a lot of shots at political things or what technology's doing or a lot of things other artists do. What kind of advice would you have for someone who has a lot of things they're feeling? Would it be something to write about, or do you think it's not important to take shots at the issues or talk about what you see happening?
Gary Snyder: To critique.

Dan Snyder: Yes, and I'm not saying all technology's evil.
Gary Snyder: Yeah, I really like bicycles [laughter]. Gandhi said before World War II, "I'm not really as much against technology as people say. I own a bicycle." That's a certain level of technology you can't beat. A lot can be said for tools, and the right tool for the right job. To critique something in general, where you put it out as an argument, where you enter into a dialogue. You make it possible for people to respond to you, to answer back, to say, "I question that." Poetry, when you start being critical, is more rhetorical, which I don't like. It's more screaming at. Robert Bly wrote a powerful poem against the Vietnam War that he read at a lot of colleges during the war. It's called the "The Teeth Mother Naked at Last," and it was about how America had revealed itself as the mother who eats her own children. That was a little extreme, but it was very enthusiastically received in its own time. But no one remembers it anymore. I think in a larger time frame, I'm not postmodern, I'm not modern, I'm premodern; I think in premodern terms, which means I think ten thousand years back and I think ten thousand years ahead, and I've been able to do that by working more with bioregional ideas than with political ideas, knowing how long an ice age lasts, knowing how long it takes for a type of botanical succession to take place. And knowing a little bit about human history. I mean long human history. I mean *really* long human history.

I visited caves in southern France about ten years ago that had these extraordinarily wonderful paintings of cows on the wall. They were thirty-five-thousand-years-old. They were really good artists thirty-five-thousand-years ago, and also, they were exactly the same human beings as we are: big skulls, totally intelligent, very handy, lots of tools, great artists, probably great storytellers. We don't know a whole lot about them, but we do know now that Cro-Magnon and upper Paleolithic human beings were hardly at all different from us; if anything they have slightly larger brains. That's true, on the average. So an artist's work is to be under the radar and to hopefully, truthfully, honestly, deeply help people with their lives and help the society with its life, and that's one job.

There are other jobs. There are the jobs of day-to-day critique; I subscribe to several magazines, and every week they are coming up with analyses on the errors of the current administration, the military flaws of Iraq and Afghanistan, and so forth. Well I appreciate those critiques. I don't do it myself because I'm not expert enough, but I learn from them and I also try to learn from the defenders. I read some right-wing stuff from time to time just to get the other position. So one can do that, but maybe to some degree it's some type of good sense not to try to do things I can't do. So I can't change public policy. Your work as a PR guy is not something I would dismiss either. I would look at it professionally, and professionally say, "how can I reach and convince people without telling lies?" There are a few Buddhist ethical rules; one rule is try not to harm things, another is don't tell untruths, another is don't take things that have not been given to you. Another is, be careful about getting intoxicated! And another is, be careful about how you use sex, and be sure that it's loving. Pretty basic. I like most of the Ten Commandments. There's only one Commandment I don't like: Thou shalt have no other God before me. Now wait a minute. What's wrong with this guy? Is he so insecure? I mean, can't I think a little bit about other gods?

Misty Dawn Shelter: Hi Gary, I'm nervous.
Gary Snyder: Hi, Nervous [laughter].

Misty Dawn Shelter: My name is Misty and I have been a fan since the early eighties, so it's really cool to be here now. I know a lot of writers go on walks, a kind of walking meditation, as a way to connect to the sacredness of it all. It helps them to open up their subconscious and connect to ideas and encourage the flow of inspiration. As a Buddhist, do you find sitting or walking meditation helps you to write? What other sort of things help to get your creative juices flowing?

Gary Snyder: I love walking, and I walk a lot; I always have. I don't ever meditate, however, thinking about poetry or thinking about creativity. The kind of meditation that I do, and the way I was taught, in Zen, is not directed toward any goal. It's goal free, so that you can simply see what your mind is doing at that time, at that day, what your feelings are. It's more basic than writing. It's like where the hell am I? And who and what am I right now at this moment? And then letting it come to you, and observing without judgment, observing what thoughts arise and pass by without judging them. Neither good nor bad. I have never found myself even close to thinking up poems while meditating. And it's not even that I made myself do that, it just never came to me. It's curious. Walking is sometimes meditation, but generally it is more like reflections. It's a little distinction there between reflecting and meditating. Reflecting is fun too. And reflecting—which means more directed examination of thoughts, memories and going over what you did again, and what somebody else said—all of that comes up a lot while walking, as well as just plain observing and seeing as you go. Walking is very much tied to the breath, obviously. There are some wonderful essays on walking; it is one of the great human activities. It is the human way to move around and get places; we ought to do it more—we ought to walk a lot. We would all be happier and healthier if we walked a lot. So we've lost something that is very precious, really. Our bodies were made to walk, that's why we have these big fat legs. And it's only a hundred years ago, or a hundred and fifty years ago that people quit walking, and they still do it in some parts of the world. So, Henry David Thoreau's essay, "Walking," and Rebecca Solnit (she is a really splendid writer who lives in San Francisco and she's been publishing a lot of books lately). Solnit wrote a book called *Wanderlust*, which is all about walking and is quite good. And I'm working on an essay myself on walking that will be part of a book about Mount Tamalpais, which is a place that we've walked a lot.

James Schulte: The first time I ever heard about you was yesterday, so I wanted to ask you what you would say to somebody who has never read any of your poetry? What would you say your poetry is about, and what do you try to convey in your poetry?

Gary Snyder: My poetry is about work, love, and nature. I try to convey a sense of affection and gratitude to the world. For someone who's never read my poetry, start with *Riprap.* That's pretty basic. Kenneth Rexroth was one of the great poets of the forties and fifties in San Francisco who nobody remembers much anymore, and somebody asked him why he wrote poetry. He said, "To overthrow the state and seduce women." People used to talk that way. They don't anymore.

Ken Fears: You say you derive inspiration from nature. How would you contrast city life with nature?

Gary Snyder: Using nature in its most basic sense which is the phenomenal world, the subject matter of science is nature. Science studies physical phenomena and the rules by which it operates. By that definition, cities are natural, and that's the definition I like to use. They're not wild, but they're natural. Make a distinction between wild nature and nature in general. To say nature inspires me is to say the phenomenal universe inspires me, and probably the spiritual universe does too. Any universe will do that we're present in. I have written a couple of really fun poems about cities, including one about New York City, Manhattan, called "Walking the New York Bedrock," which is all about walking around in New York City. I don't have anything against cities, except that they're not enough like cities. They should be more like cities are, and they'd be better. That is to say, more crowded in, tighter, more walking space, less suburbs around them, the way old-time cities used to be. And then lots of neighborhoods, lots of congeniality, lots of friendship, and public transportation. Los Angeles doesn't make it as a city; it's too spread out, and you have to have a car. So that's not a good city. London is a great city.

Amie Barnes: As someone who considers herself an environmentalist and an avid reader and writer, your writings combine my two favorite passions of nature and language. I have always felt that these disciplines are complexly intertwined. In your writings, both "Riprap" and "Claws/Cause" address the relationship between the natural world and language, which man created. What do you feel the relationship is between the two? "Riprap" was included in your first book of poetry in 1959, while "Claws/Cause" is in your most recent collection, *Danger on Peaks* (2004). Have you noticed any evolution of this phenomenon? Have your own feelings about this relationship [between language and nature] changed in the forty-five years between the poems?

Gary Snyder: The relationship between nature and language. I've written about that in some of the essays in my book of essays called *Practice of the Wild.* I'm not so sure that language is so different from nature. There's been a lot more study of the large territory of what we might think of as language, which is science symbiotics, especially among animals and insects in the last forty-five–fifty years since I first started studying language; that we aren't aware of elaborate and sophisticated communication systems in the natural world, in the non-human world, the language of bees and how bees communicate by dancing, using language through the sign system. Human language, I now believe, is biological, that we are hard-wired from birth to be able to learn a language; that our nervous system skillfully picks up, memorizes, internalizes, and becomes capable of using the language that it is raised with from the age of one on. Whatever language you are hearing in the first five years of your life you'll learn, and you'll learn it very well. And by the time you're five years old you will have completely learned that language. Completely except for additional vocabulary.

The important part of it is all structure and grammar, and if you've internalized the structure and grammar, you can create proper sentences. You know intuitively the difference between an improper and a proper sentence. Now that is a remarkable accomplishment that everybody does. And it is after that, from the age of five on, that what we do with language is more affected by culture: our talk is polite or impolite in language, and what people think beautiful language is and what people think less beautiful language is begins to emerge. All of that stuff, including literature and so forth, comes later. But the basic material of sentence production and internalized syntax comes to you absolutely naturally. However, as they have just learned, if you don't learn language by exposure to people speaking language like your parents by the time you're eight or ten, you lose it; it's very hard to learn a language. There are some very sad cases of children that were locked up and kept by themselves by crazy parents or something, for ten or twelve years and then finally discovered and finally treated, as they are permanently damaged by that inability to learn language when they were ready to learn language. So in essence, language is part of our biological heritage. Dogs can learn about a hundred words. I have an adult female standard poodle. She is so smart, and she knows a lot of words. If I'm going for a walk I have to say I'm going for a W-A-L-K or the dog will go get the leash and stand there, waiting to go with me. So, those are really interesting questions about those relationships.

Rebecca Macfife: I can't imagine the mind of a poet ever stopping for sleep: how do night-dreams impact your poetry—or does your poetry impact them?
Gary Snyder: I don't know if they impact my poetry. I've never made a big issue out of dreams in my life, personally. I have friends who are followers of

Jungian psychology, and I like Jung's writings, and I've studied Jung, but I've never been particularly inclined to pay too much attention to my dreams, except when they really force themselves on me and are so vivid, then I do look at those. But again, they don't get into poems as such, I don't think. Obviously, I can't speak entirely about my own work, because I do things that I don't understand. There's a lot I don't understand about my own work. I just trust it, that's all.

Ken Weisner: Thanks again, Gary, for taking the time to speak so generously with us—and for giving each of us the chance to ask a question. We have some cards for you, and Misty made an origami paper crane for you and your wife, on behalf of all of us, wishing her well.

Gary Snyder: Thank you; I've enjoyed being with you. [Students and Snyder clap for each other].

Interview with Gary Snyder

Junior Burke / 2011

not enough night, Fall 2012, Naropa University. Reprinted by permission.

In November of 2011, international poet Gary Snyder, came to Naropa's Kerouac School. Throughout his brief stay, he was exceedingly generous, working in a lecture, a reading, an informal class visit, and this interview. It took place in the green room of the Nalanda campus, with *not enough night* executive editor, Junior Burke.

Also included here are Snyder's responses to Burke's students (two days later) during *Kerouac's Road*, a semester long investigation into the life and work of our school's namesake. An added bonus was Snyder's perspectives on the historic Six Gallery reading in Berkeley in 1955, at which he was among the featured readers.

not enough night: A couple of interviews you have done—one for *East West* in '77 and the one in the *Paris Review*—I thought we could use those as touchstones and maybe see where you are at today. It would be a nice, almost symmetrical, sort of time frame.
Gary Snyder: I have done a lot of interviews lately but they haven't been that much in poetics.

NEN: You seem to long be aware of the need for an artist to strike a balance between inner-work and outer-work. Would you care to comment on that?
GS: Well, I thought that was perfectly normal. I mean, this is not an ideological point with me, nor is it something I think I have to give lectures about. It seems obvious. And I would say what I always have to my classes when I was teaching poetry in the Creative Writing Program at UC Davis. I had a list of things that a poet should have, and it included good binoculars, a compass; uh, very nice underwear (laughs). Things that take care of your body.

NEN: In your *East West* interview you expressed the lack of self-sufficiency among Americans. How do you see that aspect as it relates to Americans say who are between nineteen and twenty-years-old now?

GS: Can you change the oil in your car yourself? Do you know how to change the oil filter? Do you have a tool kit available? Do you have a tool kit that has several types of pliers, Phillips screwdrivers, and slotted screwdrivers? And there is a lot else. To be a self-sufficient human being at this point in history means you need to know a few things, and you can't always—especially if you are not rich—rely on calling up somebody to come and fix it for you and charge you a lot of money. I am not talking about knowing how to grow your own food or how to cast lead to make your own bullets or something like that, although that would be relevant at times; but just what everybody has to know. My older son, Kai, who lives up in Portland, is forty-three now . . . He grew up on the farm in the country, or whatever we call it, and he said to me just a couple years ago: "You know, almost none of my friends my age understand what I am talking about when I say I have got to do this with my engine, or I am going to tune up my weed-whacker, or I have got to do some more plumbing, or I have got to get a proper snake for the drain. They never learned anything about fixing things, or about tools." Everybody lives in a house, okay? So everybody should be able to do something with their house.

NEN: You also pointed out in that interview the differences between begging in China and begging in India. In China it wasn't tolerated, and in India it could be considered something of a virtue. How do you see those attitudes in relationship to the current American homeless population?

GS: I don't think it's relevant, either way. We certainly do not have religious commitment to giving money away, as both Islam and Hinduism do. They didn't solve it, but they handle it with more grace in India, like in Calcutta and in Bombay, by providing plenty of public toilets and places for people to camp. They had not just thousands, but maybe tens of thousands of homeless people in Calcutta, and they have a lot of buckets and a hose-bib so you can take a bath and do laundry. And that is what people do. But that is still not an answer. Building big homeless shelters or providing houses for homeless people will work if, in the long run, the economy gets better. If the economy gets worse, then you are just going to have more of the same.

NEN: Also from that interview: "It's actually quite impossible to make any generalizations about the past and the future, human nature, or anything else on the basis of our present experience."

GS: Well, I said that because I considered our experience to be in many ways outside the bounds of what our historic experience had been. I think that is still true. I think it's still unpredictable.

NEN: You also spoke of people's lack of commitment to any given place, being totally unnatural and outside of history. Regarding America, how do you view that at present?

GS: I think we have made some headway. The bioregional movement, as small as it is, has gotten a little traction. There are people who don't even know the term bioregional who are involved with more and more watershed groups, and they are understanding that dealing with the environment or environmental issues is often a matter of dealing with small local issues. So I think we have made some headway there.

NEN: What do you see as the current relationship between song and poetry?

GS: I don't think they have changed. Sooner or later, poetry is song. If there is any change going on, it's because of all these various recording devices . . . Every once in a while a few people turn up whose work in song is really good. And they always get respect. Joni Mitchell is doing some retrospective recordings and CDs now. She is a great singer and has some great songs that will not be forgotten.

NEN: You expressed that Zen and Chinese poetry demonstrate that a truly creative person is more truly sane than the romantic view of a crazy genius, which is just another reflection of our times. How do you see the artist's place in today's society regarding that?

GS: I still think that not all artists, but basically very good and sustainable artists, are pretty sane. When they are not sane, they are way over some other boundary that most people wouldn't know about. Things haven't changed that much in the last century.

NEN: You also said: "I always looked on the poems I wrote as gifts that were not essential to my life." How do you view your writing right now? Is it a structured discipline, or are you grabbing what comes by?

GS: What I practice is availability. That is a practice. It doesn't mean that I am not doing other things, but I am aware that I should stop doing whatever I am doing when something like a poem begins to sneak up on me. That was true then, and it's true now.

NEN: And obviously, you have long been able to recognize when that is happening.

GS: Generally, I can. I guess that is the fruit of a lot of meditation (laughs).

NEN: You once served on the California State Arts Council. What are your current feelings about government involvement in the arts?

GS: Well, that was many years ago. I was with the Arts Council of California from '74 to '78. Peter Coyote took over as the chair after me, and he was chair for probably four years. He did a lot of good. But then, subsequent governors, being Republicans, started cutting down on the budget, and then the subsequent economy cut down on the budget, and actually, with Jerry Brown back in the governor seat, he hasn't really given much more money to it, but has given support in such a way that it is still limping along, and all of that is okay. It's also interesting to see that the cultural centers right in my neighborhood . . . are getting along without any state money coming in. They are managing somehow, and are just like business people everywhere. They are actually looking to try to get a bigger audience than they ever did. And they are booking more things that will have more public interest. So the plus is people will learn to do that. The minuses—there are probably some freaky little funny things that they would have funded in the past that are being overlooked now. Those people have to figure out themselves how to get out there. Which is like poets.

NEN: What was Reed College like in the late forties or late fifties—was there much awareness of it as an alternative institution at that time?

GS: Absolutely. It's always known that it was an alternative institution and has always been left-wing. And it's always been libertarian in style and substance, and it's always been academically demanding.

NEN: Do you have any relationship with it currently?

GS: I gave the centennial speech last June, at the gathering for the 100th anniversary.

NEN: You were part of a circle in San Francisco that included Kenneth Rexroth. How did you meet him?

GS: Somebody told me about him. Well no, first I read him in Selden Rodman's anthology, *A New Anthology of Modern Poetry*, which was a Modern Library giant. That was enough to get me interested in Kenneth because the biographical paragraph said he was a mountain climber and an anarchist, and

I thought, "Well, those are two good things." And they didn't say that about anybody else. I found some of his books in the library and read them. When I got to San Francisco, I went to an Alan Watts talk and met a lady there and we got into a conversation about poetry and I said, "I am interested in meeting Kenneth." She said, "Oh, I go there every Friday night—why don't you come with me?" So that was my introduction.

NEN: This is from the *Paris Review* interview, a quote: "The first step in poetry is to make us love the world, rather than make us fear the end of the world." How does that resonate for you today?

GS: I am pleased that I said that way back when because I still think so and it's not a small point, because you can't know that the world is going to end. But that you can still love the world. If you don't love the world, well fuck it, you might as well drill at it, or do whatever you are going to do. Dump oil on it all, because you've got other things in mind. Suppose you are the kind of apocalyptic Christian who says this world is just what we are going to get away from when the rapture comes . . . you are not going to treat the world very well.

NEN: Your advice in 1992 that Americans should stay put, seems to relate to sentiments expressed by Emerson. How do you feel about that in 2011—Americans staying put?

GS: Well, I am still arguing those points. I have also added onto that particular phrase—staying put doesn't mean you can't go on trips. You do allow that people have to change places sometimes, but wherever you are, take it seriously. It's like going from marriage to marriage. You don't go through one marriage without getting to know the person you are with, because you are going to go to another one. That would be like people moving around without ever learning where they were.

NEN: As someone who has lived much of your life relating to the outdoors, what kinds of memorable encounters have you had with animals?

GS: Well, you know, I could go on for a long time.

NEN: Precarious ones, or dangerous ones?

GS: Most of the charismatic ones, I don't talk about. I mean, that is too easy. It's more interesting to think about the small things that you finally learn in the presence of animals. One of the things I have learned is they are really graceful with their bodies and they never make a move that isn't graceful, and they can curl up or sit down anywhere and look comfortable. I notice that with squirrels and with my dog. I started looking at cows and horses, and all of those animals really know their own bodies. Really know it well. They never make a wasted move or a clumsy move. I think primates are actually kind of clumsy, compared to a lot of other animals.

NEN: Those are the questions I brought with me . . .
GS: Interesting questions. I guess things haven't changed that much.

NEN: You were definitely on to something.
GS: Oh well, I am just not smart enough to change.

POETRY CHAT

GS: I was talking with Junior Burke a few moments ago about what you folks have been through so far. He said most of you are in the *Kerouac's Road* class, is that right? As one who hung out with Jack a bit and shared a cabin with him; drank a lot with him, did some hiking and climbing with him, I thought I might give you the chance to ask personal, intimate questions about Jack Kerouac. You don't get too many people who actually hung out with him—seeing as how he died pretty young . . . Anything you want to explore in that, let's do it right now.

Question: What did you like best about him?
GS: What I liked best about him was his charming naivety. And openness to things. His lack of judgment about a lot. And his ability to listen. He carried that with him everywhere. He was a non-judgmental person, which I think is a pointer for people that might want to write novels. One pointer, anyway.

Q: Did he attempt to take a bead on people, and probe them through questioning?
GS: No, he didn't in that direct way that I am reading what you are saying. He didn't seek people out and say, "What do you do?" Try to find out about their family and their children and where did they go to school. Jack was more subtle than that. He kind of circled around people and figured them out, and then by degrees got a better sense of who they were and what they were. He was an extremely intuitive person who did not operate in a hugely analytical way. Didn't need to.

Q: You say he was non-judgmental, but when then did he become such apparently a reactionary, deeply conservative and angry man at the end?
GS: Well, that was his choice (laughs). I mean, lots of people do that. I am not sure he was so angry. He was bitchy sometimes. In part that was his response to Allen Ginsberg, who was so pushy all the time. Allen really loved Jack and I think they were even lovers a little bit, just for fun. But as the years went on, Jack resented Allen assuming so much about him. What Jack ultimately was, was a French Canadian Catholic from a working class background. Jack had a mythical imagination that allowed him to enjoy the big mythologies of the Catholic Church right along with the big mythologies of Buddhism. I don't know too many people that could do that. And he was shy. He never could figure out how to deal with being a celebrity and being famous. That caused him a lot more grief than being rejected. He was used to that; he could handle it. You may have seen him in that video that has been around and available for a long time where he was there by the piano with what's his name . . . Steve Allen. It was very sweet, the way he was with Steve Allen at that time. The two of them were interesting together. That was at the point in his career when he was still not feeling jumped on or criticized and he was relaxed. But he got jumped on a lot by reviewers and had a difficult time with the big really heavy negative reviews that came out because he couldn't figure out why they were being so negative. That was part of his naivety. "I am not a bad guy," he says. Whereas some of them are saying, "Here is this Barbarian-vandal-crude-beatnik-whatever, tearing down a classical culture." It turns out he was a great spokesperson for the vernacular culture of America. Especially in my favorite novel of his which is, of course, *On the Road*. My second favorite novel, which is a better novel, is *The Subterraneans*. It's the perfect little French novel with a beginning a middle and an end. A nicely structured Flaubertian piece of prose which shows his craftsmanship, but it didn't have the panache that *On the Road* did.

One of his worst novels was *The Dharma Bums* (laughs). He wrote that as a potboiler because of the success of *On the Road*, his publisher saying, "Jack write something else, quick." That is the way publishers are. They will try to get you to write a second book right away if they have a very successful one. And *The Dharma Bums* is hasty. It segues too swiftly. It's not a relaxed story. While I am saying that, I will also say Japhy Ryder is not me. The novel is fiction. It's not journalism. I have to say that all the time. People say to me, "You are Japhy Ryder, aren't you?" I say, "No, I am not." But I might have been partly a model for him (laughs).

So some of the criticism that was aimed at Jack was actually aimed at Allen Ginsberg. That is another story, you now. You don't be a Jewish, communist, homosexual boy without getting some heat. His parents were Communist Party members. When he was a little boy he walked the streets of communist parades to demonstrate what they believed in. What you call a red diaper baby.

Q: In the time you spent with Jack, did you ever see any part of his process, or did he talk about his work in that way?

GS: Actually, I saw him work. He washed dishes a lot (laughs). He was very helpful around the place. . . . Jack's style, as far as I could make out at that time, was to be out in the world for a few weeks or months experiencing things; meeting, hanging out with people. Apparently, jotting a few notes down, but not much. Then he would jump on the various trains and cars, and head back to his home place, where his mother was. Get his typewriter out and take a lot of speed and write for three or four days. Like, that is how *On the Road* was written. It was written apparently in one big burst after he had accumulated all the narrative material he could possibly hold. I know from experience that Jack had a remarkable, almost tape-recorder memory. I was at a party in San Francisco once before I left the whole scene and went to Japan that spring . . . spring of 1956. Jack looked much of the time, especially in the evening and especially at parties, like he was really out of it and he'd had quite a bit to drink. So he was sitting on the floor leaning against the wall, eyes half-closed and some conversations were going on around him. The next day, later in the day after coffee and lunch and everything, he started telling me what the people around had been saying. And he repeated like, verbatim. So and so said, dah, dah . . . and then he would repeat what some other person said. He had it all in his mind. Well, the fact was I had heard it too and he remembered a lot better than I did. Although he had looked like he was asleep (laughs). That gave me a really good sense of how Jack could be in a situation, apparently not particularly knowing what was going on, and come out of it with a very clear picture of what had transpired. So there is another pointer for how to be a novelist. Because if you are going to write a novel, you don't want to sit around writing notes that people can see, unless you are an anthropologist and you are paying them. Somebody, one of his critics, said (of Kerouac) "That is not writing, that is typing." Capote said that . . . Jack ended up being a real alcoholic. He was just a half-way alcoholic when I knew him.

Q: Did you and Jack ever talk about women's roles in the arts or in writing?
GS: I think we talked about some women we knew that were writers; Joanne Kyger, in particular, because I was seeing Joanne at the time. Outrageously good poet, who comes to Naropa once in a while. But I don't know any men that talked about women as writers or artists in a big way back in those days.

Q: Is there anything that you remember teaching Jack, or Jack teaching you?
GS: I taught him a lot of things (laughs). I actually did teach him how to pack, how to roll a sleeping bag. How to pack a backpack, how to lie down on the ground and sleep under a tree. How to climb. One thing in *The Dharma Bums* that is pretty close to what actually transpired was the account of the climb on the peak called the Matterhorn which is on the northern border of Yosemite Park. That is pretty close to what we actually went through on that trip. It was very cold. It was late in the autumn season. It was mid or later-October when we went up there. That was my choice. I said, "Let's go, before it gets any colder." So, yes, I wanted to introduce Jack to nature and I did do that. He would have introduced me to the whole of New York City if we had been in New York, I am sure. As it was, he introduced me to the areas south of Market in San Francisco, which has now become more and more gentrified, yuppified. And Silicon Valley. A lot of places were really booming during the height of the Silicon Valley period and it declined a little bit, but in those days it was kind of a skid-row with a lot of stop-and-rob liquor shops. Cheap hotels. Jack taught me how to go in and get a couple of bottles of Muscatel, put them in a brown paper bag, go around the corner, sit in the alley with your back against the wall, and drink. And keep it in the bag. That is classic. I shouldn't have had anybody teach me that. But I did. He taught me a few other things like that. How to get along in certain situations. How to look at the railroad track, and look at where you would go, and so forth.

Q: What are some things that you felt Kerouac was really passionate about that he would want students at the Jack Kerouac School to learn or be passionate about as well?
GS: Craftsmanship. He was a seriously educated person in the craft of writing, who had initially modeled himself on Thomas Wolfe. And Thomas Wolfe was a person who read a lot, thought a lot, and practiced a very genteel kind of writing. Jack's first novel before *On the Road,* was a much more traditional twentieth century—early twentieth century style of prose

writing. Jack paid a lot of attention to writers of his era and before. And the idea of good writing. You don't find careless or sloppy language in his novels. You find vernacular. You find great vivid vernacular and colloquia maybe, but you don't find anything sloppy. He was a writer who turned his attention to the world of the people he knew and the kind of language they spoke and he took certain figures like Neal Cassady and followed them a long way because he was fascinated by Neal's fluidity with language, which you might guess. But Neal was over-the-top. He was always like he was on speed. Even when he wasn't. And he was Irish—I don't know if you can blame being Irish on this but he could talk non-stop for three or four hours. I mean, you would become exhausted. I couldn't stand it. I had to leave after Neal had been around for a while; but Jack loved that, and he lived with Neal and Neal's wife Carolyn for a while. So he took certain models to learn from and watch. For a while, Allen was a model for him. But like a model for an anthropologist. He was a kind of human being that Jack had never met until he had come down to New York City. Allen introduced him into another world, which is the early New York world and its junkies and all. Like meeting with Bill Burroughs, and so forth.

Jack was a student of the era he was living in—of the language that was spoken in depth at that time. I would hazard to guess that *On the Road* will be a signature novel for centuries to come for mid-twentieth century life and speech.

Q: What was Jack's perspective on publishing—was it important to him?
GS: He was ambitious to be published and to be received well. He hoped for that. That is one of the reasons he got disappointed later because, although he was a financial success, he was not a critical success. He wanted to be a critical success. So again, he was a writer. He wanted to be accepted as a mid-twentieth century writer. And so he talked a lot about publishing. He talked a lot about the editors at Viking Press and at other presses. He would talk about editors that had rejected his work. Editors that were supporting him. Editors that said they were supporting him, but weren't supporting him enough. Publishers he was hoping he could count on. He went through a lot of frustration before *On the Road* was actually published. It was accepted and rejected several times over and he had that problem with several other novels.

Finally, when he had a financial success with *On the Road*, he didn't know what to do with it. He didn't know what to do with the money that began to come in. Kind of threw him off, but otherwise I would say he was more than normal. He was hyper-normal, as a writer would have been at that time. It's very different now. Writers today know that there aren't any publishers that you can count on. That all the good publishers have been bought by Australians and Europeans and they are tied in with media companies. That the whole small press and medium press and big press world is on the rocks. Except for the big press world, maybe. That independent book sellers are having a terribly hard time, and even the big guys like Borders are going bankrupt. So what else is new? The new thing in publishing is self-publishing, in some cases. And another new thing is the experiment with online publishing. I say experiment because I don't know if it really does much good.

Q: So what did he do with the money?
GS: I don't know. I never saw any of it (laughs). I was living in Japan by that time. You know, that is a good question. He probably gave some to his family. Whatever did happen to it? If Allen was here, I would ask him.

Q: Would you mind talking about some of your memories of the Six Gallery Reading?
GS: The Six Gallery Reading in October of 1955 . . . came about . . . because Kenneth Rexroth had a soiree. Really, that was the word for it. A couple of Friday nights a month, at his apartment in San Francisco. You didn't drop in there without sort of finding out if it was okay. It was never more than a dozen or sixteen or seventeen people at the most; sometimes it was only four or five. It was the local writers and left-wing people's political scene. So I started going to Kenneth's Friday night get-togethers. I was a graduate student in Berkeley at the time and I very much enjoyed listening to Kenneth outrageously talk about everything in a very knowledgeable way. I learned eventually that sometimes he didn't know what he was saying, but that didn't matter. He said it with a great deal of confidence. He had a lot of very interesting and sometimes sort of toxic opinions; that was kind of a known factor.

And Allen Ginsberg came into the Bay Area, initially to go to graduate school at Berkeley; he was going to change his life and become a professor. He had decided this after being in New York in market research. And having a suit, as well as being actively gay. So Allen was at one of the soirees and he said his friend Jack Kerouac was coming up from L.A., working on the railroad. Writing while doing his brakeman's job on the train called the Zipper. And could he bring Jack over the next time we all met? So Jack and Allen were there at the next Friday's soiree—a fascinating conversation between everybody, because Jack spoke well. Somebody asked Jack, "What are you working on now?" And he actually pulled out the manuscript of . . . what was that piece called? It was about the railroad.

Q: *October in the Railroad Earth?*
GS: That's it. *October in the Railroad Earth.* He pulled out that manuscript, which was from his time on the railroad. He read a portion of it to us all, and it was very exciting to hear. Even Kenneth was impressed. And so Jack and Allen got together in the following week and kept on talking and I got to know Jack, and I got to know Allen better; and Allen had rented a little place in Berkeley, and Jack was staying with friends in San Francisco, and anyway, that is where we all started getting together . . . We all agreed we were having a hard time getting published. We all had rejected poems, etc. So Allen, or somebody, said, "Why don't we just hold a reading?" People did not hold readings in those days, although we knew that such a thing was a possibility. So we called the Six Gallery, which was a little art gallery in the Marina and they were agreeable to us putting together a little reading and somebody—maybe it was me—said, "Michael McClure has some unpublished poems . . . Philip Whalen is going to be in town . . . Who else? Philip Lamantia." And we typed up a postcard that I wrote most of. We had it mimeographed because we didn't have Xerox in those days and sent it out to several hundred people, just off our heads you know. My three-by-five card file. Allen's little book of addresses. To our amazement the Six Gallery was full of people.

In the meantime, Allen had started writing a new poem which he called *Strophes.* I went over to see it when he was still working on it. You know Strophe, in poetry? S-t-r-o-p-h-e. So Allen said, "This is *Strophes,*" and we looked at it and said, that is the wrong title for it. He said, "Well, maybe I'll call it *Howl*" (laughs). So the Six Gallery is famous for Allen reading that for the first time. And Jack didn't read anything. He just sat and encouraged everybody, but that kicked off that practice of having poetry readings virtually every night somewhere in the Bay Area ever since. It never stopped. And Ginsberg—Ferlinghetti wrote him the next day, or called him the next day, and said, "I want to publish that." And so it got into the *City Lights Pocket Poet Series* as book #2 or book #3. Eventually it got taken to court and that made the book famous, etc. And City Lights Bookstore is still going.

Lawrence Ferlinghetti and I did a poetry reading a week ago in San Francisco, in North Beach. Which is where Lawrence first read poetry in public, about 1952 or '53. So that was fun and a lot of old friends came to that. Lawrence is ninety-two years old now. He has had heart bypass surgery. Doesn't ride his bicycle the last couple of years, because he said, "My eyesight is not so good." I asked him, "Lawrence, are you still swimming?" He said, "Well, I don't swim in the Bay anymore. It's too cold." But up to a few years ago, he was, and he says, "I only swim in the heated pool, but I still work out at a gym." At ninety-two he stands perfectly straight, speaks very coherently, is a lot of fun, and has a very cute girlfriend. I always think, gee, maybe I should live longer.

That whole event started a lot of things, although Lawrence and I told the press, "Please don't call us Beat." It's very hard to stop anybody from saying that. Lawrence says—it was in the *San Francisco Chronicle* a couple days ago—"I get called Beat because I published most of them, but that doesn't mean that is who I am."

I get called Beat because they were my buddies and friends at that time, but I would say none of my writing—almost none of my writing—accords with anything that people would call Beat literature. It goes off in its own direction entirely.

A Sense of the Land: An Interview with Gary Snyder

Sean Elder / 2015

Portions of this interview appeared in *Newsweek* (July 10, 2015) and *Shambhala Sun* (November 2015), 70, 72–75. Reprinted by permission.

Shortly after his eighty-fifth birthday, Pulitzer-Prize winning poet, naturalist and all-around Renaissance man Gary Snyder read from his latest (and possibly last) collection of poems, *This Present Moment*, as part of the City Arts and Lectures program at San Francisco's Nourse Theater. He drew an interesting crowd of young techies and older hippies. Actor and activist Peter Coyote, who credits Snyder with introducing him to Zen, asked a question from the front row; Michael McClure, who had read along with Snyder and Allen Ginsberg at the legendary Gallery Six reading in San Francisco in 1955 was there; and California Governor Jerry Brown who appointed Snyder to the California Arts Council during a previous term attended both the reading and a small after party held in the poet's honor. I spoke to Snyder by phone shortly after that evening.

Sean Elder: You were introduced at the Nourse Theater by Will Hearst, who said you shared a passion for watersheds. Were California watersheds an early interest of yours? Can you say more about that?
Gary Snyder: Of course that's an interest of mine; I'm a bioregionalist. I've written about watershed consciousness, the intelligence of basing your thinking on the landscape, starting out by making sure you know what watershed you're in and how watersheds relate to each other. Which most people don't do because their thinking about place is dominated by the highways. That's all they know, really is the roads. It changes things a lot when you clear the roads out of your mind and look at the watersheds. And watershed does not mean just one big river; it's the main stem and all the tributaries at once. . . .

This is part of being an environmentalist and having a sense of the land. Watersheds generally tend to contain ecosystems and there's no difficulty about understanding the landscape. Watersheds are not arbitrary; they have been shaped by the land itself, the play of ridges and streams, whereas boundaries that are on the map, especially in North America are arbitrary lines drawn with a ruler, often by people who had no idea where they were. Which means they're temporary; five hundred years from now we won't be using those boundaries at all. So that's just part of my toolkit (laughs).

SE: Hearst produced a film that you and Jim Harrison appeared in (*The Etiquette of Freedom: Gary Snyder, Jim Harrison, and The Practice of the Wild*). Had you known Harrison before?
GS: Oh yeah, way back. We did a poetry reading in upstate Michigan when we were young, as a pilot program to see if poets if the schools might be a viable idea. To see if students would sit still and listen to poets talk about poetry. That was before Jim wrote short stories . . .

SE: Were students sitting down and listening to poetry when you read?
GS: They enjoyed it a lot. For one thing we said bad words. Poetry gives you permission to say any kind of language, using any kind of grammar. . . . One of my neighbors has being doing that for years. He says, "One of the first things I do is I tell all the children in the third grade, 'Write a lie' and they love it. They say, 'You mean we can write something down that's not true?'" . . . It's a wonderful permission.

SE: You were raised on a very small dairy farm outside Seattle in what you described as "a hardscrabble rural poverty life." Would you say that existence informed you politically?
GS: Definitely, but you have to understand, the whole Northwest was much more leftwing than it is now; the whole country was more leftwing. The west side of Washington state and western Oregon west of the Cascade Mountains, there were a lot of proto-socialists and downright Marxists. Of course the labor movement is still strong in Seattle. It was the Depression; when I say "hardscrabble poverty," I'm just talking about the Depression. Everyone was poor, everyone that we knew. My dad was out of work for eight or nine years, but we did all kinds of other things, including splitting shakes, cutting old cedar stumps off close to the ground. . . . We had chickens and cows and eventually fruit trees. But I never had a

consciousness of poverty until later when I realized there are people who have it a little easier. But compared to the kinds of poverty you see in other parts of the world, we always had a car that ran at least. It's all a matter of degrees. I sat around and listened in on a lot of conversations. My father was part of the League of Unemployed Voters, an early Seattle-wide mutual aid association that had cooperative auto repair shops, cooperative food stores; it was flourishing so well—a lot of people were Communist party members in those days—a lot of people say that was why President Roosevelt started the welfare programs because he didn't want the west coast to go Communist.

There's a guy who's working on my biography who had done a lot of research on that [period], John Suiter, who lives in Chicago. It's taking him too long.

SE: How far has he gotten at this point?
GS: He's gotten at least up to 1953. He's gotten me out of college. He's gotten completely fascinated with details, the rhapsody of facts. . . .

I didn't realize that I had a progressive background until I had to fight for my position when I was at Reed and decide whether I was Stalinist or a Trotskyite or anarchist or democratic socialist.

SE: How did you identify yourself? Your grandfather was a Wobbly.
GS: Yeah, a member of the International Workers of the World, and the IWW is still a good memory for all of us. I joined the IWW later, it still exists and I still have my IWW card. . . . Having an exact name for yourself wasn't that important. I studied the Kropotkin school of anarchism and his great book, *Mutual Aid.* And *Mutual Aid* kind of morphed into the whole bioregional project in my mind. Since anarchism is very much misunderstood I generally use the term bioregionalism these days.

SE: How would you describe yourself politically now, or do you?
GS: Self-definition is presupposed before we start talking politics, which is also to say: What picture of the world have you managed to create for yourself? One of the ways to get right at somebody is just to ask them, "What do you subscribe to?"

A poet and a writer like myself—I have six prose books, books of essays—you can't help but be a public intellectual. People ask you for your opinion whether you have one or not . . .

SE: Can you tell me about your early interest in Native American culture and traditions?

GS: Our farm was between the north end of Lake Washington near Puget Sound, still home of many Salish groups of Indians . . . That was one of the heaviest populated places in the US with native people. As heavily populated as the area around San Francisco Bay . . . When I was a kid I went out to one of my uncle's places on the Rich Passage on Puget Sound and spent the whole afternoon sitting on the beach cracking open and eating fresh oysters. Acres and acres of oysters. Other days we'd go elsewhere and dig clams all day. It's not quite that way anymore. The clams are now going to Japanese sushi markets . . . Pike Street market in Seattle is not much changed. The way the streets are laid out on the rickety hillside there is the way it was when I was a kid . . . Down at one end where the Hmong women sit now, selling embroidery, that was native Puget Sound Indians. Sitting on blankets on the ground, selling blackberries and huckleberries, dried fish. I took that as part of the world when I was a kid. And I was fascinated by the anthropology museum at the University of Washington; my parents would drop me off there when they were going shopping in that part of town. I took note of all that cedar carving and so forth, talked to Indian guys when I could. So it was a sort of easy gradual move from an interest in Native American culture to an interest in East Asia.

The first big hit on East Asia that came to me was at the Seattle Art Museum, which has a wonderful collection of East Asian and Chinese and Japanese landscape paintings . . . Looking at the Chinese and Japanese mountain landscapes my thought was that it sure looked a lot like the Cascades in Washington. I also thought, "Gee, these guys really knew how to paint!" You look at a European landscape, I don't know, maybe if you live on the East Coast it looks familiar but it was a very unfamiliar looking landscape to me. I already knew the West. East Asian painting covers a mountain landscape with ice and rocks and clouds that looks very much like the landscape of interior Washington.

And I had a definite argument about the ethics of Christianity, or the absence of what I thought was ethics, in their inability to extend concerns to non-human beings. That's when I quit going to Sunday school, when I found out that our heifers that died couldn't go to heaven. Then I learned somewhere that Buddhists and Hindus included all the different creatures in their moral concern and I said, "Well, that's for me!"

I ran onto Buddhism in college, partly through anthropology and world humanities courses and partly through the presence of one Chinese gentleman who had been in the American army in World War II and was going to Reed on the GI Bill; he was an expert calligrapher in Chinese and an expert calligrapher in the Roman alphabet. . . .

Went to Indiana University for one semester on linguistics, then I went to Berkeley and started studying Chinese full time for a while. Got a certain vocabulary, some Chinese characters and so forth . . . Then I went to Asia with the goal of studying with a Zen teacher; by that time I had run on to Buddhism and narrowed my territory to Zen Buddhism, its particular kinds of discipline and its poetry and its heart. It was accessible in Japan but at that time China was totally closed. Managed to make my way to Japan and stayed there for twelve years.

SE: How were you embraced as a Westerner?
GS: As long as you speak the language and have good manners you can go anywhere. At first they think you're a little odd and then they get used to you.

SE: Can you say more about what those twelve years were like? Were you in monasteries?
GS: I was partly in monasteries and partly living in a little place nearby; I had to do that because I needed to be able to look things up, which you cannot do in a monastery. They don't have a library or a dictionary in a Zen monastery so I had a place just a ten-minute walk away. To pay the rent I took on conversational English teaching jobs. Part of the time I was very much in the Buddhist world but also I got to know Japanese intelligentsia and various European and American expat types, the bohemian subculture of western Japan . . . Learned a wide variety of Japanese that way. Zen Buddhists speak the most learned and polite Japanese when they want to. All the way down to Kyoto dialect, the southern part of Kyoto, which has gambling and prostitution and bar zones. And they have quite a vocabulary too (laughs) . . .

SE: When did you return to the US?
GS: I made the big trip back here in '68 with my Japanese wife and my first-born son. We came back by ship and I brought my library back. Moved here a couple years later and built a house in 1970.

SE: How did you come to build a house there, in the foothills near Nevada City?
GS: It's a simple story. Dick Baker from San Francisco Zen center had been assigned the job of finding a piece of country land that the Zen Center could buy and make a country branch. He narrowed it down to some land up here

and the Tassajara land, and Suzuki Roshi chose Tassajara partly because it had a hot springs . . . So then Dick said to me and Allen Ginsberg, "I know another piece of land that Roshi doesn't want and maybe we could buy it. This is a really good deal right now and it's an interesting place." We came up here and looked at it. I wasn't familiar with this part of California; on the other hand I was familiar with what I saw when I got out of the car and started taking my handheld compass and looking at everything. I recognized ponderosa pine, incense cedar, black oak madrone and several species of Manzanita, and I said, "Oh this is just like southern Oregon. Same climate probably, same maximum and minimum temperatures, same rainfall. This is a good place to be." I would go in on this place, knowing what to expect in the West . . .

We went in on the property together, then Baker got in trouble. He and his wife brought a little Zen temple over from Japan; it was given to them because they were going to take it down. It sits up on the hill up there and it belongs to me now. Dick had to leave the Zen Center, or thought he did anyway. Now he's based in Colorado. Still in touch with him, he has students in Germany. Goes there for a few months at a time . . . He's made a big impression on people. That's the kind of guy he is. People take note of him. And in a way he's kind of scary too.

SE: Both interests (Native American culture, Buddhism) were later embraced by a lot of young people in the sixties and the seventies. Did you ever see yourself as sort of a trailblazer in that regard?
GS: I had no intention of it; most of what I see I think, "They're not doing a very good job of it." But I appreciate the steadiness of a lot of the Buddhist people. I have a current companion and she practices Vipassana; she'll probably eventually find her way into Zen. She asked me, "What is the relationship of Vipassana to Zen?" and I said, "Vipassana is like going to college; Zen is graduate school. You really get down to where you've got to make it work."

SE: After the publication of *Dharma Bums* (1958) you found yourself identified with the fictional character Jack Kerouac based on you. Was that annoying? Were you aware he was writing the book and did its impact surprise you? People were still carrying copies around in their backpacks when I was in high school, ten years later.
GS: I was away from the country during most of that . . . Jack was a novelist; he wasn't a journalist. I am only one small model for the Japhy Ryder character and a lot of what Japhy Ryder does is fictional. But some of it is

interestingly drawn on what we did together; the mountain climbing scene is close. But as a piece of writing goes it's not one of my favorite Kerouac novels. It was written too hastily, and you can see the haste. He's just banged it together because his publisher said, "*On the Road* is doing so well, let's have another novel right away." Jack sort of got into that so you have to be careful what your publisher needs. Turns out *On the Road* is the all-time bestseller in the Kerouac oeuvre and *Dharma Bums* is the second best. I think *On the Road* is a very fine piece of work; *The Subterraneans* is a wonderful book, and *Dr. Sax* is charming, a playful youthful piece. Both of those I like better than *The Dharma Bums*. But the Western Buddhist world, however it is, has to live with *The Dharma Bums*. I don't have to live with it too much; people don't talk to me much about it.

SE: Can you talk about your relationship with the Beats? Was there any sense at the Six Gallery reading (October 7, 1955) when Ginsberg first read "Howl" and you read "A Berry Feast," that this was the beginning of a movement? And how did what you were doing diverge from Ginsberg and others?
GS: There was already a movement and I was very much a student of Kenneth Rexroth. I got over and listened to what Kenneth had to say. He had an open seminar twice a month in his apartment out in the avenues. It was from Kenneth I first heard discussion of labor unions, the history of the anarchist movement, the history of West Coast communism, the history of the IWW . . . The circle of people around Kenneth were part of my continuous education in the history of the West Coast-left. Kenneth in his earlier days had been going to all the earlier meetings of the Italian Working Men's Circle on Portrero Hill . . . He had a lot of crazy opinions but also had very good insights. The first time I met Allen Ginsberg was at Rexroth's house; Allen had just come up from Mexico. The first time I saw Kerouac, Allen brought him to Rexroth's place. Because Allen was living in Berkeley I saw more and more of Allen, too. Kenneth thought of both Jack and Allen as "talented jerks."

SE: Was that his phrase or yours?
GS: I don't remember. They weren't quite grown up yet.
   The one thing I haven't said, and I should say something about is poetry: Of all the things I do, poetry is the one I think I do well. I've been watching what poetry can be and what I think it can be for a long time and part of that is orality. Poetry is very old; it predates literature and predates writing . . . That's also part of my linguistic and anthropology background; I learned to appreciate non-literature cultures and prehistory, and what is now called deep history . . .

SE: You also said that *This Present Moment* would be your last collection; does that mean you're not continuing to write poetry?

GS: You don't plan to write poetry; if it comes to you, fine, if it doesn't, that's fine too. It took me ten years before I felt like I could let this collection go. In fact I'm gearing up to do a new prose book, taken from a history of the environment of China I was working on in the seventies. Most of it is already written . . . To be called *The Great Clod,* which is a Chuang Tzu line: he was a contemporary of Lao-Tzu's—the other great creative Taoist writer. He says, "The great clod nourishes me, comforts me, chills me, feeds me. If I appreciate my life I should appreciate my death."

The Chinese communists don't talk about Chuang Tzu at all, they talk about Lao-Tzu a little bit; they decided they have to talk about Confucius after attacking him for forty years. What made China a viable culture and an interesting culture over the centuries was that it was constantly playing between the Taoist outlook and the Confucian outlook. Men used to say during your working career you're a Confucian and after you retire you're a Taoist. Taoists say, "The Buddhists meditate, the Taoists take naps."

SE: You also said you weren't sure if you liked *This Present Moment.* Have you made up your mind about its merits?

GS: Its strength is that I let it be imperfect (laughs). That's what I'm learning. There's a Japanese saying: "Imperfection is best." That's one of their aesthetic sayings. I decided I'm not going to hold it down to the line and get it just right. There are things in here I don't know what I think of myself. People like it; I can see that.

Index

CPSIA information can be obtained
at www.ICGtesting.com
Printed in the USA
BVOW03*1749030817

490481BV00002B/2/P

9 781496 811622